MODERN HUMANITIES RESEARCH ASSOCIATION
TEXTS AND DISSERTATIONS

Established in 1970, the series promotes important work by younger scholars by making the most accomplished doctoral research available to a wider readership. Titles are selected and edited by a Board of distinguished experts from across the modern Humanities.

Editorial Board

English: Professor Catherine Maxwell, Queen Mary, University of London
French: Professor William Brooks, University of Bath
Germanic: Professor Ritchie Robertson, University of Oxford
Hispanic: Professor Derek Flitter, University of Exeter
Italian: Professor Brian Richardson, University of Leeds
Latin American: Professor Catherine Davies, University of Nottingham
Portuguese: Professor Thomas Earle, University of Oxford
Slavonic: Professor David Gillespie, University of Bath

Constructing Feminine Poetics in the Works of a Late-20th-Century Woman Poet: Maria-Mercè Marçal

by
Noelia Díaz Vicedo

Modern Humanities Research Association
2014

Published by

*The Modern Humanities Research Association,
1 Carlton House Terrace
London SW1Y 5AF
United Kingdom*

© *The Modern Humanities Research Association, 2014*

Noelia Díaz Vicedo has asserted her right under the Copyright, Designs and Patents Act 1988 to be identified as the author of this work. Parts of this work may be reproduced as permitted under legal provisions for fair dealing (or fair use) for the purposes of research, private study, criticism, or review, or when a relevant collective licensing agreement is in place. All other reproduction requires the written permission of the copyright holder who may be contacted at rights@mhra.org.uk.

First published 2014

*ISBN 978-1-78188-000-5 (hardback)
ISBN 978-78188-001-2 (paperback)
ISSN (MHRA Texts and Dissertations) 0957-0322*

www.texts.mhra.org.uk

CONTENTS

	Acknowledgements	vi
	A Note on References	vii
	Introduction	1
1.	The Hermeneutics of the Body	12
2.	Poiesis	54
3.	The Poetics of Space: Reconfiguring Reality	100
4.	Love and Passion: Towards the Process of Self-Transcendence	137
	Afterword: Marçal's Feminine Poetics as a Powerful Principle of Being	188
	Bibliography	192
	Index	210

ACKNOWLEDGEMENTS

This book is a revised version of my PhD dissertation submitted to Queen Mary University of London in October 2011. It has been an adventure, and only possible thanks to the following people. I am grateful to Dr. Jordi Larios for providing most thoughtful insights on early drafts. Thanks to Professor Peter Evans for his academic and human support. Also, thanks to Dr. Fina Birulés for her comments on some theoretical aspects and for her conversations on Marçal.

I would also like to thank the following institutions that have funded part of this project. In the first place, thanks to Institut d'Estudis Catalans for awarding me the 'Països Catalans Prize'. Also, I acknowledge the assistance of the Central Research Fund at the University of London for a travel grant that financed archival work on Marçal's manuscripts at the Biblioteca de Catalunya. The British Federation of Women Graduates provided me financial support at the final stage of this book. Most of all, my sincere thanks to my supervisors Professor Parvati Nair and Professor Omar García-Obregón, for their academic expertise and encouragement, especially at difficult times. I also thank to Dr. Montserrat Lunati and Dr. Dominic Keown for invaluable suggestions and stimulating insights, which I have incorporated here.

Thanks also to my family for their support and love. I owe my gratitude to Santiago, Cecilia and Amaya - my second family and masters of knowledge. Thanks to Andreu and Pep for hosting me in Barcelona and making me feel at home. Finally, thanks to Periklis for being there.

A NOTE ON REFERENCES

The references to Marçal's poetry are indicated in the text using the following abbreviations:

Cau de llunes (1977) — CLL
Bruixa de dol (1979) — BD
Sal oberta (1982) — SO
Terra de Mai (1982) — TM
La germana, l'estrangera (1985) — LGLE
Desglaç (1989) — D

The page numbers of these references are in the publications listed in the bibliography.

References to Marçal's manuscripts are given with the full title of the paper, followed by the box number and the folder separated by a slash and then the folio number. If the author had several pages stapled and included in the same folder, 'Sheet' is written, followed by the number. It has not always been possible to provide the title and page. It has also not been possible to provide the exact date for the manuscripts except for 'el mite d'Atenea'. All manuscripts from box 16 correspond to the 1990s.

For my parents

INTRODUCTION

This book analyses questions of the female body, writing and poetry in the works of Catalan poet Maria-Mercè Marçal (1952–1998) through the in-depth study of the corpus composed between 1973 and 1988 — *Cau de llunes, Bruixa de dol, Sal oberta, Terra de Mai, La germana, l'estrangera* and *Desglaç*. It aims, firstly, to introduce the complex and innovative work of a prominent Catalan female author within a broader panorama of both Hispanic and international literary traditions, through a detailed analysis of some aspects of her work such as love, passion, the figure of the poet and the space of poetry. Secondly, this research focuses on the question of the female body, its interaction with the process of writing and its effects upon the poetic imagery in order to uncover specific symbolism representing Catalan female subjectivity. Thirdly, I offer, through a sequence of contested images, new readings on the dialogue that Marçal establishes between experience and poetry, providing a particular feminine poetics within the Catalan context.

I have chosen to study this corpus (1973–1988) exclusively, collected in the book *Llengua abolida (1973–1988)* (1989b), because it forms a complete unity not only chronologically but also thematically. The dialogue between life and poetry is intertwined in the poems with the aim of researching through poetry Marçal's identity as both woman and poet.[1] The title itself, *Llengua abolida*, evokes:

> el mite d'un suposat llenguatge 'de dona' (Llengua, en el sentit Saussurià de codi) que hauria estat abolit pel patriarcat i del qual només en tenim indicis, i és així, amb aquesta 'mancança' per dir-ho d'alguna manera, que es produeix la 'parla' de les dones. (Barcelona, Biblioteca de Catalunya (BC), Fons Maria-Mercè Marçal (FMMM), Fira-dona i literatura, 16/6, fol. 2)

This unity was interrupted after the publication of *Llengua abolida* and Marçal ceased her poetic activity to concentrate all her efforts upon the only book of fiction that she wrote, entitled *La passió segons Renée Vivien* (1994c). Marçal also wrote three short stories, two of which are published. These are 'Joc de màscares' (1995c), 'El retorn' (1995d) and 'Tronatrons' (unpublished).[2] Although she returned to the exercise of poetry after the publication of this book, her attitude towards writing projected other interests and other literary horizons, which are not at stake in this book. Marçal did not have the time to complete and develop this new poetic stage due to her untimely death in 1998. The poems written in this second brief poetic phase were posthumously collected by scholar and friend

Lluïsa Julià in the book *Raó del cos* (2000), with a prologue written by Catalan poet Pere Gimferrer.

Marçal started her career as a poet at the end of the Spanish Francoist dictatorship with the publication of her first book of poems *Cau de llunes* (1977), which won the prestigious poetry prize Carles Riba in 1976. Immersed in the rather unstructured poetic context of the time, Marçal, along with Ramon Balasch,[3] Xavier Bru de Sala and other poets, part of the young generation of the seventies, founded in 1973 the publishing house Llibres del Mall (1973–1988).[4] The purpose of this publishing house was to promote different literary postulates from those of the 'realisme social' that orchestrated the poetic panorama of the time in the Catalan context.[5] With the anthology *Poesia catalana del segle XX* (1963), edited by Castellet i Molas, these young poets, Marçal amongst them, 'practicàvem amb assiduïtat el nostre juvenil vudú estètic' (Bru de Sala 2000: 43), vehemently opposing the manipulation of poetry in favour of the state. They also disagreed with a later account that appeared in the mid-sixties connected with poetry of the 'realisme social' and conducted by Gabriel Ferrater, the so-called 'poesia de l'experiència', whose lyrical tendencies claimed a discursive understanding of poetry and a plain use of words.[6] In opposition to these miscellaneous tendencies, this young group of poets conceived poetry as a vital experience connected with a personal desire for self-construction. The poet's function was to rediscover the self, to redefine his/her own existence. Poetry, for them, was the space in which the poet reformulates language and adapts it to his/her particular needs of self-creation. Poetry offered the possibility of conjugating magic sounds with well-established lyric forms such as sonnets or sestinas. In this sense, El Mall provided a space for poetic forms and postulates other than the social or political. They published poetry from all parts of the Catalan Countries and vindicated works written by authors such as Joan Brossa, J.V. Foix or Miquel Martí i Pol.[7] They also translated Novalis, Rilke, Blake, Coleridge and Wordsworth among others into Catalan.

Amidst this effervescent environment, Marçal emerged with *Cau de llunes* and a rather distinctive poetic itinerary. The main trait that distinguishes Marçal's poetry from the rest of the poets of this generation is the gendered position she takes. Marçal's poems explore the existence of a woman poet whose subjectivity questions the contingency between corporeality and cultural inscriptions, the effectiveness of such an interaction, the interweaving of poetry and reality, and the symbolic effects of a relational being in the poems.

Since Marçal won the Carles Riba prize (1976), she has been labelled as one of the most important Catalan poets of the twentieth century. Writers such as Carme Riera have declared that Marçal is one of the best European poets: 'una de les més importants poetes de la literatura europea de la segona meitat del segle XX' (2008: 205). For this reason, she has been celebrated as a poet with a sublime treatment of poetical structures who, as Vinyet Panyella stated, has produced 'una obra poètica única, impressionant, i d'una inigualable qualitat literària' (1998: 27).

As seen, many of Marçal's critics have extolled the technical quality of the poems, her masterly talent to combine form and content in poetical production and her ability as a virtuoso in language. As a result, her literary production has been compared to those classical Catalan poets such as Ausiàs March, contemporary Joan Brossa, J. V. Foix, or Spanish poet Federico García Lorca.[8] Interestingly enough, she has even been considered a classical poet. At the time that Julià edited an anthology of her poetry entitled *Contraban de llum* (2001), as part of the collection *Clàssics Catalans* from Proa publishing house, Andreu Gomila in the newspaper *Avui* declared: 'Aquest pas que fa Proa dins la seva nova col·lecció no ens hauria de provocar cap conflicte perquè Marçal és veritablement un clàssic, un dels millors autors catalans del segle passat' (2002: 10). These words are surprising if one reads Marçal's poems. The central poetic themes engage with rather problematic issues distant from classic tenors, such as same-sex love or woman-identified eroticism in the book *Terra de Mai* (1982c), later included in *La germana, l'estrangera* (1985a). She also manifests her heterodox vision of maternity and her conflict with traditional models of motherhood in *Sal oberta* (1982a) and *La germana, l'estrangera* (1985a). She even openly questions the figure of the symbolic father and his Law through the poetic display of the death of her real father Antoni Marçal in *Desglaç* (1989d). Despite this innovative form and content that I find in Marçal's poetry, the critical reception of her work has been rather complex and peculiar. Mainstream criticism has not engaged with some aspects of her work, which are essential to understanding the aims of her poetic project. Aware of this situation, Marçal gave the following answer to how most critics, mainly male, have considered her work:

> La crítica masculina, en canvi, poques vegades ha calat el nucli de la meva poesia. En força ocasions tinc la impressió que els ha servit per a fer un desplegament molt sincer i visceral de la imatge de dona que tenen i que, és clar, connecta d'alguna manera amb allò que apareix al text. Un tipus de crítica masculina ha estat força superficial i externa, no s'ha implicat gaire; altres crítics, en canvi, han buscat en el text una imatge de dona que ha resultat, fins i tot, massa idealitzada. (Nadal 1989: 28)

In this passage Marçal refers to how male critics have barely understood the core of her poetry. From a superficial approach to an idealised configuration, she laments how, despite some considerations by female scholars such as Julià or Mercè Ibarz, the importance of her work as a woman poet and feminist thinker mingles with the exaltation of a great poetic craft. Marçal was not only a poet, she was also a woman poet with a conspicuous feminist position towards women's presence in public spaces, particularly in Literature.[9] The disregard of her poetic aims reveals the lack of consideration given to feminist, female and feminine positions by male-dominated institutions. Marçal herself, in a paper entitled 'Entre dones',[10] lamented how critics have not only diminished some points in her work but have also contributed to protecting her public image.[11] This supposed protection thwarts the profound poetic elaboration of extended themes, symbols and images that Marçal used to explore the connection between women and writing in the process of recapturing female subjectivity. Both poetry and feminism are entangled in her discourse in which theory and practice continuously oscillate to provide explicit alternatives to the images and representations that she builds upon the category of woman. Marçal says:

> És molt curiós, i m'agradaria tenir-ho més analitzat, l'estrany 'proteccionisme' cap a la meva persona, o cap a la meva imatge, que ha funcionat en els altres casos, fins a forçar interpretacions de poemes d'una forma increïble: pura miopia o voluntat de neutralització d'un discurs 'dissonant'? (1995–96: 203)

What does such protection hide? To what extent can protection be considered as a double-edge sword? As she suggests, this 'myopia' (in the full sense that the Oxford dictionary offers as 'lack of intellectual insight')[12] discloses an intention to consign to oblivion some aspects of her work, by a well-established critical apparatus hostile towards particular feminist positions and practices within the socio-political space of the peninsula, particularly in the Catalan context. It also masks a disregard of women writers as intellectuals, showing a supposed discrepancy between a feminist perspective and the subsequent means of composing poetry. As seen in the passage above, Marçal herself was aware of this fact, and she never abandoned her task as a woman writer and the possibilities that poetry could offer to redefine the space and place of the feminine subject. On the contrary, this situation was decisive in igniting in Marçal the fearless need to put forward her creativity. Her position, as a female writer, becomes a revolt against male-dominated discourse. As critic Ibarz has suggested:

> Algú podria dir que la naturalesa obsessiva de l'escriptura i, en ella, dels seus temes la van fer hiperconcentrada, però en paral·lel cal dir que els amos de la paraula pública no l'escoltaven. I, davant el mur, la Marçal tímida i insegura era tossuda i decidida, valenta. (2004: 18)

Although she enjoyed certain recognition during her life, especially after she was awarded several prestigious prizes for her novel *La passió segons Renée Vivien* (1994c), it is only recently that Marçal has received great attention and interest from other writers and critics. Several monographs have been edited in some of the most prestigious Catalan journals, such as *Lectora*, which in 2004 published a brief dossier with a few articles edited by Marta Segarra. In winter 2006, Adrià Chavarria and Ivan Favà in the literary magazine *Rels* edited a brief monograph 'Miscel·lània Maria-Mercè Marçal' that included some out of print articles. The journal *Urc* published a rather more extended monograph in homage to the thirty years since the first publication of Marçal, 'Traginera, de llunes i cançons. 30 anys de la irrupció poètica de Maria-Mercè Marçal', edited by Julià (2007a). The latest publication, edited by Josep Maria Sala-Valldaura (2008a), is the journal *Reduccions*, which offered to its readers a considerable volume entitled 'La poesia de Maria-Mercè Marçal', with poems inspired by her poetry and articles by critics. And yet, no substantial piece of work has been published on her poetry, with the exception of a book by Laia Climent, *Maria-Mercè Marçal: cos i compromís* (2008a), which appeared when this research was well-advanced. Prior to this study, the material available on Marçal's poetry was limited to interviews and brief articles published in newspapers and journals and the recent donation of her manuscripts to the Biblioteca de Catalunya as *Fons Maria-Mercè Marçal*.[13]

The publication of her essays in 2004 by Ibarz in the book *Maria-Mercè Marcal. Sota el signe del drac: Proses 1985–1997* was another important step in consolidating not only Marçal's figure as a feminist intellectual but also the theoretical threads that mark her thought. In the introduction to the book, Ibarz captures Marçal's feminist postulates not only as theoretical writings but also as reflections on her experience of writing. Both poetry and theory address the question of the female body that foregrounds her activity as she states: 'Tot parteix del fet de tenir un cos diferent, crec que això marca molt' (Montero 2004: 273).

The question of the body in Marçal's poetry and its interaction with language has been substantially examined by Climent in her book *Maria-Mercè Marçal: cos i compromís* (2008a). In this study, Climent uses a psychosomatic approach and understands Marçal's poetry as a research of the psychological self. She understands the presence of the body in Marçal's poems as an unlimited dimension: 'en la lírica marçaliana, l'espai corporal és entés com il·limitat tot i que és concebut com un microcosmos independent' (2008a: 180). In order to discuss her arguments she uses a wide range of theoretical frameworks, which range from feminism — with theories by Luisa Muraro and Luce Irigaray — to philosophy, with texts by Maurice Merleau-Ponty, Pierre Bordieu, Gilles Deleuze and Félix Guattari, Michel Foucault or Simone de Beauvoir. She also uses writers such as Julia Kristeva and David Glover and Cora Kaplan. Climent highlights the importance of Marçal's private life and her biography without taking into account the relevant poetic effects of such relations in the texts. Also, my own work published in 2004, *Maria-Mercè Marçal: An Exploration of the Feminine Poetics in the Work of a Late 20*[th] *Century Catalan Poet*, explored these questions from the perspective of French Feminism through the analysis of two poems from *Terra de Mai* (1982c) and *Desglaç* (1989d). I focused primarily upon the main traits of *l'écriture féminine* to discuss the fluid interaction between the female body, language and creativity. Although no further substantial piece of written work has been published there are some studies on women and poetry that include her work as a reference such as Dolors Sistac's *Líriques del silenci*.

La cançó de dona a Safo, Renée Vivien i Maria-Mercè Marçal (2001). Sistac provides a general overview of Mediterranean poetry written by women. Her scope ranges from ancient Greece to the twentieth century, where she discusses how women poets display the experience of love and their desire for freedom in their texts.

In this book, I seek to demonstrate critically that Marçal's poetry is inextricably linked to her personal experience, through the acknowledgment of the body, to the extent that the poems are composed from and mark different important moments of her life. Marçal's poems reflect how the embodied experience challenges and even displaces patriarchal mechanisms of signification. Her woman-centred poetry offers the site for reconstructing, re-writing her being, her *ser dona*, a topic which I shall address in Chapter One. In her own words:

> què és ser dona? És ser com la mare o no? Com es compaginen unes tries 'no femenines' amb el fet de continuar essent dona? Totes aquestes qüestions afecten molt el nucli de la personalitat; per això en mi és central el tema de la dona. (Nadal 1989: 26)

Her poems tackle this *ser dona* not only as a starting point for her creativity, but also as her principal poetic aim, to the extent that writing becomes for Marçal a vital intellectual exercise that gives shape to life: 'en mi caso, escribir es dar forma a la vida' (Barcelona BC, FMMM, 17/5, 'Sheet' 20, fol. 3). In this book, I pay attention to how Marçal's poetry unleashes the need to address the following questions: how does Marçal engage her poetic writing with the embodied vision of a female subject? How is this embodied vision to be understood in poetic terms?

In developing my arguments, I draw primarily upon discourses of difference, particularly the Italian understanding of *differenza sessuale*. This theory, derived from the works of French philosopher Irigaray, has yet to be exploited fully in academic analyses of feminine subjectivity. The use of this theoretical framework in relation to Marçal's poetry offers a novel approach to the limited criticism published to date. I also utilize Maurice Blanchot's theoretical knowledge on literary action, writing, and the purpose of literature. Marçal was influenced by Blanchot, whom she read deeply during the last years of her life. A file on her computer, found among her manuscripts and entitled 'Blanchot-literatura', reveals how she recasts his thought and adapts it to her own poetic needs. Taking Marçal's words derived from her readings on Blanchot: 'el món deixa de donar-se per suposat' (Barcelona BC, FMMM, Blanchot-literatura, 16/6).

My purpose in approaching Marçal's feminist discourse from the Italian angle of sexual difference draws on several points. In a broad sense, the mutual connection between Italian and Catalan feminist academics, especially Libreria delle donne di Milano and Diotima, is established via the figure of Muraro, who collaborates in both groups and whose work is regularly published in Catalan feminist journals such as *Duoda*.[14] Also, Marçal collaborated with the group 'Philosophy and Gender' ('Filosofia i gènere')[15] at the University of Barcelona, directed by Catalan philosopher Fina Birulés. During these years, Marçal established an intellectual connection with Italian feminism through the friendship of Muraro, in 1991. Secondly and more importantly, Marçal's understanding of feminism and her act of writing connects with two specific points developed by women from *il pensiero della differenza sessuale*: the perspective of sexual difference and the socio-symbolic practice of entrustment.

These points do not constitute the whole Italian perspective of sexual difference. Italian feminism is characterized by the heterogeneity of its development. Intimately linked with the complexities of the political history of the country, the Italian debate has been evolving into different perspectives according to the different explorations carried out regarding the relationship of the sexes. In Italy, there are several groups that work separately around the country. They form a network whereby they collaborate and exchange their experiences. Such diversity, with members of groups spread around the country, makes it difficult to talk about a homogeneous perspective of Italian thought. However, despite all these numerous views and practices, I shall mainly use the theories elaborated by Libreria delle donne di Milano and Diotima.

On a conceptual level, there is a fundamental commonality between the precepts from *il pensiero* and Marçal's poetry: both discourses foreground the principle of 'starting from oneself' as a translation of the original Italian term *partire da sé*. This term does not strive towards an essentialist perspective. It implies, rather, a political position, which embraces the questioning of subjectivity, representation and social visibility of women in discourse. Its main traits, inherently configured in connection with language, are examined in the book *La sapienza di partire da sé* (1996b) written by the group Diotima. According to this book, *partire da sé* sustains the importance of researching the possibilities of language in constructing a female identity. The Italian feminism of *il pensiero* strives towards the elaboration of thought whose basic principle is centred on the female self. In this sense, *partire da sé* entails the narration of a female identity, whose origins emanate from female desire. This connects with the aesthetic principles proposed by the young generation of poets of El Mall, whose aims were to approach poetry with the purpose of self-creation, in other words, to shape the self through words and redefine new forms of signification. Thus, *partire da sé* entails a displacement of linguistic signs that have defined the identity of a woman in patriarchy. The elaboration of feminist thought from the basis of *partire da sé* proposes: 'una vía que se sustrae a las muchas oposiciones que están inscritas en el simbólico dominante: la que hay entre subjetivo y objetivo, entre individuo y comunidad, entre local y general. Abre otro camino' (Zamboni 1996: 2).

The ethos of this theoretical background coincides with Marçal's mode of understanding feminism and the act of writing. This is particularly relevant to understanding the kernel of her discourse. Feminism for Marçal is not only a theoretical approach, but a vital position that encompasses all levels and aspects of her everyday life and her intellectual activity. Feminism and poetry are inextricably entangled in what constitutes her life:

> el Feminisme, no només com a ideologia, sinó com a actitud vital, quotidiana, ha de determinar el com i el què dels poemes. I ha determinat des de la meva pròpia relació amb la llengua fins als temes més diversos que han sorgit, estretament lligats a la meva vida: la meva relació amb el país, la vivència amorosa amb els homes, la solitud, la maternitat voluntàriament soltera, la solidaritat, l'amistat, i més tard també l'amor, amb les dones, el dolor i el plaer, la mort del pare. (Barcelona BC, FMMM, Fira-dona i literatura, 16/6, fol. 2)

Furthermore, neither discourse is based on a specific institution; therefore, they are not conditioned by particular political demands. The production of thought, based on the principle of *partire da sé*, is derived from the 'practice of doing', whereby language gives shape to the embodied experience. In order to overcome the discrepancy found between the personal and the political — experience and collective reference — women from Libreria delle donne di Milano have proposed establishing practice as a priority in relation to theory. In their book *Sexual Difference: A Theory of Social-Symbolic Practice* (1990), they have explained in one chapter how the excessive ideology found in most prominent feminist discourses pits against personal experiences and modes of interacting with cultural collective references.

Taking this into account, in this book I apply a methodology based upon a theoretical and practical model, adopting a reflective perspective in my own procedure, as was used by Marçal herself in her literary project. The reasons why I apply my theoretical approach in this way lie in the following points. Marçal was a writer who worked independently from any particular academic or intellectual network. The parameters and references she develops come from her intellectual experience and subsequent meditation. She was a woman writer with a particular and defined position that provided her with a specific perception of reality and its effects on poetry.

I shall finish this introduction by considering a relevant aspect of Marçal's biography needed to understand some aspects of her poetry and the perspective of her thought. This is the figure of her father, Antoni Marçal, to whom Marçal dedicated her complete *oeuvre* published in *Llengua abolida*: 'si bé vull dedicar *Llengua abolida*, així, sense paraules, a la memòria del meu pare, perquè ell fou qui, paradoxalment, m'obrí portes que em durien a qüestionar la *seva* llei' (1989b: 11, her italics). According to Balasch, her ex-husband, there was an event that considerably increased the tension between Marçal and her father. In 1972,

Marçal's father irrupted into his daughter's flat where he found her with her boyfriend Balasch. Marçal's father, considering this behaviour as shameful and indecent, forced them to get married. This almost anecdotal passage in Marçal's life increased the tension between father and daughter, and bestowed relevant poetic consequences, to which she refers in the quotation above. The presence of the father becomes a figure recurrent in her poetry. This symbol, whose judgment continuously follows Marçal, lies in her particular use of poetic forms and contents and her mode of finding signification. It is life that induces poetry in Marçal. In Balasch's words:

> la relació pare-filla experimenta un terratrèmol de conseqüències difícils d'avaluar amb justesa. Sense por d'exagerar es pot afirmar que la figura del pare s'esberla a l'interior de la futura escriptora i serà una magnitud constant en la seva relació interpersonal i en la seva obra. (Balasch 2007: 38)

In Marçal, poetry faces the facts that life brings and questions its modes, its sanguine effects. Poetry reflects the life of a fragmented self who seeks the image of her identity. Based on this interaction between language and the body, the chapters that comprise this book present my interest in discussing the tension unleashed between both parameters in Marçal's lyrics. They aim to shed light on the way in which, for the poet, poetry holds her mode of being. Considering that her poetical mode of being lies in assuming the condition of sexual difference, I divide this book into four chapters, whilst at the core of the research is the oscillation between theoretical postulates and poetic praxis.

Chapter One focuses on mapping the field of the theoretical framework that I use. I introduce the paradigm of the body in relation to language and writing in order to tackle perceptions of female identity. It examines the conceptual and structural connections between the Italian feminist theory of *differenza sessuale* and Marçal's theoretical reflections, outlining the relationship between feminism and poetry. This connection is based on the acknowledgment of the space and place of the female body. In order to do this, I put the theory of Italian sexual difference and Judith Butler's distinction between sex and gender into dialogue, in order to assert that the position of the body in Marçal's poetry needs to be acknowledged neither via essentialist connotations nor in terms of cultural constructionism.

In Chapter Two I present the act of writing poetry as a process of constructing the self. I use the Aristotelian term *poiesis* as a mechanism whereby Marçal poetically articulates her *ser dona*. I examine this matter from her cultural and biological position as a woman, considering how Marçal writes about her experiences using existing iconography. I apply *poiesis* to Marçal's poetry, also foregrounding this mechanism alongside the very act of creation in order to show how creativity attempts to provide positive results for the feminine subject. I then explore Marçal's particular historiography, through the main icons that she uses to find her own mode of symbolic significance. Using Butler's theory espoused in the book *Giving an Account of Oneself* (2005), I consider critically the validity of such a process by discussing it in relation to Butler's proposal on the strict limitations of engaging with this mechanism.

Chapter Three enquires into the spatial conditions that foreground the process of *poiesis* presented in Chapter Two. In this sense, and taking the theory of *mettere il mondo al mondo* formulated by Diotima as a starting point, I claim that Marçal's poetic horizons reconfigure the codes of reality. I deal with action and its relevance for poetic activity. I show how Marçal as a poet engages with the activity of literature and emerges as a poet from patriarchy through the exploration of different images and cultural symbols. This issue precedes my further discussion on the position of the woman poet and creativity as birth. All in all, the idea behind this chapter is to recast biological contentions of the female body and their metaphorical implications for creativity.

In Chapter Four I analyse the question of love and passion in Marçal's poems. I end my project by examining the structure of the world that Marçal has put forward lyrically in the preceding chapter. In order to do this I offer a detailed account of the poetic display of same-sex passion and its understanding as an approach of the self towards the other. I seek to prove that to write about the love for the other as the same (resemblance) bears upon expanding the limits of the self and fortifies novel configurations of self-definition.

Notes to the Introduction

1. The understanding of poetry as a mode of research, influenced by poet J. V. Foix, is explored in detail in Chapter Three.
2. See Riera 2004: 251–58.
3. Ramon Balasch's *nom de plume* was Ramon Pinyol.
4. Other poets were part of this group: Miquel Desclot, Jaume Medina, Miquel de Palol and Josep Albertí. See Marçal and Julià 2006.
5. Representatives of this generation are the poets Pere Quart or Salvador Espriu. Xavier Bru de Sala confessed that they used to call Espriu 'orellut i narrador.' See Bru de Sala 2000.
6. Poets of this group were Narcís Comadira, Marta Pessarrodona and Francesc Parcerissas among others.
7. Poets from Valencia connected with them and also published in Llibres del Mall (Bru de Sala 2000: 43). They are Joan Navarro, Josep Bonet, Josep Piera, Gaspar Jaen i Urban and Salvador Jàfer.
8. See Pàmias 1986, Gimferrer 2000a and Castillo 1989a.
9. I use Literature with capital L to indicate 'the institution of Literature' and to differentiate it from literature as the process of creating texts. This emphasizes the political dimension of the former.
10. This paper was found by Mercè Ibarz among Marçal's unpublished papers. Ibarz, as the editor of her prose, decided to include it in the final edition of her complete theoretical works *Maria-Mercè Marçal. Sota el signe del drac: Proses 1985–1997* (Barcelona: Proa) with the title 'Entre dones'. The date of composition is reliably thought to be between 1995 and 1996.

11. This protection towards her persona can be extrapolated to an extended understanding of the position of the woman writer. In Chapter One I connect this 'protection' to the analysis of the myth of the birth of Athena, which Marçal used to explain the position of the woman writer in patriarchy.
12. See Oxford Dictionary on-line: http://oxforddictionaries.com/view/entry/m_en_gb 0545380#m_en_gb0545380.
13. This recent interest in the figure of Marçal as a woman poet has been also underpinned by the creation of 'Fundació Maria-Mercè Marçal'. Among various literary activities and cultural events it is important to highlight the 'Jornades Marçalianes', celebrated three times, once in 2007 entitled 'Llavor de cant, lluita en saó', with a second one, 'Saba vella per a fulles noves', in 2008. The third, 'Jo no sé pas on són els meus confins. Obertures teòriques i polítiques en l'obra de Maria-Mercè Marçal' was held in November 2010. In my first project on Marçal, published in 2004, I already refer to the lack of critical engagement with her poetic works at the time. No considerable piece of critical work had been produced at the time I published this.
14. *Duoda* is the Research Centre for Women's Studies at University of Barcelona that regularly publishes a journal of the same name. Muraro collaborates as an academic researcher alongside Diana Sartori, Chiara Zamboni Antonia de Vita, Anna Maria Piussi (University of Verona) and Marirí Martinengo (Libreria delle donne di Milano). This women's research centre and its magazine are referential points to locate the development of sexual difference in Spain. Since 1987 and through María Milagros Rivera Garretas, the centre DUODA introduced the thought of *il pensiero della differenza sessuale* in Spain. For a historical account of this, see Rivera Garretas 2003.
15. This is a seminar founded in 1990 at the University of Barcelona coordinated by Catalan philosopher Fina Birulés. In these seminars Marçal met Italian philosopher Muraro, establishing a friendship until her death in 1998. The group 'Filosofia i gènere' collaborates with Italian Universities of Verona, Florencia, Padua, and Salerno. Italian feminists such as Luisa Muraro publish regularly. Other Italian feminist thinkers such as Wanda Tommasi, Angela Putino and Zamboni are also related to this group.

CHAPTER 1

The Hermeneutics of the Body

In this chapter I examine Maria-Mercè Marçal's distinctive feminist thought and her contribution to the scope of Catalan feminism. I also argue how this feminist dimension results from a profound meditation on her experience as a woman and the consequent dialectic relationship with the process of writing. I attempt to demonstrate how in Marçal's aesthetics, feminism and poetry become inextricably linked and interdependent, and how both converge in a profoundly heuristic process of the place and space of the female body. In her own words: 'Que hi ha una relació entre el fet de tenir un cos de dona i la manera com et situes en el món, la manera com et situes davant del fet d'escriure, això em sembla gairebé obvi' (Sabadell 1998: 15). My purpose in linking feminism and poetry in Marçal is to prove that the importance of her theoretical reflections on women and writing create a new feminist space, whereby poetry as praxis contributes to the alteration of pre-established images and references to the identity of woman.

Despite the clear aims of Marçal's feminist project and the as yet unexplored presence of such features in her poetry, it is important to underline specific problematic questions that arise from such a perspective. Acknowledging the position of the body and the experience derived from it calls into question certain controversial presuppositions regarding the legitimacy of the body and its consequent consideration for the process of subjectivity. One of the most important theories regarding these issues is Judith Butler's critique of sexual difference and the category of woman. I explore Butler's critique which problematises the interaction between the position of the body and the performance of subjectivity in order to present a full account of the dangers involved in considering the body as a source of knowledge. This provides the necessary framework with which to unmask prescriptive understandings of the body and a gendered subjectivity.

Although I emphasize the vicissitudes of engaging with corporeality and the embodied subject, my intention is not to strive towards an immediate inherent relationship of a sexed body and a determinative, constrained and fixed specific gendered identity, but rather to demonstrate that Marçal's understanding of 'body' underpins the need to reconsider universal and neutral parameters of discourse at various levels and performances. In this chapter, I propose that in Marçal's writings the concept of 'body' reclaims a further profound consideration that goes beyond corpo-reality as a fixed and monolithic dimension.

The purpose of this chapter is not to debate the interaction between sex and gender as a result of a discontinuity between body and experience — Butler has given a magnificent account of this problematic issue in her acclaimed book *Gender Trouble* (1990). Rather, this chapter will deal with the possibilities of the female body, which hitherto have been constructed upon a plethora of paradigms that clash with Marçal's own experience. Also, I will investigate the extended possibility of new configurations of the female subject and the category of woman that her poetic production may offer.

Within this framework, Marçal's distinctive work connects experience itself with theoretical postulates as a result of experience. The oscillation between both dimensions implies an exploration of other related areas such as images, language, and symbolic place. Marçal's experience as a woman provides her with the starting point from which to develop her specific feminist discourse. Her poetry results as a practice of 'being'. Relying on several dimensions of 'being', including Jacques Lacan and Butler's theoretical accounts, I demonstrate how, in this sense, Marçal's awareness of the socio-historical position of women is important to understand both her theoretical reflections and her poetry. This dialectic process between both spheres connects with a specific feminist perspective: the Italian understanding of *differenza sessuale*. This movement has influenced not only some theoretical considerations in Marçal's writings and configuration of thought but also has contributed to the scope of Catalan feminism. Furthermore, I will prove that Marçal's aesthetics enacts theory and practice — through the literary exercise of poetry — and that this practice finds an intimate link with the Italian perspective and its theories of 'entrustment' (*affidamento*) and 'socio-symbolic practice'.

Given the connections that I find between Marçal's discourse and the Italian perspective of sexual difference, I offer a brief outline of the main points raised by this specific feminist movement, particularly those developed by the Italian groups Libreria delle donne di Milano and Diotima, both led by Italian philosopher and feminist Luisa Muraro whose theories of entrustment as a socio-symbolic practice connect with Marçal's perception and creation of a feminist discourse. Prior to debating this matter, I offer a general panoramic overview of the problematic of the body in the development of feminist thought that will serve as an introductory section to understanding the theoretical contingency of Marçal's theoretical proposal.

Engaging with the Body: Tradition, History and Poetry

Is there any need to theorise the body? What are the consequences of such theoretical claims? Will they contribute to the democracy of feminism? Or would they simply imply a step backwards in the redefinition of non-male, hence non-hegemonic, subjectivities? The controversy surrounding the possibilities of theorizing the body or acknowledging its position for the development of a specific epistemology lies in how, historically, culture has constructed thought and how this has been developed exclusively around the concept of mind, conspicuously opposing it to the notion of body and determining respectively the disassociation between culture and nature. Marçal meditates on this dichotomy. She writes:

> No debades tenim un cos diferent. Ens movem en una cultura que ha mini-mitzat molt el cos; el cos és la natura, l'important — sembla — és la raó i la raó no té sexe! Penso que hi ha, de segur, una vivència concreta de les dones, una vivència específica diferent. (Montero 2004: 268)

Two discourses have historically reinforced the disassociation of body from thought (mind), both inherent in the formation of different hierarchies. On the one hand, the beginning of Western culture with the Greek formation of the *polis* and the political system of democracy was important in determining the virtues of the subject to be performed in the public arena. On the other hand, religious discourses, especially those of Christianity, have negated the instinctive nature and finitude of the mortal body in favour of the eternal soul.

Within these two frameworks, the binary of mind/body has been associated with that of culture/nature. The consideration of the body as an instinctive organism formed by fluids and flesh conferred upon the mind a privileged status in the analysis of the subject, producing, thus, disembodied thought. Hence, taking into account the limitations of the body, the development of gendered subjectivities were subject to the parameters that configured this disassociation.

In response to the long Western tradition that has neglected the body as part of any intellectual exercise, Western feminism has elaborated its main discourse around the concept of the body. The body is constantly in dialogue in feminist perspectives, and therefore engaged with the mind. This connection between the body and the feminist project has been a matter of disagreement among feminist scholars across different fields. Furthermore, this disagreement has evolved into a variety of positions and perspectives, which either reject or acknowledge corporeality as a source of knowledge in the production of feminist thought and the subsequent consideration of identity and performing subjectivities.

Numerous feminist thinkers have analysed the classical postulates that conferred a privileged status upon the mind in order to grasp the origins of the identification of women with the body and men with the mind. Examples include Luce Irigaray, whose philosophical work engages with the distinction between woman equals the body and man equals the mind in texts such as *Speculum of the Other Woman* (1985a) or *This Sex Which is Not One* (1985b), and with readings of 'Plato's *Hystera*' in *An Ethics of Sexual Difference* (1993a) where she engages with the binary through readings of Plato and Aristotle's physics and its relation to the matrix. Other writers who have also examined such issues include Julia Kristeva, who explores Platonic conventions of the *chora* and other related issues in *Revolution in Poetic Language* (1984), Butler, who uses the classical understanding of this matter, particularly from Plato, to deal with the materiality of the body in *Bodies that Matter: On the Discursive Limits of 'Sex'* (1993), Elizabeth Grosz in *Volatile Bodies: Toward a Corporeal Feminism* (1994) and *Space, Time and Perversion: Essays on the Politics of Bodies* (1995). In addition, many other feminist thinkers such as Italians Adriana Cavarero in her book *In Spite of Plato: A Feminist Rewriting of Ancient Philosophy* (1995) and Muraro have also drawn on classical understandings of body in opposition to the mind.

Some feminist thinkers have considered the body as the centre of their epistemological development. The acknowledgement of the body and its configuration not only problematizes the interaction between the female subject and cultural perspectives but also limits, according to some postmodern theorists such as Butler, gender performances. Such a view, which involves the acceptance and consideration of the materiality of the body, is intimately linked with the way in which tradition shores up the biological predisposition of women and has devalued and dismissed the female body in favour of the male mind. To acknowledge the body and its corporeal dimension as part of the development of feminist thought may cause some controversy, especially in regard to feminist positions such as those of Butler in *Gender Trouble*, or Monique Wittig in *The Straight Mind and Other Essays* (1992), which find the engagement of the body and the consideration of the corporeal as problematic. They see the need to go beyond the biological perspective in order to de-construct the dichotomy of mind/body, which has had deleterious consequences for women historically.

One of the main consequences arising from such a problematic view is precisely the association of the body with biological determinism and the consequent consideration of a body exclusively as corporeal, predisposed to reproduction, static, ahistorical and fixed in opposition to the mind, and without a specific place and space within the intellectual, therefore, political sphere. Thus, in order to dismantle general conventions, it is important to contextualize the development of the female subject in order to grasp the complexities that have surrounded it. In Catalan culture, the body has also been relegated to the two dimensions mentioned previously: secular discourse with the elaboration of a disembodied thought from the origins of classical thought, and religious discourse, with a long tradition of Catholic practice in the peninsula, especially during the Francoist dictatorship, where the body was considered as limited, mortal and ephemeral. As Marçal states:

> A la nostra cultura la diferència s'estableix de manera evident. Fixa't com fa variar la perspectiva tenir un cos de dona o d'home, que és un punt de partida. I és que em sembla que la nostra cultura gira l'esquena al cos, perquè és limitat, és el límit, és mortal i, com que estem molt abocats vers el que és transcendent, cap a la idea d'eternitat. (Sabadell 1998: 15)

In this passage, Marçal recaptures the body as a starting point for reconsidering the perspective whereby the subject can negotiate particular experiences. These experiences become available through the limitations of culture, as she suggests, and the body. In this sense, the body inserted within a definite context provides the specificity whereby such experience can be perceived. These suggestions concern certain parameters that amplify the relationship between body, writing, and their subsequent interaction for the development of a feminist space. The challenges involved in the questioning of the body and its possibilities for the elaboration of a specific female experience open up the debate on poetic composition and the elaboration of thought. Marçal's suggestion that the body is considered limited and mortal as opposed to transcendent and eternal highlights the controversy regarding the concept of the body.

Another problematic consequence derived from the fact of pursuing embodied thought is the supposed direct connection between sex, gender and identity, which theorists such as Butler have explored in depth in their willingness to go beyond the binaries. I shall draw on Butler's view of the discontinuity between sex, gender and identity in order to analyse problems arising from the consideration of the body in Marçal and the Italian account as a starting point for their intellectual and political feminist project. The aim of the following section is to present an overview of the similarities and connections I have found between Marçal's embodied practice and the Italian conceptualisation of the female body in its socio-symbolic practice of entrustment.

The Italian Connection: *Differenza Sessuale* and Socio-Symbolic Practice of Entrustment

Although the term of *differenza sessuale* in Italy is indebted to Irigaray, the Italian feminist understanding of *differenza sessuale* becomes a distinctive one. It is necessary therefore to trace the evolution of feminism in Italy in order to understand why sexual difference shifts slightly from Irigaray's scope and why it becomes distinctive. Inextricably connected to politics, the first feminist text which appeared in Italy concerning women's rights was the *Manifesto Programmatico del gruppo Demau* (1991, first published in 1966) by the group Demau (Demystification of Authority). This text, which recalls the *Comunist Manifesto* (1848) by Karl Marx, was considered as the manifesto of the need for revolution, the need for establishing the female subject as a participant in political and social structures. Some years later in 1970, following the publication of vindicative texts, Carla Lonzi published the controversial text *Sputiamo su Hegel* (*Let's Spit on Hegel*), where she explored the situation of women at the time and clearly exposed how the question of sexual difference had been taken as a negation of the self for women. In this text she highlighted the urgency of considering the female subject as a specific subject, different from the male and with her own particular identity, and rejected equality as an ideological framework for considering women's identity.

Along with the political experience of women from the Communist Party, the invitation to Irigaray by women of the PCI (Communist Party) to give a talk at the women's festival in Tirrenia in 1986 asserted and changed the course of the feminist debate in Italy.[1] As a result of Irigaray's participation in this event, the book *Il tempo della differenza. Diritti e doveri civili per i sessi. Per una rivoluzione pacifica* (1989) was published, and was later translated into English as *Thinking the Sexual Difference: For a Peaceful Revolution* (1994). Irigaray's involvement in this event linked sexual difference to discourses of 'the universal' and 'the neutral', both being analysed from a linguistic point of view.[2]

Universality and Neutrality in Discourse

The traits of universality and neutrality of discourse and the subject influenced the Italian concept of *differenza sessuale*, and especially the women from Libreria delle donne di Milano. Irigaray's understanding of sexual difference is not perceived in Italy as a sign of essentialism but as a political problem, which engages women and their representation within the socio-political arena. They see Irigaray's work as a call to celebrate women's differences and establish a dialogue with political and social institutions, which Irigaray labelled as 'symbolic practice'. The emphasis on difference as a distinctive discourse to dislocate the universal and neutral subject becomes the ground where *il pensiero della differenza sessuale* is elaborated.

Furthermore, the exploration of sexual difference becomes a positive starting point from which to expand and apply this perspective for a concrete alteration of symbolic processes. To examine sexual difference positively implies to take into account the qualities of the corporeal not as a deleterious consequence for women as tradition has stated — through the oppression and objectification of their bodies — but as a productive dimension, which inevitably differentiates one subject from the other. The perspective of sexual difference must not remain within the constraints of theoretical discourses but must transcend into the social and political sphere.

Italian feminists denounce the fact that the modern political system develops a mechanism where the subjugation of female sexual difference is performed not by exclusion but by inclusion. Thus, in this process of assimilation 'women are not *another* subject — with an equally genuine origin and therefore equal dignity and empowerment — but are a sort of empirical specification of the sole male subject' (Cavarero 1992: 33). Hence, women's subjectivity cannot be conceived from the premises of equality. They reject equating 'the woman question' with an egalitarian dimension. To consider 'equal' as 'the same' keeps women's bodies subjected to patriarchy. This sense of sameness carries an unfortunate consequence for women's difference and a sexed thought. From the beginnings of the feminist movement in Italy, the term equality and its understanding have been neglected as a way of performing feminist knowledge.[3] As Lonzi (1970), translated by Paola Bono and Sandra Kemp in *Italian Feminist Thought: A Reader* (1991), suggests in her writing *Sputiamo su Hegel*, at the beginnings of the Italian feminist movement:

> Equality is a juridical principle. To the common denominator of all human beings justice should thus be rendered. Difference is an existential principle which concerns the modes of being human, the peculiarity of one's own experiences, goals, possibilities, and one's sense of existence in a given situation and in the situation one wants to create for oneself. The difference between woman and man is the basic difference of humankind. (41)

On these premises, Lonzi establishes the importance of celebrating women's difference in contrast to the fallacy of equality, which becomes a sophisticated way to keep women's desires within a phallocentric dimension. Sexual difference foregrounds the importance of acknowledging the perspectives of the body. Being a man or being a woman is not neutral as it offers different bodily perspectives of the world that surrounds each sex. This is not to say that the two biological corpo-realities develop a dual perspective of subjectivity. It suggests that the parameters, which have structured these two sexed beings, have not operated similarly. In this sense, the task is to identify the different postulates that have traditionally developed those processes of identity, insofar as the laws governing both spheres are diverse, and hierarchically established. In the course of fragmenting the monolithic discourse of patriarchy, the first step is to acknowledge the unequal premises that have operated for both sexed beings, establishing only these two subjectivities as politically recognized.

In this interpretation, the universal concept of 'man' as 'human' does not include sexual difference. There is only one form of signification, which has been categorised as objective, even though it does not represent the different possibilities of being. Italian feminist thought calls for a deconstruction of the 'apparent' universality and neutrality of the thinking subject, reconsidering the need to specify the existing different subjectivities and appealing to the specificity of the female subject. In 'The need for a sexed thought' Cavarero formulates that:

> The greatest danger lies in not acknowledging the *need* for a sexed thought, in acknowledging instead its superfluidity. If western culture is not put into question, not in its specific features, but in its deep and founding male

essence; if on the contrary its neutral-objective value is recognized, culture produced from women's point of view becomes an adjunct, a production alongside the other. (1991: 184)[4]

Cavarero advocates that there is an imperative need to (de)neutralize Western culture and its system of thought, which is shaped as neutral, universal, objective and exclusively male-referenced. In this article, she critiques the fact that women's perspectives are still unrecognized. To follow an objective, universal system of thought contributes to negating the existence of a female subject as the subject is exclusively male. In order to disentangle such a universal framework, there are some concepts and understandings which must be revised and redefined such as 'mankind', 'humanity', 'human' or 'the self'. On this point, Cavarero proposes developing a heuristic process, whereby the female subject can interact with the system of thought. She states: 'I want to make a very simple point, but very important for us: the *need* for thought of sexual difference, a need not only born of desire, but founded in theory, and ready to bear the strain of conceptualisation' (1991: 183). She draws upon the problematic of the subject of discourse, specifically upon the interaction of women with the symbolic when they try to speak, or even simply to think. The dominance of this neutral-male subject transcends from his own specificity to the universal. As a result, the female subject does not have a place from which to complete the same process; her own specificity cannot transcend and be considered as an actual subject of the universal. It is in this sense that the Italian concept of sexual difference vindicates the female cogito and the need to give meaning to the female body: 'sexual difference is an originary human difference. We must not enclose it in this or that meaning, but must accept it along with our being-body and render it significant: an inexhaustible source of ever-new meanings' (Libreria delle donne di Milano 1990: 125).

The idea of needing to overcome universal and neutral male-dominant discourse raises the following issues: firstly, to assume that the specificity of the female subject enacts some considerations of universality of the identity of woman at the same level of abstraction. Secondly, such an assumption engages with the understanding that there must be an identity *a priori* or a pre-given identity following, or determinant from, the body, which adds to the confines of conceiving the binary discourse of masculine/feminine that results from splitting the male-dominant structure. Using Butler's perspective on cultural constructionist thought on the performance of subjectivity, I shall focus on providing a critical account of this problematic that the Italian understanding of sexual difference may reveal in its conceptualization of the female cogito as a strategy to thwart patriarchal discourse. I question how the universal dimension contributes to providing an ahistorical disembodied subject. Also, I examine how the theorization of a supposed given identity does not consider the plurality, diversity and particularity of different subjectivities attending the context which surrounds them and excludes again certain performances of subjectivities. There is a need to acknowledge not only the disparity of differing discourses but also different experiences among women. For now, it is compelling to approach the issue of fragmenting the structure of the male discourse from a variety of dimensions that problematize such stipulations. It is precisely this critique that the following section will focus on.

Universality versus Particularity

The problematic concept of acknowledging the female body and claiming the need for sexed thought raises some controversy concerning parameters of identity and representation. How can we demand the acknowledgement of the female cogito without falling into the trap of universalizing such female cogito? Will this reinforce patriarchal parameters which subjugate, limit, and constrain different possibilities of 'being'? To split the epistemological account and knowledge into the structure of a sexed thought opens up a debate, involving various stages and levels, and provokes a certain anxiety within the feminist movement. Using Butler's theoretical postulates of the sex/gender dimension, I critically examine the dangers of acknowledging the body as a starting point for an epistemological development and a specific means of political representation. Butler writes:

> Universalistic claims are based on a common or shared epistemological standpoint, understood as the articulated consciousness or shared structures of oppression or in the ostensibly transcultural structures of femininity, maternity, sexuality, and/or *écriture féminine*. (Butler 1990: 14)

With the critique of universality that the category of woman involves, Butler, in her acclaimed book *Gender Trouble*, opens the question of identity and the controversy of gender performance. The quotation above reveals the conflicts she finds in certain feminist positions, especially those which are more intensively engaged with bodily perspectives such as sexual difference. According to Butler's statement quoted above, the perspective of sexual difference reinforces a unity which includes all possible representations of subjectivity within a fixed category. In this sense, concepts such as femininity, maternity, sexuality and *écriture féminine* have an abstract quality that makes them common to all sociohistorical contexts regardless of place and time. Consequently, such displaced, decontextualized and disembodied frameworks establish a new hierarchy within the consideration of subjectivities and reinforce the performance of the heterosexual female subject. But to what extent can we consider such concepts as universals? For Butler, the problem lies in considering the category of woman as a universal identity with the common aim of freedom from patriarchy. In this sense, Butler equates feminism to a universal subject: woman. She criticizes the category of woman and universal discourse, which the perspective of sexual difference seems to vindicate based upon its premise of a common project.

She tackles this allegedly apparent universal conception of woman and its monolithic consequence for gender perspectives and the politics of representation. In addition, she states that such specificity is not only exclusionary but also reinforces the binary of masculine/feminine. Butler finally suggests that the recognition of such specificity decontextualizes and displaces the female subject from other singularities such as class or race, also inherent to the subject. However, despite Butler's formulation, the position of the female subject within patriarchy does not exclude other points of interaction within the political landscape. Surely, what Butler suggests is that the acclaimed specificity of sexual difference enhances traditional postulates which have equated the female body with a sort of specific subject that does not enjoy the benefits of the complete and rational male subject.

Perhaps this is part of the problem of attempting to theorize a subject who has never been the subject of her own theory, and who has always been conceptualized as an appendix to the main discourse. Perhaps this is also why Butler starts her critique by positing the importance of the *historical present*, taken from Marx (1990: 5), and has centred her work on the politics of gender representation. The difficulty of interacting with a subject that is still fragmented theoretically brings up the possibility of failing to theorize it. Yet how can a starting point be based on a historical present without grasping the structure which has been governing social and political contexts hitherto? How can we guarantee a redefinition of multiple subjectivities without analysing the points used to constrain specific political identities so far? Is it safe to start a deconstructive process without being familiar with the roots that have traditionally constituted such a political basis?

Indeed, the purpose of calling for a sexed thought and the acknowledgement of sexual difference entails the inherent danger of providing the reversed answer to the questions formulated, and the imperative need to establish a sexed thought may reinforce patriarchal parameters. However, sexual difference needs to come into dialogue with the discourses that orchestrate the patriarchal structure, in a way that seeks to convey a reformulating of the specificity of the female body and grasps the possibilities that the fragmented subject of woman may encounter, as a source of establishing an effective female experience. By demanding a rupture of the universality of thought and epistemology, Italian feminists took a step forward in the globalized dimension of politics. My intention, therefore, is not to come to terms with the parameters of an essentialist and cultural constructivist debate, but to draw — through the specificity of the theoretical framework of women of *il pensiero* — a specific methodology that provides an alternative reading of women's experiences and which establishes, as one of its main points, the unmasking of the presumed commonality amongst women by positing as a starting point the particular experience of each embodied subject within the socio-historical present that surrounds the female subject. Furthermore, this book seeks to contribute in this way to the voicing of the silenced experiences yet to be spoken. It is not the purpose of the Italian feminists and Marçal's aesthetics to establish a set of limitations and fixed experiences which correspond to a unique subject. To assert this would be a mistake and would thwart the purposes of feminism, gender thought, and the aim of this research. The mechanisms that operate in the process of establishing such signification are developed in the practice of entrustment which offers an alternative space to give symbolic existence to female difference, the vicissitudes of which will be explored further in the next part of this chapter.

Socio-Symbolic Practice of Entrustment

The social and political practices that some Italian women were carrying out in terms of double militancy foregrounded the problematic relationship of women within patriarchy.[5] The socio-symbolic practice of *affidamento* became the specific and distinctive practice of Italian feminism. It appeared as a result of such particular practices being carried out by Libreria delle donne di Milano. As a result, they published a book entitled *Non credere di avere dei diritti: la generazione della libertà femminile nell' idea e nelle vicende di un gruppo di donne* (1987) that emphasized the 'need to make sense of, exalt, and represent in words and images the relationship of one woman to another' (1990: 25).[6] This wish to represent women's practices is derived from the need to search for the space of a female symbolic, yet unnamed and inexistent, but still part of the project of the socio-symbolic practice of entrustment: 'we believe that to write theory is partly to tell about practice, since theoretical reasoning generally refers to things which already have names. Here we are dealing partly with things that had no names' (1990: 25).

The issue of a sense of inadequacy first appeared immediately after the publication of '*Piú donne che uomini*' ('More women than men') in the journal *Sottosopra*.[7] In this text, women described problems encountered in their practices in social and political affairs despite legal achievements in civil rights:

> We have fought, effectively, against the social poverty of women's condition. We have discovered the originality, which goes with the fact of being women. Through the political practice of relations between women, by spending time with other women, by loving other women, we have to come to value ourselves. But at the moment we have no way of translating the experience, the knowledge and the value of being women into social reality. (Libreria delle donne di Milano 1991: 110–11)

As this passage states, these women were demanding the essential need to discuss and open up the question of why women were still experiencing a feeling of inadequacy, despite their efforts to perform in social life. Italian thinkers take this sense of failure not as a fault of the individual but as a starting point from which to work on women's own needs and wants. This feeling of inadequacy was described by women from the Libreria as a feeling of 'estrangement'.[8] In this publication, they describe the feeling of estrangement that a woman experiences when she cannot find social representations of her own desires. This problematic evolves into what they called 'the wish to win through', which expresses women's desire to surpass this difficulty and to find a female symbolic. As a result, both 'estrangement' and 'the wish to win through' become two important consequences of the vicissitudes of expressing female desire within the symbolic order. However, these need to be explored in order to change women's place in society and to find a possibility for self-definition. Women from Libreria devoted themselves to developing a socio-symbolic practice, which connects theory and practice and involves an interaction between the symbolic structures and the web of social images and representations that historically and politically determines women's identity. This implies an exploration of sexual difference and the mechanisms and devices that operate in such process.

According to their descriptive text of entrustment, there are several issues that contribute to women's feeling of estrangement within the symbolic dimension. One of the problems results from the complex interaction between the female body and the linguistic system. On this point, Cavarero has stated that in the process of significance the speaking subject (male) interacts actively and directly with the system of language. In contrast, the relationship of the female subject with the linguistic realm becomes a stark process, as Lacanian postulates have demonstrated. Women from *il pensiero* have worked on this uncertainty experienced by women within the linguistic space and have manifested their 'estrangement' in the system of language:

> Uncertainty about our sexuality separates us from any order of discourse we don't have a language of our own, and are forced to use the words of others if we want to express any part of our new knowledge. The 'contradictory ambiguity of our knowledge' derives from this. (Libreria delle donne di Milano 1990: 108)

In response to this uncertainty, they have worked with the linguistic implications of the female subject. As their only possibility to grasp the roots of such uncertainty, they conceive the system of language as a 'symbolic structure of mediation' between their experience as speaking subjects and the socio-symbolic context. The suggested discontinuity between women and language endorses the absence of a symbolic place (*collocazione simbolica*) within patriarchy. The vagueness and consequent conflictive interaction of women within the linguistic dimension destabilizes the position of women writers in literary practice:

> Without a symbolic placement, the female mind is afraid; exposed to unpredictable events, everything befalls it from outside the body. Neither the laws nor rights can give a woman the self-confidence she lacks. A woman can acquire inviolability by creating a life which has its starting point in herself and is guaranteed by female sociality. (Libreria delle donne di Milano 1990: 31)

This lack of female mediation reveals not only the difficult situation of women writers but also the absence of a female reference to which women writers can have free access in order to identify their subjectivity and thus contribute to the construction of a feminine genealogy.[9] Therefore, the practice of entrustment aims to provide the symbolic placement needed. This dimension of symbolic practice can only be configured if there is a previous theoretical fragmentation of the patriarchal order. That is to say, to work from a position of sexual difference is not to describe a process whereby we establish a myriad set of rules to depict the relationship between man and woman. Rather, it is to engage with the specific purpose of offering the alternative of searching for a multiform existence and varied participation in the world. The emphasis on considering differences and disparity amongst women as a central point for sexual difference practices is explained by *il pensiero*'s suggestion of *affidamento*, entrustment. It is for these reasons that women from the Libreria proposed the practice of *affidamento*.

The actual process of entrustment consists of an interaction between two women, where one of them becomes the guide to the other and, through interaction, she 'entrusts' her desire to her guide. The guide then becomes her reference between herself and the social sphere. This mentor is considered as a figure of empowerment and gives value to the other woman. She finds her symbolic mediation precisely in the heterogeneity and disparity between them. Their different positions provide them with the necessary changes in symbolic relations between women, creating exchanges and rejecting equality in every way. Entrustment thus becomes both the space that bridges the feeling of estrangement and the construction of a new female symbolic order. *Affidamento* is therefore a mediation between women's desires and the representation of these in a transformed symbolic dimension.

The practice of entrustment celebrates the possibility of a female genealogy. Not only does it offer a critique of patriarchy and the situation of marginality suffered by women historically but it also provides an alternative space in which women's desires can take shape and transcend into the social dimension both synchronically and diachronically.

Marçal's Aesthetics

Marçal's understanding of feminism is dialectically fused with the production of poetry. For Marçal, the poetic exercise is intimately linked with her experience as a woman. The intellectual activity of poetry cannot be extricated from her experience of the body and the socio-historical space of her *ser dona*. As the scholar, and Marçal's friend, Julià has stated: 'manifesta i aprofundeix en la doble exclusió que viu la dona: exclosa de la història, estranya de la pròpia identitat' (Julià 2000: 354). Marçal's writings become the result of a profound cognitive exercise of her experience as a woman and her relationship with language and the act of writing itself. Both feminism and poetry form an inextricable binary whose oscillation affects both spheres. Marçal explored her own creativity and poetic production in relation to different processes of signification. Such processes are developed on two levels: the symbolic, which posits woman in relation to language and writing; and the historical, where Marçal analyses and uses poetry as a discourse that flows from individual to collective images and diachronic fragmentations of such images in the public space of Literature. For Marçal, feminism:

> lliga molt l'espai privat i el col·lectiu. N'és indestriable, perquè com deia abans el problema principal és el tema de la identitat de les dones, i això és absolutament una barreja d'afirmació individual, d'aprofundiment en la teva experiència, i de vinculació col·lectiva. (Montero 2004: 263)

Both levels of exploration described above — symbolic and historical — aim to elaborate, to construct a new feminine space necessary for a woman writer in order to shape her experience and contribute to the creation of a female genealogy. Her work as a writer, thus, can be placed at the intersection of these two levels. Marçal engages her symbolic placement as a woman with her historical position as a writer. Her aesthetics are grounded upon a dialectic interaction of her position as a woman both historically and symbolically.

Marçal's feminism evolved gradually from the activist militancy of the early years of the post-dictatorial period to a more cognitive practice, with a poetic engagement and profound thought. Marçal's disenchantment with the new socio-political system culminated in a change in her manner of involvement with the process of feminism. After an active political and social militancy during the period of transition,[10] Marçal devoted herself to contributing to feminism from a more intellectual perspective, whereby experience and the subject of such experience elaborate her own discourse. This discourse is the poem, whose space gives shape to new configurations and images that enhance collective representation of the female experience. Julià has suggested that Marçal's feminism comes from a disappointment with the political stage where 'the emancipated woman' cannot resolve the problem of equal rights: 'emancipation puts us into a social game with words and desires which are not our own' (Libreria delle donne di Milano 1991: 115).[11] In this sense, feminism for Marçal is understood in literary terms, where tradition and her particular imagery intersect:

> En certa manera el feminisme ha determinat també algunes de les meves influències de caire literari i formal, com per exemple la de la cançó popular tradicional, on l'emprempta de les dones és ben perceptible. I ha determinat també el meu món simbòlic que s'ha alimentat en gran part de símbols i imatges lligades tradicionalment a la feminitat (la lluna, la bruixa, la mar, la sal, la sang) però que una consciència feminista ha sotmès a un procés de redefinició, n'ha forçat els límits fins a fer-los dir coses diferents, d'acord amb la meva realitat. (Barcelona BC, FMMM, Fira-dona i literatura, 16/6)

Poetry for Marçal becomes a form of research, an investigation of her body and her identity. Her literary production evidences an inherent intention to find novel and alternative modes of expressing female desire. In this sense, poetry becomes the space in which new configurations of the female subject can be explored. In her study of poetry, *Filosofía y poesía* (1993b), philosopher María Zambrano has stated that in poetry 'las cosas se nos aparecen sumergidas en el flujo del tiempo; se nos muestran como naciendo y tornando a nacer. Su presencia es un milagro, el milagro primero de la aparición de las cosas. Poesía es sentir las cosas en *status nascens*' (120–21). The genre of poetry with its combination of synchronic experiences and its capacity to represent these experiences, as Zambrano suggests, bridges Marçal's attempts to recapture the past and re-write it. In this sense, her writing:

> implica una posició inèdita en la poesia catalana, s'alça com a revolta i descriu una indagació: revolta, des del moment que assumeix explícitament la identitat de dona més enllà de tot clixé; indagació, perquè la seva escriptura esdevé recerca incessant de la identitat femenina, i gradualment del seu lesbianisme. (Julià 2000: 355)

Marçal's feminism and poetry incessantly aim to recover the female body from historical silence. However, she rejects traditional female images and references. In her poems she goes beyond the limits of the biological body, which has been traditionally exiled from the cultural sphere. Her understanding of feminism is based on a heuristic process in which she constantly rereads other women's writings, analyses them, studies them, and tries to discover the fragments dispersed amidst the history of philosophy and literature. In order to do so, she revisits the myths of ancient classical literature. In the following section, I shall explore how these myths offer a symbolic route to understanding how the identity of woman has been created both historically and culturally in Western tradition.

Defining the Methodology: Revisiting the Myths

For Marçal, the interaction between woman and writing cannot be understood if the parameters that connect women with culture or the symbolic space have not yet been clarified. In this sense, Marçal developed her task of reconfiguring the ancient myths as a process of returning to the roots of Western civilization where the category of Woman was constructed. Marçal considered myths to be the representation of collective images. The introspective exploration of myths became one of the backbones of her discourse. She finds a connection between the linguistic fragmentation of women's writing and the interpretation of these myths as the origins of Western culture. According to Irigaray, Western civilization is based on an original matricide.[12] The myth of Clytemnestra shows how the law of the father is imposed through the death of the mother. Clytemnestra was killed by her son Orestes, who, after his mother's murder, had to restore order. Previously, Clytemnestra had killed her husband, Orestes' father, Agamemnon, because he sacrificed his daughter Iphigenia to the gods. Orestes was judged and finally pardoned by Athena. This demonstrates that a return to order and the laws of the *polis* can only be possible if the son kills the mother. However, despite committing this crime, he is forgiven by Athena — another woman — goddess of Attica.

Marçal returns to these origins and analyses how women, body and language are represented in the myth. This revisionary work allows her to investigate the mechanisms involved in the equation of woman with Literature. Her study of myths reveals a more profound understanding of the ideas and meanings connected to the construction of the category of woman from its very foundations in the historical patriarchal approach.

In her book *Women in Ancient Greece*, Sue Blundell sees the study of myths as particularly important in investigating the mechanisms whereby meanings are brought together in order to shape a specific understanding of women from the male perspective:

> These stories can help to reveal to us the response to women experienced by men living in a patriarchal society: what makes myth a very different source from, say, a philosophical treatise on the duties of a wife, is the fantasy element. Through myth we can reach the unconscious, rather than the logically-argued, notions which men entertained about women. In this way we can gain an insight into the symbolic value accorded to women — into what, in fact, the term 'Woman' meant to men. (Blundell 1995: 16)

There is also an intimate connection between myths and the genre of poetry. Myths were transmitted through poetry, since poetry was the first form of written expression in Western civilization with poets such as Hesiod, who wrote the *Theogony* about the formation of the world, and Homer, who wrote the *Iliad*. Marçal rereads the myth of Athena's birth in order to analyse the particular relationship of women with literature: for her, the birth of Athena reveals the first contact of women with the cultural sphere. The poet herself confessed to being fascinated by this myth, and, in her talk about women and writing 'Més enllà i més ençà del mirall de la Medusa' (1996a), recited an unpublished poem:

> Del cap diàfan
> del pare et creies néixer
> closa i armada.
> Des de l'escut et fita
> i t'emmiralla en pedra
> -esdevinguda monstre-
> la nuesa negada. (163)

Athena's birth represents the first encounter of women with culture and the arena of knowledge. It narrates the construction of female identity through patriarchy. I will thus offer a brief account of this myth and how it explains the relationship of woman with literature.

Metis was the first wife of Zeus, and, when she was pregnant with Athena, Zeus swallowed her whole in order to assume her power. Athena was born from Zeus' head. She was born without her mother and completely dressed 'sense contacte inicial amb la seva pròpia nuesa' (Marçal 1996a: 163), wearing a helmet and holding a shield with the face of the Medusa (a Gorgon).[13] This myth shows a clear desire to celebrate the triumph of male rule over the female with an inverted delivery: a man giving birth to a woman. Like Athena, the woman writer is literally born from patriarchy, the force and power of which has swallowed female strength and knowledge, leaving women's creativity and authority unacknowledged. Marçal interprets this birth in these words:

> Protegida pel llegat patern de l'armadura que l'embolcalla, que li estalvia, potser, recordar que el seu cos és com el de la Metis espoliada i invisible, la imatge d'Atenea evoca, a primer cop d'ull, la dona que assumeix un arquetip viril, però també pot ser, simplement, la dona revestida de Dona, és a dir, la feminitat entesa com a construcció conceptual masculina. (1996a: 164)

In this reading of the myth of the birth of Athena there is a polarized set of images of women that correspond to the two different concepts which have been constructed upon women's subjectivity. On one hand, we have the figure of Athena conceived from a patriarchal point of view: the androgynous figure, visually represented as a warrior — the guise she wore when she was born.[14] This androgynous figure of Athena blurs the specificity of her sex and demonstrates the assimilation of woman into patriarchy. Her image seems to be neutralized with a male façade, covered with men's clothes. Athena cannot be connected with her own nudity, and as a consequence she cannot have contact with her body as a woman:

> Imatge de la nuesa negada d'Atenea, d'allò que queda exclòs de la construcció cultural, de l'ordre simbòlic del patriarcat: la no-accessibilitat des de la cultura a l'elaboració de la pròpia diferència sexual. Aquesta part de si mateixa ha quedat alienada, expulsada fora de si mateixa, convertida en pedra. (1996a: 164)

On the other hand, we find the presence of another female figure: Medusa the Gorgon, who symbolizes chaos and monstrosity. In Greek mythology Medusa is a snake-haired figure who has the power to turn men to stone with a glance. On Athena's statue, Medusa's face appears on the shield. The power of Medusa symbolises man's fear of women in ancient Greece, which Marçal reads as: 'dona monstre, el femení indomenyat, salvatge i perillós. Mirada petrificadora d'allò que es exclòs, no dit, que, encarada al mirall, s'ha petrificat a si mateixa' (1996a: 164). Both images of woman appear to represent the neutralized, assimilated body from the male perspective, and the exile of the woman poet from her own experience. As a result, the images of women available within the cultural sphere are those which represent excess, irrationality and monstrosity ('la dona monstre'), or those which show the deficiency of women through a woman who enters the cultural dimension 'being like' a man: dressed up in men's clothes and alienated from her nude body just as Athena is.

Marçal and the Practice of 'Difference'

Marçal understands the intellectual act of writing poetry through the elaboration of the writer's experience. She appropriates the specificity of the individual experience of the poet as part of a chain that constitutes the common experience of Literature and thus of a particular culture. Thus, both individual experience and the final production of literary texts are components that create historical testimonies of a specific context. Marçal examined the transcendence of this process for women writers and deplored the absence of women poets in the literary arena. Her critique of patriarchy and the institution of Literature lies in denouncing the silence, which women writers, and particularly women poets, continuously face:

> El moll de la qüestió sembla residir en la incapacitat de concebre la diferència si no és en termes jeràrquics. . . i hi ha diferències fins ara irreductibles i gens banals: un cos diferent, una vivència diferent del temps i de la sang, una forma de respirar diferent en la reproducció humana. . . fins a quin punt la meva escriptura diguem-ne 'de dona' es veu condicionada i/o alimentada per aquesta pertinença estrictament de sexe? (1995a: 191)

In Marçal's essay, 'Llengua abolida: Poesia, gènere, identitat' (1995a), she states that historically one half of human experience has not been represented, as there is no chain of written evidence of it, only fragmented images. The analysis of a fragmented female genealogy becomes the cornerstone of her intellectual work. Yet, as she has suggested in another essay, 'Per deixar d'ésser inexistents' (given at the series of seminars 'Women and Catalan literature'): 'em caldrà, doncs, moure'm en el camp de l'experiència i de les reflexions quotidianes entorn de la pràctica d'escriure, amb cos i ment de dona, dins d'una societat i una cultura de signe — no cal que ho digui — masculí (1986: 33). Marçal laments the recognition of only one gendered experience understood universally as human: 'es posa de manifest la fal·làcia que suposa identificar gènere masculí i gènere humà: identificació absolutament vigent encara en la majoria de textos històrics i d'història literària, en els manuals, en les antologies, etc' (1995a: 191). Due to the historical relationship of women with culture, this situation affects the perspective of the woman poet.

Statistical evidence shows that one part of human experience, the female, has been less elaborated upon than the other, the male, raising certain questions. Does this mean that women do not write poetry? Is this significant in terms of the non-recognition of different, that is, non-male experience? Is the sex of the poet considered when writing, and is this a criterion for analysing poetic texts? The oscillation from individual subjectivity as a woman to a collective identity as a writer is produced in Marçal's work through the consideration of her body as a woman and the practice of her *ser dona*:

> Crec que és molt important, que el cos hi és en tot, que en definitiva no som res més. Per això, si hi ets al text, el teu cos hi és d'alguna manera i, quan no hi és, també aquesta absència és una manera de ser-hi. (Sabadell 1998: 15)

The consideration of the body, however, is no longer used in Marçal's work to establish a political and social order, but, rather, is a category implied in the signification of the body as the representation of this order. In other words, for Marçal, sexual difference considers the body as an open space, which intersects with the cultural realm. Being a woman is not a metaphysical understanding but the historical and political position of the flesh, which transcends directly into a symbolic performance.

The concept of difference brings together two elements that Marçal inextricably interlinks: body and experience. Starting from a different biological body, Marçal develops all her writing around the female experience, derived from this specific *ser dona*. As a result, the process of meaning in Marçal's work occurs through the interaction of the body and the experience derived from it, subsequently performed in the socio-symbolic context. This process integrates the body as a biological organism within cultural practices, with a transcendent result in the political dimension. The female subject for Marçal becomes a body; that is to say, the woman achieves subjectivity in her own body, which occupies a place in space and time, synchronically and diachronically, and thus historically and functionally. In the following section this interaction will be examined.

Delimiting the Configuration of 'ser dona'

One of the most important considerations for understanding Marçal's perspective on feminism and poetry is to posit the origins of her production as a result of the vicissitudes she experiences as a woman. Despite the vagueness of such an assertion, this is particularly important in order to foreground Marçal's theoretical development and her feminist projection in poetry as a revolt against male-dominated discourse. In her own words:

> Encara circula la idea que ser dona és menys que ser persona i per això sembla que hi ha la necessitat d'afirmar que jo sóc abans que res una persona. En canvi, jo considero que el fet de ser dona (o home) és més, afegeix alguna connotació, alguna coloració al fet de ser persona i, per tant, no és una restricció, sinó una addició. (Sabadell 1998: 15)

Similarly, *il pensiero* takes the realm of sexual difference beyond the limits of the body and the cultural paradigm of gender and considers the interaction between these two spaces within the symbolic dimension. That is to say, *differenza sessuale* goes beyond theoretical premises and establishes a practice of 'being'. The purpose of this section is to delineate the limits of 'being' that determine such a practice. What are the premises that allow Marçal to establish her *ser dona* as a standpoint for her writings?

The mechanisms whereby the legitimacy of the subject and of sexual identity are formed in the Lacanian perspective reveal the patriarchal constructive mediation of such understanding. In positing the phallus as the signifier and mark of identity, Lacan establishes the formation of the sexed subject based on two disembodied structures. On one hand, there is the ontological predisposition of the resulting beings: those, who 'have' the phallus and those who 'are' the phallus. The subject who 'is' the phallus functions as the desired object of the 'one', leaving the space of the 'other' for the one who 'is' the phallus. On the other hand, the validity of such account can only be possible if one of the subjects — the woman — serves as the object that reasserts the existence of such structure. To formulate this in linguistic terms, 'being' stands for not interacting with the linguistic system; women, therefore, become the subjects who stand for this understanding of 'being'.

Women writers, Marçal in particular, challenge such presuppositions by re-appropriating the linguistic system as a mediation for reconfiguring certain pre-established notions of what constitutes the category of woman. In the following pages, I intend to show that *ser dona* does not remain as a marginal position of the symbolic but as an intervention in such symbolic scope through the appropriation of language as a writer, and her irruption into male-dominated discourses.

According to the binary division of 'being' and 'having' the phallus in Lacanian ontology, 'being', as I have stated, upholds patriarchal structures which consider any subjectivity other than the masculine as outside, as a marginal object of desire with no possibility of interaction within the linguistic dimension and, therefore, within social and cultural structures. Hence, can *ser dona* be productive for the reconfiguration of such specific subjectivity? How can it be considered in terms of praxis?

Taking such Lacanian postulates on the formation of the sexed subject and the process of significance, the question of 'being', as we have seen, finds its meaning through the linguistic parameters of the 'phallus' as a signifier. In this way, subjectivity and the process of a sexual identity come to terms with the presence and/or absence of the phallus. As confirmation of this, Lacan establishes a clear difference between those who *have* the phallus and those who *are* the phallus. In this sense, to 'have' the phallus and 'to be' the phallus determines clear, divergent sexual positions, which also follow different processes of signification and, thus, disparate categories of identity.

Butler revisits this Lacanian ontology that suggests that the process of identity is established through the binary between 'having' and 'being' the phallus. According to her, the contrast between this binary is established in oppositional and hierarchical terms. That is to say, there is a primacy of 'having' the phallus over 'being' the phallus, both positions being culturally constructed through the symbolic. This is articulated when, in Lacan, 'being' the phallus is a direct consequence of 'not having' the phallus, which marks the process of signification in oppositional terms, and, as Butler says, 'every effort to establish identity within the terms of this binary disjunction of "being" and "having" returns to the inevitable "lack" and "loss" that ground their phantasmatic construction and mark the incommensurability of the Symbolic and the real' (1990: 44).

Consequently, 'being' in Lacanian terms is equated with occupying the position of the repressed subject, who is characterized by lack, loss, and absence, as a result of 'not having' the signifier. And it is in this sense that the divergent positions of the different subjects involved in the process of signification result from the construction of structure itself. Thus, women, who are those who do 'not have' the phallus, occupy the place of 'being'. According to this postulate, 'being' is identified merely as a function in favour of the masculine subject who has the phallus and finds his subjectivity as a result of configuring his own desire. The place of 'being' in Lacan remains equated to the place of 'woman-being', which is relegated to the object of desire and to what Lacan denominates *masquerade*.[15] Yet, according to Butler, in Lacanian terms, women are said to 'be' the phallus and men to 'have' the phallus:

> Women are said to 'be' the Phallus in the sense that they maintain postures of the masculine subject, a power which, if withdrawn, would break up the foundational illusions of the masculine subject position. In order to 'be' the Phallus, the reflector and guarantor of an apparent masculine subject position, women must become, must 'be' (in the sense of 'posture as if they were') precisely what men are not and, in their very lack, establish the essential function of men. Hence, 'being' the Phallus is always a 'being for' a

masculine subject who seeks to reconfirm and augment his identity through the recognition of that 'being for'. (1990: 45)

One of the problems of 'being' is that, as Butler has suggested, women in their 'being' reinforce the power established by patriarchal law. By this means, *ser dona* becomes a mere process of transference, as its space is controlled by male-dominated desire. If the subject is constructed through language, then 'being' becomes a characteristic inherent in women as lack and loss.

One might argue, thus, that the subject of 'being' becomes a disembodied subject. Furthermore, the loss, lack and absence become possible exclusively through the repression of the maternal body and the continuous rejection of the mother by the female child. In the process of identity and signification in Lacanian narrative, the repressed maternal body is that which permits the subject to acquire her identity. When the father intervenes and breaks the unity of mother and child, the child, who experiences the loss immediately, will try to bring the mother back — in Lacan's terminology, the 'phallic mother'. In this way women 'are' said to 'be' the phallus and assert patriarchal laws with their woman-being.

Despite establishing the limits of 'being' within the linguistic structure, the debate has now been reopened by Italian feminist thinkers of *il pensiero* whose theories, centred on the female cogito, provide the theoretical space to revise, analyse and redefine the processes whereby the *ser dona* can alter the paternal law of the symbolic.[16] Taking the Italian perspective of sexual difference and socio-symbolic practice, I suggest that *ser dona* does not represent a functional fixed position. Rather, woman-being challenges the position of the woman as object by embracing the linguistic dimension as a mediating space. By these means, when she decides to write the woman writer alters the Lacanian laws that govern the linguistic dimension and the cultural performance of subjects. As a consequence, the woman writer breaks the dichotomy established by Lacan and the symbolism of the phallus. The interaction between the woman writer and the linguistic realm challenges Lacanian structures of the process of signification. To connect women with language through the process of writing means to dislocate a prescriptive understanding of 'being'. In this sense, 'being' cannot be constructed as the opposite of 'having' the signifier.

If one of the difficulties of Lacan is found in the fixed production of a theory of identity that encompasses the effects of a disembodied thought, to what extent does the acknowledgement of the body in the process of identification affect the performance of *ser dona*? Is it necessary to take into account the materiality of the body in such a process? Given the problematic of *ser dona* in linguistic terms, it is imperative thus to provide a critical perspective on the limitations of the body, and the boundaries of corporeality in the process of a gendered subjectivity. These related issues will be explored in the following section.

The Meaning of Corporeality in the Process of Developing a Poetic Gendered Identity

What is a 'body'? Do we 'have' a body? Or 'are' we a body? To what extent does the body interfere with the substantiation of the subject? The question of the corporeality and the materiality of the body assume a highly controversial position in Marçal's poetry. Marçal's poems and subsequent theoretical reflections correspond to the idea of a corporeal subject and an embodied thought. Yet, to what extent does the materiality of the body regulate subjectivity or cultural representation of identity? Or, is identity shaped within the limits of the body? What is the place of the body?

In the introduction to *Gender Trouble*, Butler addresses the materiality of the body within the process of a gendered subjectivity. She reconfigures the submissive, underestimated female body and woman from a cultural perspective, which allows her to redefine the body without falling back into categories that limit, constrain and universalize it. Butler tackles the vicissitudes of the subject and its political representation and criticizes the monolithic structure of feminist thought which seeks to expand the exploration of woman as a subject within the limitations of such a category. She starts her critique by arguing materiality as an irreducible and fixed category. In *Bodies that Matter* (1993), Butler also analyses the materiality of the body and the extent to which such materiality intervenes in the process of subjectivity. Revisiting philosophical discourses and the binomial mind/matter, Butler engages with the masterly discourse of philosophy in order to grasp the debates which have contributed to division of mind and body and have examined the supremacy of the former over the latter. She considers conceptions such as *chora* and *mater* in Plato and Aristotle, as well as Irigarayan configurations of such philosophical accounts. Her critique argues that such materiality works as a prescriptive condition for feminism. She says:

> against those who would claim that the body's irreducible materiality is a necessary precondition for feminist practice, I suggest that prized materiality may well be constituted through an exclusion and degradation of the feminine that is profoundly problematic for feminism. (Butler 1993: 30)

To link the materiality of the body with theoretical bodily perspectives, according to Butler, connects with the biological predisposition of the female body to reproduction. In this sense, this association becomes problematic for the female subject. Butler refers to Greek notions of *mater* and *matrix* to establish the process of signification, the origins of which lie in classical configurations of matter. If one of the main critical points to be addressed is the consideration of the materiality of the feminine body within the dimension of matter, we must consider the controversial subject of the biological capability of women to give birth. In this sense, Butler explores corporeality as an effect of power, whose normative works in favour of considering 'sex' as a pre-given category. She states:

> 'Sex' is, thus, not simply what one has, or a static description of what one is: it will be one of the norms by which the 'one' becomes viable at all, that which qualifies a body for life within the domain of cultural intelligibility. (Butler 1993: 2)

Despite the complexities of exploring the vicissitudes of matter and its critical meanings, as elucidated by Irigaray, Butler reasserts that both thinkers have conceived their critiques within a phallocentric perspective, and that their investigations are based on the binary masculine/feminine, since the starting point for both is the consideration of the feminine as a subordinated category in opposition to the hegemony of the masculine. However, one might argue that if to consider the materiality of the body means to deconstruct it through a degrading or exclusive process, as Butler has previously suggested, where is the reconfiguration of the female subject within the socio-political dimension if we take as a starting point the marginal position to which patriarchy has historically relegated women? Derived from this problematic lies the question of feminism, as we have previously analysed, that inevitably intersects with the dimension of the body.

Also, it is important to question the limitations of the body, as we know that the body is malleable and it can be altered — although the legitimacy of the transformations suffered by the matter of the body is arguable. However, this is not to assume that the body is a fixed, monolithic discourse with natural origins. This would only be possible if the subject remains an abstract, ahistorical and atemporal entity, and this is not what is at stake here. Rather, it is imperative to consider the materiality of the subject within the specificity of its own context as well as to acknowledge the demands of analysing the dynamics involved in this position.

Such dynamism, which is inevitably subjugated to the political laws that structure the social contextualization of the subject, determines, from one side, that the materiality of the body becomes the physical presence of the gender performance required, and, on the other side, the social position of the subject synchronously and politically. What determines identity is the experience derived from such embodiment. And it is in this sense that the socio-symbolic practice of entrustment functions, and it is this matter that the politics of sexual difference makes central. Prior to investigating these, I shall further discuss the materiality of the body in the construction of a specific subjectivity, and how the acknowledgment of the female body does not provide a direct equivalence between sex and gender.

Sex/Gender Perspective

Marçal's feminist project of reconfiguring the woman's body as a theoretical device with which to redefine her position as a woman poet within the cultural dimension not only refutes certain structures that question the legitimacy of the body but also establishes the limits of that sexed body in terms of a rethinking of subjectivity. This duality comes to light at a time when there is a theoretical framework that gives the body the necessary primacy to posit such a perspective as the starting point from which to develop the process of subjectivity and the means whereby identity takes place.

Within this perspective, the question of the need for a sexed thought raises the problematic of determining the extent to which 'sex' is implied in the formation of a gendered subjectivity. If Marçal's theoretical postulates, underpinned by the perspective of *differenza sessuale*, call for the need to acknowledge the original sexual differences within the species, is she reinforcing the binary structure of identity? Is she encapsulating subjectivity within the sexed body? And, an even more important question derived from this would be, is Marçal contributing to the delegating of fixed, dual, disembodied thought derived from a supposed 'natural' pre-given subjectivity of the sexed body?

In this sense, it is important to investigate the limits and boundaries of the materiality of the body and to envisage the extent to which it can provide a new alternative grounded subjectivity. In so doing, I shall approach the matter from two different angles: the divergent positions of sex and gender, and the confrontation between biological determinism and cultural construction upon the corporeality of the subject. How then does Butler understand the process of subjectivity and gender identity? And how does she relate it to the bodily dimension?

On the basis of such problematic, Butler gives a new perspective to the reconfiguration of sex and gender. Taking Simone de Beauvoir's famous statement: 'One is not born a woman but becomes one' (1988: 3), Butler endeavours critically to destabilize the relationship between sex and gender, stating that whilst there is no intrinsic connection between sex and gender, nevertheless they are not independent from one another. Any relationship is established in oppositional terms:

> sex does not cause gender, and gender cannot be understood to reflect or express sex; indeed, for Beauvoir, sex is immutably factic, but gender acquired, and whereas sex cannot be changed — or so she thought — gender is the variable cultural construction of sex, the myriad and open possibilities of cultural meaning occasioned by a sexed body. (Butler 1990: 112)

If we consider gender exclusively as a cultural construction, how can one seek political intervention without considering the materiality of the body? How can performativity take place without the materiality of the body? Therefore, is there any possibility that gender 'as a matter of doing', albeit performatively, may encounter in its volatility a correspondence between the body and the specificity of that gender performance? Based on Michel Foucault's understanding of 'power', Butler in *Gender Trouble* presents us with a myriad of questions that destabilize the boundaries of the 'heterosexual normative' which, according to her own investigation, is what the approach of sexual difference precisely undertakes:

> If gender is the cultural meaning that the sexed body assumes, then a gender cannot be said to follow from a sex in any one way. Taken to its logical limit, the sex/gender distinction suggests a radical discontinuity between sexed bodies and culturally constructed genders. (1990: 6)

As previously discussed, in Lacanian postulates the sexed subject acquires a position in relation to the linguistic signifier: the phallus. This position entails strongly patriarchal postulates as the performance of the phallus can only take place upon the repression of the maternal figure. Yet, Butler's critique of this psychoanalytical understanding entails the process of identification and gender formation from the monolithic scope of positing the maternal perspective and the implication resulting from the category of woman, which, in her own words, 'tends to reinforce precisely the binary, heterosexist framework that carves up genders into masculine and feminine and forecloses an adequate description of the kinds of subversive and parodic convergences that characterise gay and lesbian cultures' (Butler 1990: 166).

This sacrifice of the maternal figure in favour of the success of paternal laws is not only portrayed in Lacanian postulates of the formation of the sexed beings. It is furthered in the revisions of Lacanian positions held by other feminist thinkers such as Irigaray and Kristeva. Butler's most fierce critique of Kristeva foregrounds the assumption that heterosexuality is the only possibility of the symbolic, leaving other possibilities as a kind of psychotic process of self-loss. For Butler, the controversy is found in Kristeva's conceptualization of the Semiotic dimension of language. She laments how Kristeva, despite her strong critique of the Lacanian symbolic, reinforces the hierarchy of the paternal structure, which, according to Butler, in Kristeva, takes the shape of the Semiotic, apparently still subordinated to the Symbolic.[17]

Considering such formulations, two problematic issues arise in Butler's understanding of sex and gender. In the first place, the gender performativity she pursues as a valid structure in the process of subjectivity may encounter some challenges. The first challenge lies in the presence of a disembodied subject that seeks political intervention. The second is that to acknowledge a complete discontinuity between cultural constructionism and the body would be to negate the materiality of the body, which causes great anxiety in political terms.

Another point I would like to argue is that if biology does not operate in the cultural and political participation of the subject, why is it important for some people to reconstruct their bodies in order to find social and political recognition? Under the terms by which Butler has directed her investigation, it is important to mention the possibility of a process of a specific gender identity within the form of the materiality of the body. Regardless of what the performance of the subject might be, it would inevitably interact with corporeality for purposes of political recognition. In this sense, I propose Marçal's feminist discourse, as an example of praxis within an oscillation process, which becomes possible through the intellectual practice of writing poetry and theorizing an interactive specific gender performance.

Linking Theory and Practice: Marçal and the Socio-Symbolic Practice of Literature

Having established the importance of the female body in Marçal's poetic production, I analyse in this section how specific debates on the body foreground further considerations of 'being' and a more extended definition of identity in poetry. Firstly, I will establish the paradigms that structure such a body in a continuous oscillation between theory and praxis. The sense of exile derived from Marçal's experience as woman writer, particularly as a woman poet, marks the axis of her discourse. Her main task as a feminist and as a woman writer is not only to examine the mechanisms whereby this sense of exile has been historically produced but also to unmask all the experiences that have been silenced, neutralized and dissolved into the alleged universality of the symbolic.[18] This section thus, contains the core points of Marçal's feminist postulates. I shall explore how she relates the fact that she has a woman's body with the linguistic dimension, and the intersection of both within the process of writing and signification in her texts. In this sense, literature as a socio-symbolic practice offers alternative references and images whereby Marçal tackles the possibilities of elaborating an alternative female symbolic: 'Precisament la literatura, com totes aquelles pràctiques que apel·len a la capacitat imaginativa, i que alhora són eines de coneixement, d'elaboració de l'experiència i de redefinició de la realitat, pot tenir un lloc, modest però no negligible, en aquest procés' (1986: 36).

Towards an Understanding of the Socio-Symbolic Practice in Marçal's Literature

Il pensiero della differenza sessuale elaborates its discourse within the specificity of its historical and political context, in which the feminist movement in Italy emerged. As I have previously examined, feminist discourse in Italy emerged from the political engagement of women in the left-wing parties and their wish to partake in social activities. Due to the previous difficulties experienced in political performances, Italian feminists, specifically women from the Libreria delle donne di Milano, established a debate, which bridged theory and practice, as a response to the inadequacy felt in their experience in the social arena. This debate was called the 'socio-symbolic practice of entrustment', the purpose of which was to establish a dialectical relationship among women in a search of self-affirmation both historically and symbolically. This connection between both dimensions — theory and practice — becomes the distinctive perspective developed by the Italian feminists of *il pensiero*. Their socio-symbolic practice enacts two words: 'social' and 'symbolic' in an enmeshed dialogue. The 'symbolic' describes women's problematic relationship with language, inherited through Lacan, and the 'social' aims to restructure the laws that govern the order of things in external reality and, as a consequence, re-elaborates upon the order of signification.

As I have mentioned in the introduction to this chapter, it is important to stress here that the scope of Marçal's literary project connects the social participation of the woman poet with the practice of literature. Therefore, the main point of Marçal's feminism is posited within the space of writing. For her, writing is an intellectual practice derived from the manifold, dynamic and fluctuating relationship of her *ser dona* and the experience derived from this. She conceives the practice of writing as a potential way of articulating new points of view. In her own words: 'A través dels mots, i dels mots escrits, és a dir, més o menys perdurables, s'articula una visió del món, una veu pròpia que es presenta als altres per a ésser reconeguda' (1995a: 192). Taking into account the activity of attempting to articulate with words the yet unspoken, how can writing poetry as praxis constitute an intervention in the socio-symbolic structure and contribute to its alteration?

Writing as a social and political activity requires the involvement of the poet in the social realm. This participation can modify the existing symbolic reference only if a dialectical relationship between other women's writing is established. Marçal explores the relationship of women with culture in order to challenge the structures that govern the hegemony of the symbolic. As Marçal suggests, there is a difference between the female and the male poet as there is a difference in their experiences and interactions within the cultural space:

> en concret, una dona que vol fer cultura, d'entrada ja s'ha de plantejar què té a veure la cultura amb ella, cosa que un home no s'ha de plantejar. Un home està instal·lat en la cultura; el corrent, l'aigua és masculina, i en aquesta cultura hi ha unes quantes dones flotant, relacionant-se d'una forma bastant estranya'. (Montero 2004: 268)

It is this interaction that the next part will deal with.

Marçal and the Estrangement of the Woman Poet

In the paper entitled 'Meditacions sobre la fúria', Marçal explores her interaction with literature as a woman poet. She narrates how she feels a sense of uneasiness, which she called 'la fúria', when exploring the sphere of woman and writing:

> Però l'obstacle seguia persistint: aquest obstacle que al principi he qualificat d'informe i que cada cop se m'apareixia com a més insidiós i obscur, i que de mica en mica vaig anar localitzant, no pas fora de mi, vull dir, per exemple, en una objectiva — o subjectiva — disparitat entre allò que se'm demanava i allò que jo podia fer, sinó endins de mi, com un buit fossilitzat, sense identificar, en algun lloc imprecís de mi mateixa. (1993: 137)

Marçal's experience with the practice of writing echoes the concepts developed in the text 'More Women than Men'.[19] This text is the result of the actual interaction of women in social spaces. As a result of their years of militancy against social structures that mediate between women's experience and public recognition, women from the Libreria conveyed their 'estrangement' towards social practices: 'What can it be this something which says "no", this stumbling block? It can't be named, because it hasn't a name. Our estrangement consists precisely of this, that something inside has no means of expression or self-realization but still exists' (1991: 113). This feeling seems to be the result of the impossibility of expressing women's desire. There is no place in the existing symbolic dimension for female desire: 'Un desig que no troba la seva mesura a través dels codis culturals, de l'ordre simbòlic vigent. Aquesta fora la mancança irreparable, el buit?' (Marçal 1994a: 179).

Marçal and women from La Libreria, although from different perspectives, engage with this sense of blockage and uneasiness that goes beyond the wish to participate in the social arena. In their paper 'More Women than Men', they describe this phenomenon as 'the wish to win through' (1991: 112). This is the wish that every woman feels when taking part in society without relinquishing her own identity. 'The wish to win through' attempts 'to find every now and then the gestures, the words, the behaviour, which correspond to our feelings and are appropriate to the external situation, to follow our thoughts, our desires, our projects, through their end' (1991: 112). Although Marçal wishes to participate in the sphere of literature, and despite the fact that she desires to disentangle the spider's web that involves women with writing, she feels a sense of blockage that hinders her wish to 'win through':

> Sí, era la fúria, un sentiment massa intens, violent, de fúria, que em feia un nus a la gola i no em deixava parlar, el que s'interposava entre jo i el text i m'impedia que el pensament anés fluint sense traves i ordenadament a través de les paraules. (Marçal 1993: 137)

She relates this sense of blockage to the ancient mythological creatures of the Erinyes. This vacuum is identified by Marçal as a feeling which finds its roots in a gap, in a void (*buit*), that was unknown to her but, despite this, is located somewhere between the dialectics of the sequence: woman and writing. The question is thus to grasp the reasons why women feel this sense of estrangement, described by women from Libreria and experienced by Marçal in her intellectual act of writing, when they try to be involved in the public sphere.

In Marçal, this estrangement is conspicuously produced as a knowing intervention of two opposed forces represented by the only two images of women available in patriarchy. On the one hand, there is the figure of Marçal as a woman poet, who like Athena is born from her father's head and assimilated into the male discourse. On the other hand, there is the image of the 'Fury', the monstrous. Marçal herself confessed the temptation and the danger of becoming involved in the trap of patriarchy, if the woman poet herself searches for an acceptance and acknowledgement of her social intervention in the cultural space:

> en un primer moment vaig percebre la fúria com a obstacle, vol dir que l'altra força, la que se li oposava, es camuflava eficaçment darrere del pronom 'Jo'. Aquesta 'Jo', que en darrer terme havia estat invitada a aquest curs en virtut d'un cert consens masculí sobre el valor de la meva paraula, volia presentar-se davant de vosaltres com Atenea, sorgint del cap de Zeus: completament armada. (Marçal 1993: 141)

Marçal identifies this inadequacy in terms of a vacuum inside herself as a result of these two unfortunate consequences that patriarchy imposed to women's identity as destiny: 'El fat inexorable?',[20] says Marçal; it is articulated under the premises of maternity, the discourse of which has served to keep women outside the socio-cultural dimension. Writing, thus, in Marçal, becomes an activity that goes against the supposed destiny (*el fat*) of her subjectivity: she suggests the concept of writing 'against life', but which life?:

> Només em fixaré en un aspecte: cap home, que jo sàpiga, no s'ha vist impel·lit a la tria dolorosa entre paternitat i escriptura: al marge de les dificultats materials que ara i aquí pot comportar encara la compaginació de la maternitat amb les tasques artístiques, culturals, etc. — totes aquelles que es desenvolupen en l'espai públic. (Marçal 1993: 143)

The sense of estrangement comes from the fact — through male-dominated discourse — that women are alienated from their own bodies: 'If we want to name what it is in which a sense of estrangement resides, all that can be said is that it is being and having a woman's body' (Libreria delle donne di Milano 1991: 113). If such disregard for and lack of acknowledgement of the female body develops into a feeling of estrangement, it is through recapturing these embodied images of female sexuality and bringing them into discourse that such feelings of estrangement can be conquered.

Wavering Spaces: the Woman and the Woman Writer

How does Marçal, through the exercise of poetry, bring the body into the text and alter the symbolic structure? There are only two possible positions that women writers can assume in terms of images and representations of the female subject: either they identify themselves with existing images or they reject them by proposing a new alternative. Marçal does not accept prescriptive images and her desire to go beyond existing meanings and symbols leads her to search for new references. In this sense, her poems become the battlefield where particular experience and collective references confront one another.

She fluctuates between her position as a woman and her production as a writer in a dialectical conversation. As previously explored, Marçal rereads the myth of Athena in order to examine the essential images which have preestablished the interaction of women with Literature as a cultural space. The woman poet neither accepts prescriptive images of the feminine nor does she remain encapsulated in silence: the fact that she decides to write breaks the space of silence and:

> Més aviat se situaria a mig camí, sempre en un espai híbrid entre Atenea i la Medusa, excavant túnels subterranis entre una i altra, sense ser capaç de triar entre totes dues encara que una o altra pugui predominar. Movent-se entre la Llei del pare que organitza el món tot excloent-la i/o inferioritzant-la en tant que dona, i el femení inarticulat, caòtic. (Marçal 1996a: 164)

Spatiality and temporality interact in the process of transgressing from the space of the woman to the space of the woman writer. The woman poet finds a discordance between her physical being and her 'conceptual being'. The woman writer refuses to recognize herself in the space-time dimension that the symbolic order has defined for the category of woman. The woman writer and specifically the woman poet reflects her disagreement with previous societal norms in her texts, where the search for the space-time needed becomes possible: 'as a symbolic placement, a space-time furnished with female gendered references, where one goes for meaningful preparation before work, and confirmation after' (Libreria delle donne di Milano 1990: 26), where the fragmented body can find a unity. In this sense, Marçal configures the space of the poem using the symbol of poetry as a 'mirror': 'Crec que és una recerca de la identitat, però d'una identitat completa. Ens hi reconeixem sencers, en el mirall. Aquest construeix i reflecteix la imatge d'una certa aparença de coherència' (Muñoz 1998: 170).

Marçal extols her different position as the woman writer in relation to her position as a woman. As she suggests, there is a difference between a woman and a woman writer: 'ni dona com les altres ni, evidentment home' (1996a: 165). The bridge between these two positions is language, the semiotic system, words. The woman writer, the woman poet, uses language in order to create new ways of representation. Literary activity becomes a social and political act, because the woman poet decides to transgress the boundaries of her traditional image and to inhabit the space of language. Her experiences, through her words, become public. Literary practice involves the use of language with the embodiment of the sexed subject. The unexpected participation of the woman writer within the logocentric space challenges, consequently, the laws that govern such a dimension. Her presence, thus, in the space of writing is, as she notes, unnecessary; intellectual writing is not an activity that women were/are entitled to carry out:

> Més ençà o més enllà, doncs, tota escriptora, tota dona poeta ha traspassat el llindar d'un món — el de la paraula en la seva dimensió pública i social — que no li estava destinat, i en el qual la seva presència és suspecta i, en el sentit que no és vista com a necessària, prescindible: supèrflua. (1996a: 165)

Mediating Images: Between Body and Language

It is clear from the above that there is an imperative need to explore the vicissitudes between both spaces: language and body. A dynamic structure becomes essential in order to succeed in bringing female experiences into the symbolic order:

> Molt més determinant, en canvi, és tenir un cos, una situació, una història de dona, o l'altre element, que continua sent molt important, el lingüístic. No puc establir una separació entre aquests elements i jo. (Sabadell 1998: 16)

Marçal thus establishes a dynamic movement within the system of language for the intellectual purpose of writing poetry, in terms of the process of meaning, and as a contribution towards representing women's experiences. The question then arises of how can writing be considered as praxis for the elaboration of a female symbolic structure if language is already historically inherited from patriarchy? Within this connection the perspective of sexual difference becomes the position whereby the body participates in and affects the social sphere. For Marçal, writing poetry endorses an intimate activity of her inner self. Writing is conceived as part of her body, a connate space in herself. In Marçal, writing becomes an extension of the space of the body, since the body is the dimension where specific experiences interact within language. Writing embodies an immediate connection to external reality, that is, writing becomes the practice whereby the body achieves signification in the socio-symbolic sphere.

Marçal's linguistic project becomes a distinctive one: she reconfigures the linguistic system by means of two different practices. Firstly, she reappropriates certain words and she redefines their meaning, altering them by providing new signification through the images such words evoke in the poems: 'i d'aquesta manera m'he anat fent una mena de diccionari propi en el qual aquesta paraula[21] s'anava tornant molt important, perquè s'havia anat omplint i enriquint, i cada vegada que la utilitzava en un context diferent hi donava un nou espai (Sabadell

1998: 18). Secondly, Marçal tries to reconfigure the language — with songs and poems — that she learnt from her mother and 'és per això que per a mi la poesia popular és, en part, com una mena de placenta que em genera seguretat' (Sabadell 1998: 17). She explores how both ways of examining the realm of language enact her subjectivity in the socio-symbolic dimension, and implies an actual performance in the literary space, because, through her exploration of linguistic structures, she attempts to alter socio-symbolic prescriptive images of women.

Language for Marçal is not only a mediation between the individual/private/inner self and the collective/outer/public. It also becomes the space where meanings, symbols and linguistic devices can be renegotiated and manipulated. In this sense, Marçal uses language not only to translate the internal, individual experience but also to represent such experiences with a plethora of symbols that are comprised of a web of collective forms. This twofold dimension of language enables Marçal to renegotiate the semiotic web of meanings and symbols and adapt them to her own needs: 'allò de què vull parlar, ho estiro i ho adapto a les necessitats d'expressió del meu poema' (Sabadell 1998: 18).

Writing poetry constitutes an important socio-symbolic practice. The poetic space provides language and words with a certain mobility. Writing, and the play between language and symbols, allows Marçal to reflect her experience of 'being'. The codes and values that shape each symbol with its meaning are framed within specific spatial and temporal conditions. As for the question of participation, the woman poet as Marçal states, seeks to provide a singular experience limited by the context in which she performs: 'i d'aportar a aquest "laboratori d'experièncices possibles" que és, segons Paul Ricoeur, la literatura, té molt a veure amb el lloc des del qual es parla, amb el sistema de valors compartit o discutit' (1996a: 160). In this sense, individuality and collectivity coexist in the composition of images; the performance of both spheres as an internal and external activity is necessary to complete the semiotic process. Without the inscription of the internal image on collective representations, female subjectivity will not be manifested or positioned both historically and symbolically.

The transgression of both spaces — individual and collective representation — becomes thus a complex process. One of the main problems that the woman poet encounters when she decides to write is the absence of female references that can provide her with the necessary space to configure her identity as a woman. It is in this sense that Marçal proposes the creation of a female symbolic order without the intervention of the father. Such a project echoes the socio-symbolic practice of entrustment and the figuring of authority by women from the Libreria, and it is the connections between these two proposals that the next section will consider.

In Search of the Female Symbolic Reference: the Literary Practice of Entrustment

Here, I engage with the question of how the socio-symbolic practice of entrustment aims to provide the space for the female symbolic reference. I also offer an overview of the way in which this practice delineates the creation of a female genealogy and the recovery of feminine authority. In Marçal's words:

> Perquè en el silenci femení normatiu que el patriarcat va decretar des dels orígens, l'autoimatge de la dona que escriu té una secreta vinculació amb el monstruós, amb un sentiment de mancança o d'excés — o no hi arriba, o bé sobrepassa el límits i no hi cap. Luisa Muraro diria que li falta la 'justa mesura', aquella que només pot donar la confrontació amb les pròpies semblants i la figura — encara negada i gairebé inexistent — de l'autoritat femenina. (1993: 153)

The figure of the monster, which Marçal relates to the woman poet, elucidates the lack of a referential point that can help women to achieve signification in social spaces. Her remarkable interest in searching for references and historically recovering female poetical voices lead Marçal to develop the task of critically analysing other women writers, translations and anthologies, in order to establish a vinculum whereby these women writers could contribute to a female genealogy. Aware of the non-existence of a cultural tradition of women writers, she lamented that:

> no existeix una cultura 'femenina' en el sentit d'aquella cultura que les dones haurien pogut crear a partir d'elles mateixes i dels seus propis interessos, sense interferències coactives. Allò que sovint s'anomena cultura 'femenina' només pot designar un espai conquerit i/o permés i/o assignat a les dones a *l'interior* de la cultura masculina que, pretensiosament i abusivament, s'anomena general o universal. (1986: 35, her emphasis)

The inadequacy of these images in patriarchal society and the need to express the specificity of female desire creates tension in the woman poet (as I have explored earlier). Socio-symbolic practices appeared as a feminist exercise first in Italy in the 1983 edition of *Sottosopra verde* (*'Piú donne che uomini'*). Since its beginnings, the project has evolved into not only a critique of actual symbolic space, but also a transformation of the symbolic with the necessary implication of a social performance. The socio-symbolic act involves a political exercise between women. It involves the functioning of a specific mechanism that alters their subjectivity and their way of relating to each other. Socio-symbolic action was introduced through the practice of entrustment.

This practice endorses a dialectic relationship between the symbolic and social conditions that aims to find signification within the symbolic without the intervention of the father, and as a result, to create a new symbolic order adequate to manifest women's desires without the feeling of estrangement. The practice of entrustment involves two women in a hierarchical position where one of them entrusts herself to the other. It is an individual practice, which emphasizes the disparity between and diverse experiences of women. Marçal envisages the practice of entrustment as a new space of interchange through the experiences recaptured in her texts:

> una escriptora es pren seriosament i interroga l'obra d'una altra escriptora, avantpassada o no; o quan dues autores contemporànies poden posar en comú la seva relació amb el món i la literatura, i una esdevé per a l'altra mesura i font d'autoritat; o quan una crítica s'enfronta de forma no inadequada amb el text d'una escriptora; i quan tot això es fa visible i operant. (1996a: 162)

The criterion for entrustment establishes that only through such a process can signification and meaning be found within the symbolic order. Marçal pointed out that to recognize authority in another woman, through the celebration of her writings, provides her with the necessary meaning to recognize the creative feminine force in its plenitude: 'només revisitant els textos de les escriptores que ens han precedit amb una mirada altra podem "desemmascarar" i "revelar" tot allò que resta fora dels paradigmes crítics pretesament neutres, construïts al marge d'aquest "plus" que no té lloc en l'ordre simbòlic patriarcal' (1996a: 165). That is to say, that the bond established by such a recognition determines the complete acknowledgement of her authority without the intervention of the father. The lack of a female authority results in the lack of an appropriate place and space for the woman writer.

Women from the Libreria began to search for references and words which could provide them with any traces or fragments of any kind of evidence with which to construct a feminine symbolic mediation:[22]

> Reading or rereading of women's writings; taking other women's words, thoughts, knowledge and insights as frames of reference for one's analyses, understanding, and self-definition; and trusting them to provide a symbolic mediation between oneself and others, one's subjectivity and the world. (1990: 2)

The Symbolic Order of the Mother in Literature

These symbolic references take up once again the idea of the mother-daughter relationship, which patriarchy has neglected to see as a positive relationship. The practice of entrustment posits the mother-daughter relationship at the core of the alteration of symbolic references and provides a new space for a new order of meanings. The original relationship to the mother is explored by the women philosophers of the group Diotima, especially by Muraro. She brings in the relationship with the mother as part of the practice of entrustment to the extent that, according to her words, she suggests that the first experience of female symbolic mediation occurs when a daughter is born from her mother, that is, when the mother delivers the daughter into the social sphere.

This experience can be replicated by the figure that they called *La madre simbolica* (symbolic mother). According to women from the Libreria: 'women need maternal power if they want free social existence. The mother is the symbolic figure of gendered mediation that puts women in relation with the world, opening a vital circuit between the self and the other-than-self in their experience' (Cigarini et al. 1991: 127). It is important to recover the mother, to recapture her figure, in order to bridge female-gendered significance and the space of a female symbolic. Marçal acknowledges the need to search for literary mothers as a practice with which to unmask and reveal the fragmented images, which are part of the female experience still silenced: 'Hem d'anar doncs, a la recerca i captura de les "mares" literàries escamotejades' (Marçal 1993: 142).

Marçal illustrates the situation of the mother within patriarchy by using the short story 'La llet de la mort' ('The Milk of Death') written by Marguerite Yourcenar. Included in the paper 'Meditacions sobre la fúria' (1993), it narrates the story of three brothers who are building a tower. In order to avoid the tower falling, they decide to underpin the building with a corpse. This corpse is that of one brother's wife, who has had a baby. At the moment that she is being immured, she asks them to leave her breasts and eyes free in order to be able to feed the baby and see if her milk is good. She is able feed the baby for two years, even after her death. The mother, in this narration, is kept behind the wall, silent, absent from her own body, with only the possibility of feeding the baby with her milk. In this sense, the body of the mother, conceived as a corpse, results from the action of the phallic function, of patriarchy. The 'death' of the body of the mother is not only the theme of this short-story, but also elucidates the way in which the mother is present in the symbolic:

> Aquesta mare sense rostre, darrere els maons que l'enclouen, nodridora, do d'ella mateixa fins més enllà de la mort, espectadora invisible morta-viva, ossada i fonament de l'edifici fàl·lic, és el bell i mític cadàver que el patriarcat ens ha ofert en el lloc de la Mare. (1993: 139)

In her book *L'ordine simbolico della madre* (1991b),[23] a key text for understanding feminism in Italy, Muraro develops in detail her theoretical perspective of loving the mother as the way to enter into the symbolic. She points out how philosophy has the power to return to the origins and establish an alternative symbolic order where we can give existence to the mother in her pure sense. As she states:

> Ahora veo que el reino de la generación y el mundo natural de que hablan los filósofos no es la naturaleza, buena o mala, ordenada o caótica, poco importa, sino la posibilidad de otro orden simbólico que no despoje a la madre de sus cualidades. (1994a: 11)

When analysing the situation of women in philosophy through the stages of history, Muraro stresses that male philosophers find the connection between 'language' and 'thought' owing to their recognition of and an intrinsic relationship with the womb of life; as she says: 'ellos demuestran haberla frecuentado y haber aprendido de su arte' (Muraro 1994a: 12). Following her critique of patriarchy, Muraro approaches philosophy since its beginning, and using the metaphor of the kitchen, she states that the mother has taken care of the son and 'todo parece confluir allí' (Muraro 1994a: 13).

Muraro reclaims the relationship of the daughter with the mother in the pre-Oedipal stage, positing the mother as the origin of both life and language. Therefore, the problem arises here of how we can establish the dialectics between language and thought and the symbolic order without the need for the intervention of the father? According to Muraro, these origins are dependent/based on knowing how to love the mother:

> es cierto que lo es porque no existen otros principios posibles para mí: solamente este, en efecto rompe el círculo vicioso, haciéndome salir de la trampa de una cultura que, al no enseñarme a amar a mi madre, me ha privado además de la fuerza necesaria para cambiarla, dejándome sólo la de lamentarme, indefinidamente. (Muraro 1994a: 13)

In 'Love as a Political Practice: the Example of the Love for the Mother' (2000), Muraro suggests the importance of producing critical thought but always followed by political action derived from the first stage. It is not enough to elaborate a critique of how female subjectivity intersects with patriarchal laws, as from that critique must emerge a response to this problematic. However, it is in the book *L'ordine simbolico della madre* (1991b), particularly in the prologue, that Muraro laments the few possibilities of significance that patriarchy can offer to the female subject. She emphasises how feminist theory in general has not yet provided an alternative to patriarchy and she states that analysing the figure of the mother and blaming society for her situation is not in fact any different from what patriarchy has been doing to women throughout history:

> de la crítica del patriarcado he obtenido autoconciencia, pero no la capacidad de significar libremente la grandeza femenina, que encontré y reconocí plenamente en mis primeros meses y años de vida en la persona de mi madre, y que luego perdí tristemente de vista y casi renegué de ella. (Muraro 1994a: 21)

The line between intellectual practices and political activity is in question here. Muraro explores, besides this, the relationship between a woman and her mother, which is still 'unthought' and therefore 'unrevealed'. Muraro considers this process as a very important step in order to achieve symbolic freedom, and, once it is established, a woman can love the mother. In her own words: 'it was a beginning, from which we started towards a new productive politics of female freedom, rendered possible by the fact that we had found a way, as it were, to "enlist" the mother on our side' (Muraro 2000: 82). The final results will lead to women being able to open the structure of patriarchy and be liberated from the symbolic patriarchal order. Muraro says:

> female love for the mother is that greater need for mediation which can bring to an end, to a good conclusive end, the critique of patriarchy, rendering it superfluous. When a woman *knows* the love for the mother, and *knows* how to love the mother, she is outside the symbolic order of patriarchy — which for her was rather a symbolic disorder. (2000: 82, emphasis added)

Muraro establishes an interrelation between being and logos, and this interaction is also linked with the origins of the human being and the world. In such terms, the opposites of binary thought do not fit in her theory because, according to her, the dual system is a merely descriptive methodology of the position that the subject already occupies. Thus, she proposes the embracing of a new perspective which is able to link women's bodies to the body of the mother as a process in order to inhabit the space of words. In her words:

> se trata de pensar que el origen de la vida no es separable del origen del lenguaje, ni el cuerpo de la mente, y pensarlo desde un punto de vista en el cual su vinculación no es objeto de una demostración, sino *un modo de ser* un hábito. (Muraro 1994a: 49, my italics)

Recovering Authority: The Presence of the Other Woman

The symbolic relation with the mother opens up a different channel of signification. The basic principle that upholds the legitimacy of this alternative symbolic order is the figure of feminine authority. Considering its function as analogous to the *affidataria*, its presence is crucial for the successful completion of entrustment. Feminine authority attempts to resolve the cultural and political effects of this practice. These effects, based on an interaction of entrustment, consist in providing recognition to feminine desire. This issue particularly concerned Marçal during her last years. The paper entitled 'Ordre simbòlic, ordre social', found among her manuscripts, asserts the poet's interest in this matter. For her, authority becomes the mediation of exchange and reassurance. It bridges the social and the symbolic through language and guarantees the cultural visibility of desire: 'l'autoritat dóna els ponts per travessar i acceptar tals coses no dites mitjançant la fe/confiança' (Barcelona BC, FMMM, Ordre simbòlic, ordre social, 16/7, fol. 2).

In feminist discourse, there is still much work to be done on feminine authority, and political and cultural effects. Women from *il pensiero* have found the key to open the door to the existent symbolic in the feminine figure of authority. Based upon Hannah Arendt's understanding of authority, women from Diotima and Libreria have investigated the ways in which the presence of this figure reasserts the function of the symbolic order of the mother that they propose.[24]

One of the main characteristics of the figure of feminine authority is its distinction from power. Power does not necessarily recognize authority. And yet, the figure of authority is not exerted in terms of enforcement, oppression or hierarchichal predisposition. This is possible because authority, according to women from *il pensiero*, is not rooted in the person who incarnates this function but in the person who entrusts this function by addressing her desire to its presence. In this sense, authority is acknowledged and not imposed; it is fluctuating and not fixed: 'l'autoritat garanteix la continuïtat dels vincles. Autoritat no és coercitiva, com el domini' (Barcelona BC, FMMM, Ordre simbòlic, ordre social, 16/7, fol. 4).

In her article 'Sobre la autoridad femenina' (1992) Muraro differentiates between the concept of authority and any implication of power. Also, Marçal in her paper 'Fragments del discurs sobre la autoritat femenina' (1997) meditated on the means by which feminine authority transforms any action of power into an action of entrustment, propitiating the function of the other woman as: 'la dona "autoritat" esdevé, doncs, punt de referència central, mediació inestimable, palanca eficaç per al propi desig' (169). This is important in order to bestow upon the female subject a sense of direction and freedom which patriarchy cannot contain, and which relegates women writers to become merely 'portadores d'una carència insuperable o d'un excés in-decent' (Marçal 1997: 167).

Due to its distance from the exercise of power, the figure of feminine authority can be applied to any context or situation, it is not only strictly political. In literature, and especially in poetry written by women, this figure marks the difference between what is said and what is yet to be said. If one seeks cultural visibility in what is to be said through language in poems, there will be the need to encourage this desire in another woman, whose presence provides a referential point to underpin its content. Therefore, in literature the image of feminine authority becomes 'influence' or 'literary precedent'.[25] Marçal also reflects on the importance for women writers of what she labels as 'mestratge' and 'influència'. The importance, thus, of recognizing and giving value to literary texts and poetic compositions written by other women is not only to confer authority to their work, but also to increase the value of one's own. Marçal gives a very peculiar anecdote in order to illustrate this exchange of enhancement. The story occurs between the Russian poets Anna Akhmàtova and Marina Tsvetàieva, whose poems were translated by Marçal into Catalan.[26] In 1915, as Marçal narrates, Tsvetàieva and Akhmàtova were invited to a literary event but Anna could not, in the end, attend. Popular criticism and the general public soon declared them rivals and competitors, but Tsevetàieva in her attempt to dispute such claims answered them with the following words, which Marçal found fascinating:

Tot el que he escrit després ho dec a Akhmàtova, al meu amor per ella, al meu desig d'oferir-li alguna cosa més eterna que el amor ... Si hagués pogut simplement oferir-li el Kremlin, no hauria escrit poemes. Perquè hi havia en mi una certa emulació amb Akhmàtova, però no era pas per 'fer-ho millor que ella' — fer-ho millor fóra impossible. Sinó per posar aquest 'no es pot fer millor' als seus peus. Emulació? Força! (1997: 169)

It is clear from this passage how feminine creative force is weakened by patriarchal forms of interaction. Furthermore, it elucidates that these words not only shed a positive light on Akhmàtova but also Tsevetàieva herself. The hegemony of the existing symbolic, based on the exclusive interaction between father-son, has kept women writers outside of the cultural construction of the values and representation of the literary canon. As Marçal says: 'les dones escriptores hem estat "ex-cèntriques" a aquesta construcció' (1997: 167).

In this sense, the figure of feminine authority acts as a mirror that reflects and recognizes female creativity, expanding its value and conferring a visible place in culture. Marçal, aware of her situation of 'orfenesa maternal crònica' (1997: 167), not only aimed to recast other feminine voices in order to broaden her own horizon through translations, papers and poetry: 'hem d'anar, doncs, a la recerca i captura de les "mares" literàries escamotejades' (Marçal 1993: 142). The figure of feminine authority is important not only diachronically, as we have seen, but also synchronically. To take another woman as the point of reference for composition offers the possibilities of novel images and meanings. It also expands the limits of existing words and creates alternative symbolic spaces. The Latin etymology of the word *autorictas*, derived from *augere*, which means 'to enhance, to increase'[27] contains the meaning of authority as expansion, opening and enhancement. Marçal's poems are intoned between a recurrent dialogue by an 'I' and a 'you'.[28] She entrusts the major part of her desire poetically to the figure of the other, who from *Bruixa de dol* (1979) is another woman.

We have seen how the distinctive feminist discourse elaborated by Maria-Mercè Marçal is constructed through the concept of *differenza sessuale* and how this discourse emphasizes the need to acknowledge such difference in terms of revaluating female experience. I have also explored the structure of the existing symbolic reference and its mechanism whereby meaning is created. From poetry to theoretical postulates, the body in Marçal's discourse occupies a central position that enables the immediacy of her particular experiences as a woman to transcend from the particular to the symbolic. In this sense, corporeality contains the specificity for self-representation. This is not, as I have shown, a return to an essentialist overview of subjectivity, but rather a proposal for a methodology with which to unravel the neutrality and universality of discourse, the male specificity of which has transcended into the privileged status of the universal.

My purpose here has been to argue that, despite inevitable essentialist connotations of the acknowledgement of the body for an elaboration of a feminist epistemology, in Marçal, the body does not signify a correspondence between sex and gender, but rather the specific condition of her own *ser dona* through writing poetry. I have used Butler's view of the problematics involving the category of woman to demonstrate not an immediacy between corporeality and identity, but to show that the process of subjectivity needs to take into account the dynamism of the body in order to overcome binaries. In this sense, the Italian perspective of *differenza sessuale*, and the socio-symbolic practice of entrustment have elucidated the importance of linking theory and praxis in Marçal's literary project. It is in the next chapter that I shall analyse how the process of constructing the self strives towards the practice of *ser dona* via the act of writing poetry.

Notes to Chapter 1

1. Irigaray's contribution to the Italian perspective of sexual difference set a precedent for the distinctiveness of her theory of patriarchal discourse as universal and neutral, in contrast to the partiality of the existing male dimension.
2. See the introduction of Irigaray's *Thinking the Difference: For a Peaceful Revolution* (London: Athlone Press, 1994).
3. It is important to point out that this statement is formulated exclusively within the parameters of *Il pensiero*. There are some groups in Italy and some feminists who work on the perspective of equality.
4. Cavarero was co-founder of the group of women philosophers Diotima. Although some years after the foundation of the group her ideas on the question of sexual difference in language differed from those of both Diotima and Libreria delle donne di Milano, she is one of the most important women philosophers in Italy.
5. During the 1970s in Italy some women were part of the Communist Party and at the same time were taking part in the first feminist groups of *autoconscienza* (self-awareness groups), a practice introduced in Italy by Lonzi in 1970 from the US.
6. This book was edited by Patricia Cicogna. The English version was translated and edited by Teresa de Lauretis in 1990; it is entitled *Sexual Difference: a Theory of Social-Symbolic Practice*. Quotations from this book correspond to the English translation. The title of this book is taken from Simone Weil. Towards the end of her life Marçal read this book with a special enthusiasm and interest. Among her manuscripts, we can find a file entitled 'Ordre simbòlic, ordre social' (Barcelona BC, FMMM, 16/7, fols. 1–5).
7. Published by Libreria delle donne di Milano in 1983 and translated in Bono and Kemp 1991.
8. This term is borrowed from Marx's concept of 'alienation'. For Marx, alienation is a form of objectivation that has neither positive nor negative consequences. It is a consequence of man's power to control nature. It is not inherent to the human condition. In this sense, it creates a conflict with the individual's existence. For full details see Marx 1975.
9. The concept of freedom is explored by women from *Il pensiero* as well.
10. Marçal joined the PSAN (Social Party for the Liberation of the Catalan Countries) in 1975. She was elected in 1976 as part of the executive board and was politically active until 1980. She participated in the first feminist meeting that took place in Barcelona in 1976.
11. 'The loneliness of the emancipated woman' is one of the first texts written by the Italian

feminist group Libreria delle donne di Milano, whose leader is Muraro, a former member of Diotima.
12. We can also find this reference to matricide in Marçal in 'Més enllà i més ençà del mirall de la Medusa' (a paper delivered at the conference "El cànon literari", Universitat Rovira i Virgili, 22/04/1996) and 'Meditacions sobre la Fúria' (originally entitled 'Woman and Writing' and delivered at the Summer School at the University of Gandia, València, in 1993, and published in Ángel San Martín (ed.) *Fi de segle. Incerteses davant un nou mil·leni* (Gandia: Ajuntament de Gandia, 1994). Both papers are reprinted in Ibarz 2004.
13. Blundell, in her analysis of the images of women in myth, suggests that in myth there are three types of women depicted: divine, human and monsters, to which the Gorgon Medusa belongs. The etymology of the word Gorgon from the Greek (Γοργόνα) reveals its meaning as 'terrible'. For more information about women in mythology, see Blundell 1995. It is relevant to note here that the Oxford English Dictionary includes a second meaning for the word Gorgon: 'a fierce, frightening and repulsive woman'. See Oxford Dictionary on-line: http://oxforddictionaries.com/view/entry/m_en_gb0343660#m_en_gb0343660.
14. In classical thought Athena was representative of both masculine and feminine activities. She was the Virgin goddess and never married nor had children.
15. Lacan establishes the relationship between the female subject and the phallus as a *masquerade*. That is to say that in terms of desire, the female subject encounters in 'the Other' the signifier that causes her desire. Consequently, she finds in herself the absence of the phallus, feeling as a result a vacuum, a lack, which is underpinned by the rejection of her own femininity. The fact that she fulfils her demand in 'having' the object of her desire in 'the Other', is a condition that reinforces her feeling of absence (lack of phallus). For a detailed account of this process, see Rose and Mitchell 1982: 84.
16. See Bono and Kemp 1991.
17. For a detailed account of the Semiotic and the Symbolic, see Kristeva 1984. For a critique on this, see Butler 1990.
18. Italian feminists adopt the Lacanian concept of the symbolic introduced in Italy by French feminist philosopher Irigaray.
19. Translated from the Italian text *Piú donne che uomini*, in Bono and Kemp 1991 (first published 1983): 110-22.
20. I recall here Freud's psychoanalytical postulates about the biological destiny of women. Some feminists have explored such postulates; for instance, Toril Moi in her article 'Is Anatomy Destiny?: Freud and Biological Determinism'. See Moi 1999: 369-96.
21. Marçal is referring specifically to the word 'moon' (*lluna*), one of the key images in her poetry. This word is especially important in Marçal's works for its connotations of femininity, passivity and submission in the Mediterranean world.
22. For a full account of the search for traces and fragments of women's writings and ideas in philosophy and literature, see Birulés 1997.
23. There is an implicit reference here to Lacanian ontology of the Symbolic. I shall quote from the Spanish translation, *El orden simbólico de la madre*, tr. Beatriz Albertini (Madrid: horas y HORAS, 1994).
24. See Arendt 1987.
25. An important male-oriented theoretical contribution on this issue is Harold Bloom's *The Anxiety of Influence* (1997).
26. With Monika Zgustova, Marçal translated poems by Anna Akhmàtova, *Rèquiem i altres poemes* (1990) and *Poema de la fi* (1992) by Marina Tsvetàieva.
27. See Arendt 1987. Women from Diotima and Libreria delle Donne di Milano took Arendt's understanding of authority to develop their theoretical proposals.
28. This is discussed in detail in Chapter Four.

CHAPTER 2

Poiesis

The preceding chapter has explored the theoretical framework and direction that the paradigm of the body takes in relation to language in Marçal's poems. Through various perspectives and insights, I have explored how the body connects poetry and feminism in her work and how feminism is based on praxis rather than theory. By juxtaposing *differenza sessuale* with Judith Butler's theorization of gender, I have discussed the means by which the body conditions Marçal's composition and how its presence in the texts should be taken as the poet's particular experience of being.

In this chapter, I turn to how Marçal's literary practice conveys these specific experiences of *ser dona* as a poetic theme, enabling the construction of her particular female subjectivity. By considering writing as a practice, Marçal establishes a literary contact between experience and poetry. I read this as a process of *poiesis*, where embodied experience is taken as a central theme for poetic composition. Taking these precepts into account, I shall now argue that Marçal's poetry, via her poetic historiography,[1] becomes a process of *poiesis*, whereby she attempts to 'make herself'. Marçal's understanding of the act of writing reveals the function of poetry connected to *poiesis* as the mechanism that brings forth the original act of creation: the movement that oscillates from chaos into light; as she explains:

> L'escriptura ha estat, és per a mi una activitat vertebradora [...] Durant molts anys he escrit només, o fonamentalment, poesia, i la poesia ha estat el meu esquelet intern, la meva manera de dir-me a mi mateixa, d'ordenar provisionalment amb la paraula el caos que l'imprevist desencadena. (Marçal 1995b: 21)

The term *poiesis*, which translates into English as 'making', was first introduced by Aristotle in his treatise on poetry, the so-called *Poetics* (c. 335 BC).[2] *Poiesis* is the technical term that Aristotle used to explain the act of poetry. Although *poiesis* is usually translated as poetry, it does not accurately reflect the concept that Aristotle elaborated as the 'art of poetry'.[3] Instead, *poiesis* implies an exercise that goes beyond the creative connotation of the poetic genre itself.

It refers to the action of elaborating the poem itself; it designates the process of making rather than the final product (that is, the poem). *Poiesis* entails a dynamic interaction between the writer and the act of writing. Of these elements, Aristotle highlights the function of the poet as the central constituent for depicting the sequence of actions in the poem. Thus, taking Aristotle's notion of *poiesis* and the dynamism implied in this definition, I posit that Marçal's poetic project endows *poiesis* with a form of return: 'camí de retorn, de reveure, de retrobar, de reidentificar, de reanomenar, de refer-se' (Marçal 1989a: 10).

In these terms, poetry as 'remaking' connects with one of the theoretical frameworks articulated by the Italian perspective of *il pensiero della differenza sessuale*: the need for a *collocazione simbolica* (symbolic placement). In order to pursue my contention, I divide this chapter into three parts. In the first one I consider how the Aristotelian concept of *poiesis* can be applied to Marçal's literary project, the premises involved in this process, and the extent to which *poiesis* can be taken as a methodology for the articulation of a feminine *collocazione simbolica*. I start by providing a brief account of the concept and how it can be applied to her specific feminist poetic space.

The unfolding process of *poiesis*, which I shall examine in detail in the second part, is developed diachronically and connects poetic themes and topics with personal experiences. This second section will follow a rather different approach compared to previous one. Since I attempt to demonstrate that Marçal's aim with poetry is to remake herself (*poiesis*), it is the purpose of this part, firstly, to reveal the mechanism that Marçal follows in order to undertake her symbolic construction. Secondly, this section aims to engage critically with the limitations involved in making herself. In highlighting the importance of tracing her biography, I seek to place Marçal's project in a critical position by examining her aim of writing poetry as a form of articulating her *ser dona* within the space of culture.

Then, I consider the legitimacy of *poiesis* and the engagement of a corporeal experience with the exercise of poetry as the making of oneself. I do this through Butler's rereading of Theodor W. Adorno, Michel Foucault and Emmanuel Lévinas concerning the agency of a presumed subject in the emergence of its own identity, positing the subject in relation to the set of norms that challenge the process of self-making. Taking Foucauldian perspectives of the formation of the subject and the way in which this subject can conduct her own narration, theorist and academic Butler has stated that the construction of subjectivity takes place in relation to a specific set of codes, structures, or norms that reveal that 'there is no making of oneself (*poiesis*) outside of a mode of subjectivation (*assujettisement*) and hence, no self-making outside of the norms that orchestrate the possible forms that a subject may take' (2005: 17). Throughout this chapter, I shall put Marçal in conversation with the iconography she uses — through her lyrical works — in order to show how poetry and experience oscillate in the making of oneself. The concept of *poiesis* is relevant here, not only because it reconciles poetry and experience in order to elaborate feminine poetics, but also subverts prescriptive understandings of poetry, woman and writing.

Approaching Aristotle's *Poiesis* to Marçal's Poetic Scene

The concept of *poiesis*, first formulated by Aristotle and later re-considered by Butler, carries important insights and values that connect the space of poetry and its aims with the responsibility and conditions of the poet and her actions. My purpose in approaching Marçal's literary works as *poiesis* mirrors her understanding of the act of writing poetry and her re-appropriation of poetic space as the locus of elaborating the specific discourse of her identity. This creates, as a result, an intimate link between poetry and identity: 'en el meu cas, la poesia va molt lligada a la meua història personal. Em fa d'esquelet intern, per fer-me un discurs sobre la meua identitat' (Civil 1995: upaginated).

Taking this conceptualisation as a starting point, I begin by referring to Aristotle's writing in part IX of his *Poetics*:

> From what we have said it will be seen that the poet's function is to describe, not the thing that has happened, but a kind of thing that may happen, i.e. what is possible as being probable or necessary. The distinction between historian and poet is not in the one writing prose and other verse [...] it consists really in this, that the one describes the thing that has been, and the other a kind of thing that might be. (Ross 1924: 8)

Derived from Aristotle's words, the function of the poet is determined by 'making' actions that have not yet found a poetic definition. This action, based on the possibilities of what can be said or what needs to be said, connects with the function that poetry acquires for Marçal:

> En el meu cas, la poesia ha estat sempre molt lligada a l'experiència vital; per això fer poesia és per a mi, una manera d'articular l'experiència, de donar-li forma. De construir-la de tal manera que tingui sentit. (Nadal 1989: 26)

Marçal understands that writing poetry is a form of 'making sense'. In contrast, for Aristotle:

> Poetry is something more philosophic and of graver importance than history, since its statements are of the nature rather of universals, whereas those of history are singulars. By a universal statement I mean one as to what such or such a kind of man will probably or necessarily say or do — which is the aim of poetry. (Ross 1924: 8)

He refers to the 'universal' as the statement that the poet, as a particular subject, has to determine as probable or necessary. By these means, the deeds characterized as universal should be narrated and reflected by the poet in the poems through the sequence of actions; this is, according to Aristotle, the aim of poetry. Aristotle makes here a rather problematic statement, especially from a feminist perspective. To use the term universal to refer to a poetic statement goes against feminist accounts of *differenza sessuale*. However, there is a point in Aristotle's words that provides a positive vision of this statement. This is the reference to temporality. Aristotle confers on the poet the function of anticipating the chain of events if the poet traces a logical sequence of actions without contradictions and with a clear structure that should be reflected in the correct use of language and images. To suggest this is to equate the function of the poet with that of a prophet, and to value her words as prophetic. This does not refer to the poet's role in anticipating events in the future. Rather, it presents the dynamism of poetic language, which displaces any sign of stability or fixity in the events it communicates.

For Marçal, the purpose of poetry and the poet's work is to provide order, to rewrite the chain of actions that have not yet found a logical sequence within the present interval of time: 'la poesia refà, crea, pas a pas, encara, un nou ordre amb les paraules' (1995a: 197). As a result, *poiesis* in Marçal not only dismantles the universality of statements and the neutrality of actions but also elaborates a feminist epistemology. The following words reveal that the function of the poet and poetry in Marçal correspond not to the need of formulating universal statements but to providing a place for the particular needs and probabilities of the female subject:

> Els meus poemes provenen d'una dona que és conscient de ser-ho i que hi ha pensat molt. Em sembla que el fet de ser dona és central i determinant en la manera d'estar al món. En sóc conscient, i aleshores lògicament la poesia ho reflecteix. (Sabadell 1998: 16)

Marçal's understanding of poetry displaces any sign or effect of universality. Rather, Marçal takes up the specificity of *ser dona* with the act of writing poetry. This need for anticipating universal statements as the principal aim of poetry reinforces the fact that the male poet transcends the particularity of his own experience into a universal form of signification. As I have explored in the previous chapter, this is precisely one of the main objectives of women from *il pensiero*,[4] the need to de-neutralize and de-universalize discourse in order to bring sexual difference into existence. They have stated in their critique of the existing discourse that 'women experience their existence as being spoken of and denied at the same time. Their ontological integrity, their being-there, is split between the correspondence to the discourse that speaks of them and a remaining with themselves, wordless' (Diotima 1987: 12).[5]

As this passage shows, women's existence is reduced to a mere object of thought. The two possibilities stated above — being spoken of and being silenced — stress the need to create a language for articulating sexual difference.[6] This is of primary importance for the development of a female subjectivity. I shall later offer a detailed exploration of body and language in the reconstruction of Marçal's embodied experience. For now, I am interested in pointing out the deleterious historical consequences of both dimensions, that is, body and language, which have limited women's existence within the symbolic. This, as we shall see, comprises a rather limited iconography. Such a situation has developed into a discontinuity between experience and social signification. As explored in the previous chapter, this is what women from the Libreria delle donne di Milano, in their text 'More Women than Men' (1991), have identified as the feeling of 'estrangement'.[7] This discontinuity results in a limited space in the existing symbolic order, and creates, in consequence, an anxiety in the woman poet since she, whose subjectivity is neither expected nor needed in the intellectual production of poetry, experiences a vacuum in terms of symbolic signification.

According to Patrizia Violi, the symbolic 'is what mediates between private experience and the general forms in which individual experience is inscribed' (1992: 157). Thus, the process of *poiesis* offers an alternative methodology for Marçal with which to overcome the prescriptive conditions of the patriarchal symbolic order. The subjectivation mode of the act of writing provides her, as a female poet, with the possibility of reappropriating language and investing her experiences with symbolic significance, presenting herself as a subject of her own desire, and allowing herself to rethink and reconfigure her *ser dona*. As Adriana Cavarero makes clear in 'The Need for a Sexed Thought':

> The female subject can emerge when she decides to be her own subject, to think about her subject taking herself as her starting point, here and now. The assertion of sexual difference through symbolic self-representation is needed, in order that she who seeks herself may know her image, and thus find and recognize herself. (1991: 185)

In light of this, I propose *poiesis* as a valid form of *collocazione simbolica* (symbolic placement) and as the site for engendered signification. I suggest that this process of making is a methodology that allows Marçal to bring her sexual difference into existence. *Poiesis* insists upon her condition as a subject and recreates her gendered experience through the poetic exercise. Next, I shall explore the specificity of the mechanisms involved in Marçal's *poietic* process as her way of bringing her female sexuality into existence, that is to say, as her way of being.[8] I will also analyse its power to achieve symbolic placement.

Transgressing Spaces: from Chaos to Order

As mentioned above, the interaction between the female body and the existing symbolic structure causes a discontinuity between theoretical contentions and social performances. The conflict arises when the subject emerges from a marginal position and finds no place for any possible signification in the existing symbolic order. This void ushers in a lack of recognition, as Cavarero suggests: 'she cannot recognise herself in the thought system and the language of a neutral subject which does not contain her — and indeed excludes her — without accounting for that exclusion' (1993: 193). The complexities of female subjectivity have ignited the need for rewriting, for reconstructing, which in Marçal entails transgressing from darkness into light. She writes:

> Quan el que visc m'és complicat o conflictiu o complex, quan necessito, diguem-ne entendre, aclarir, aleshores la poesia és una forma, a través de la qual el que és fosc, no es que es torni clar, perquè el poema és fosc, però en certa manera s'ordena. (Montero 2004: 264)

If the female body has been given a marginal position, it also mediates the space between experience and poetry, as Marçal suggests. She equates such experience 'el que visc' with the adjective 'fosc' (dark) and lends to poetry the space for 'understanding', 'making clear'. Poetry offers Marçal the place to reorder her own experience, in other words, poetry provides the transition from 'darkness' to 'light'.[9] Such a premise suggests that literary creation can function as a place for symbolic transformation. Poetry and the act of writing allegedly bring into the 'light' the specificities of the concrete female subject, thus dislocating the universal parameters said to be the aim of poetry by Aristotle. If we take 'darkness' as a trope that designates the part of experience that has no symbolic signification yet, then it is possible to confirm *poiesis* as the process that permits the transition between 'darkness' and 'light' and the conspicuous configuration of a new symbolic structure. In the following, I show how this mechanism functions in Marçal's writing.

As Marçal adumbrates: 'una de les funcions del llenguatge i de la literatura és donar sentit, articular allò que prèviament era balbucejant i desestructurat, ordenar l'experiència arrencant-la del caos i oferir miralls on reconèixer la vivència elaborada' (1995–96: 201). This suggests that literary creation implies an emergence from chaos as the space prior to structure. In this sense, chaos becomes the part of the experience that therefore precedes the *collocazione simbolica*. Given the importance of the analogy of the transition from chaos into light in Marçal's conception of creativity and poetry, I shall offer a brief explanation of the dimension of chaos and how it transgresses from invisibility to significance. In Hesiod's *Theogony*, Chaos is the condition of pre-existence:[10]

> Chasm it was, in truth, who was the very first; she soon
> was followed by broad-breasted Earth, the eternal ground of all. (2006: 26)

Chaos precedes the birth of Gaia: Chaos is the necessary condition for order (Gaia), for creativity — without Chaos there is no order. Furthermore, without Chaos the possibilities for the subject to emerge are minimal. The exegesis of the

Theogony indicates that order is paramount in bringing each participant 'as it first came into being', that is to say, into existence.[11] Chaos is the space of pre-existence, darkness — as mentioned above — the void that precedes any act of creation. This not only connects with Marçal's understanding of poetry: 'és una mica com ordenar el caos' (Montero 2004: 264) but also accounts for the process of *poiesis* since chaos always resurfaces when the pre-established order is altered. Chaos designates the stage where specific actions have not been mediated by the symbolic order. In other words, Chaos in Marçal is equated with the stage of pre-linguistic articulation: 'el caos sempre es dóna quan apareixen fantasies, fantasmes molt lligats a l'inconscient' (Montero 2004: 264). However, this idea should be taken cautiously, since the discussion of the existence of a pre-linguistic stage incurs controversy, and it implies the dissolution of the human being.[12] By approaching the space of Chaos in Marçal as a pre-linguistic perspective, I am seeking to convey that the boundaries which permit the subject to find linguistic configuration and, therefore, symbolic circumscription, operate differently for the female subject. As Cavarero has reconfirmed: 'the unspeakable, the non-representable is precisely the being a woman. A lived experience, from the very beginning to the very last hour, not spoken, or rather, spoken in *his* language' (1993: 197). The pre-linguistic dimension for the female subject, thus, corresponds to silence, to darkness and to chaos in the non-correspondence between subjectivity and *collocazione simbolica*. This correspondence, however, is determined by the cultural context that the female subject inhabits:

> Com a dona no puc oblidar que el femení, més enllà de la pobra representació de la donzella salvada per l'heroi, ha quedat exclòs històricament de la nostra civilització i es troba, també, a la banda del monstre, de tot aquell pany de l'experiència caòtic — el continent negre — en va dir Freud — que no s'ha deixat dir del tot pel llenguatge colonitzador. (Marçal 1996b: 37)[13]

Poiesis combines Marçal's experiences with the structures 'that in a given society at a given time, give shape to the culture of the moment' (Violi 1992: 162). These collective images act outside of the concrete reality of the subject, since they are inscribed into the specific cultural system where the female subject seeks representation. It is in this sense that *poiesis* accounts for the making of the self, since it puts Marçal's own individuality in confrontation with collective representations that define her gender identity. She says:

> saps qui ets tu, entre altres coses barallant-te amb tot allò que en tu és descontrolat i en allò que és descontrolat hi ha moltes vegades actituds culturalment apreses. (Montero 2004: 264)

As we have seen, *poiesis* implies a transgression from the invisibility of the female subject to existing sexual difference. The conception of writing poetry and creativity as an intervention into the existing symbolic order entails the consideration of this process as a way of going beyond a merely linguistic articulation of the female experience. It also elucidates an interaction between individual experience, collective images and symbolic signification. In the following part, I shall explore *poiesis* as the method of 'making herself' that allows the poetic subject to mediate between her own individuality and the images that form the web of collective representation.

The Making of the Feminine Self, Towards a New Methodology

This part focuses on the process of *poiesis*. The synchrony of the individual experience of the female subject transcends into a historical diachrony at the time that it becomes linguistically articulated and poetically structured. This is necessary for the success of *poiesis* since the experience of the female subject transgresses the space of the private and enters the dimension of culture, mediating between her own individuality and collective images. The individual experience of the female subject, thus, precedes and determines the act of writing in Marçal:

> Escrius sobre la teua experiència vital, que, alhora, condiciona l'experiència posterior. Et vas donant un relat sobre tu mateixa a través dels poemes i tot i que després puguis replantejar-lo d'alguna manera ja està marcant la teva trajectòria. En aquest sentit, doncs, trobem una interacció. Primer seria la vida, però la literatura després torna a influir en la manera com es viuen els esdeveniments. (Nadal 1989: 26)

This is what women from *il pensiero* have determined as bringing sexual difference into existence, since 'subjectivity cannot but be engendered, and that any expression of our subjectivity will exhibit traces of our membership of one gender' (Violi 1992: 155). In this sense, the experience of the female subject 'is fundamental for the constitution of subjectivity, since it allows us to objectivize our individual experience' (163). This objective character of experience results from the transition between individual experience and collective representation. As Marçal suggests: 'Quan escric és com si allò que he formulat tingués un cos, com si es trobés fora de mi. Escriure objectiva les coses' (Nadal 1989: 26).

Following a diachronic line based on these embodied experiences, this part is divided into two sections. Firstly, I focus on Marçal's first three books, composed between 1973 and 1981:[14] *Cau de llunes* (1973–1976), *Bruixa de dol* (1977–1979), and *Sal oberta* (1979–1981). In this period, Marçal draws poetically upon three factors: the poetic subject, the moon and the shadow. With the participation of these three elements, she 'temptava la construcció d'una identitat des del cor mateix del conflicte' (Marçal 1989a: 8). Secondly, I examine the poems written between 1981 and 1988 in *La germana, l'estrangera* (1981–1984) and *Desglaç* (1984–1988). During these two periods of poetic composition Marçal also wrote a book of fifteen sestinas entitled *Terra de Mai* (1981). *Terra de Mai* is the first book of poetry written in Catalan that poetically narrates same-sex love. In addition, it marks the turning point of *poiesis* where the poetic subject relinquishes the existing symbolic order as the locus for self-representation and explores the possibilities of female desire in its abundance via the eroticism of the body. In what follows, I attempt to show that *poiesis* can help to dismantle the internal structure of collective images by establishing the experience of the poetic subject as a starting point from which to achieve symbolic existence.

Beyond Feminine Destiny

In this part I focus on the first three books of Marçal's poetry. In these books the poet uses specific images: 'the moon', 'the witch', 'fairies', 'salt', 'the snake' and 'ivy'. Among these, the moon is one of the most important symbols, not only in this first part of *poiesis* but also in Marçal's poetry. As I will show, the moon limits the subject, and attempts to extend her signification within the arena of shadow. Female subjectivity refers to the images and symbols that patriarchy has established and associated with the identity of woman. In her own words: 'des de l'herència i contra l'herència, des d'uns arquetips mítics i contra l'arquetip: una identitat *de dona* enllà i ençà del femení que confina amb tornaveu de fat' (Marçal 1989a: 8, her italics).

This is particularly relevant, since Marçal's identity is articulated within the particularities of her historical presence, that is to say, from the images that have been culturally available in her concrete socio-political context. In light of this, Violi has suggested that:

> the way we become women, the way we establish an identity as women which is at the same time individual and social, internal and collective, depends precisely on how we work out the images of what it means to be a woman that we are bequeathed to us by a particular culture at a given time. (1992: 162)

It is within the particularities of the context of the poetic subject that the moon and shadows are intertwined in the space of poetry for the process of *poiesis* and symbolic representation. This part is divided into three subsections: the poetic subject, the moon, and shadow.

The Poetic Subject: 'des de l'herència i contra l'herència'

In Marçal's poems, the poetic subject is always identified with Marçal herself. This subject is available in the poems by the personal pronoun 'jo' ('I'). Marçal, aware of the difficulties involved in equating the poetic subject with the real author, has declared several times that 'en el meu cas, sempre el *jo* del poema sóc jo, que tampoc no passa sempre, en poesia' (Batista 1986: 3, her italics). This 'I' intervenes in *poiesis* on two different levels: poetic and socio-symbolic. The former, as the backbone of the *poietic* significance, leads Marçal to anchor the development of *poiesis* in relation to the axioms of 'the moon' and 'shadow'; the latter plunges the poet into the dynamics of the intellectual activity of writing and the social and cultural position of her specific female subject.

This involvement is intimately related to the vicissitudes she was encountering with her *ser dona*, as has been discussed in the previous chapter. This difficulty discloses the inadequacy she encountered between her conceptual being and her social signification. Marçal started writing poetry only one year after getting married to Catalan poet Ramon Balasch.[15] Her first book *Cau de llunes* was dedicated to him: 'A Ramon Pinyol, en penyora / d'un paisatge comú' (Marçal 1989b: 21). Of this period of time she says:

> Vaig passar un temps amb la impressió de viure com a 'consort', de no ser prou jo ... Fou estrany, fou un temps de molts enfrontaments, i a mi em desagraden moltíssim ... A la reunió de Roda, a El Mall mateix, hi era més com l'acompanyant del Ramon, que no pas com jo mateixa. (Busquets i Grabulosa 1980: 217)

These words reveal Marçal's sense of conflict arising from particular practices of her female subjectivity in the social and the literary space, coinciding with her marriage to Balasch. This uneasy situation inspired in Marçal the need to explore the social and cultural forms of female experience through poetry. This sense 'de no ser prou jo', implicit in the lines above, reveals the interrelation of the powers that anchors both subjectivities: male and female, as fixed categories in hierarchical terms. Women from the Libreria delle donne di Milano in their text 'More Women than Men' (1991) have analysed this feeling of insufficiency that women feel when they enter the social, therefore symbolic, dimension. They have claimed that:

> this sense of inadequacy must therefore be brought into the open and questioned on its own account as a more profound stumbling block than any which derives from an unjust social order. We are therefore discussing the failure of our social performance in terms which do not attribute it to discrimination. We are relating our sense of blockage to what we want for ourselves, not to what others want of us against our own interests. (112)

The poetic result of this feeling of lack of self-representation in social performances appears in her first book *Cau de llunes* (1973–1976), where Marçal sees herself trapped in a bird cage: 'Roja d'enyors encastellada xera' (CLL 35, line 2) in a space where she does not have a voice. This failure to speak reflects a female subjectivity dislocated from the existing socio-symbolic order, since female difference 'was left without mediation and therefore silent and ineffectual' (Libreria 1990: 127). This is explicit in the second part of the book *Atzeituní*[16] with the poem 'Xera',[17] which is structured in the Sapphic lyrical form:

> Xopa de cants orba sirena muda
> muda de cants te'm bado sol m'enartes
> nàufrag altiu vaixell salvat de l'ombra
> > blat a les veles (CLL 35, lines 13–16)

The following lines, imbued with a sense of melancholy, show Marçal's resistance to being defeated:

> M'alço del vent lluny de presó d'arestes
>
> [...]
>
> Nada del rou incandescents de xarxes
> i teraranys   Jo me'n desfaig   A lloure (CLL 36, lines 2 and 9–10)

Her subjectivity is blurred between atavistic categories and personal involvements. The ambivalence of her cultural and social position as a woman poet, and the still uncertain possibilities that poetry may offer coexist, as the last lyric of the first part of the book 'Núvols amb corc' shows: 'Tot era una selva de paraules / i era tot una paraula embullada entre arços gegants' (CLL 32, lines 12–13). This insecurity is derived from the lack of symbolic placement. Ida Dominijanni has stated that 'what a woman suffers from is being put into the world without a symbolic placement' (1991: 129). Despite this situation of uncertainty, Marçal clamours for her voice to be heard: 'Folla de seny folla Cassandra clamo / Cega vident contra el vaixell atàvic / Sang a les veles' (CLL 36, lines 14–16).

In *Bruixa de dol*[18] (1976–1979) the poetic subject has overcome this sense of discomfort experienced in her social existence: 'cadenes són presons / i jo en fugia' (BD 91, lines 17–18). These lines reveal Marçal's change of personal circumstances: she separated from her husband in 1977. This decision resulted from the ambivalence she experienced in her relationship, which disappointed Marçal's expectations of a heterosexual relationship and the conception of love: 'L'amor hi clavava / negres ganivets / i jo, sola, / entre albera i alba' (BD 86, lines 27–30). This rupture brings the poetic subject to a sense of defeat and bitterness: 'quin esquer m'arrapa / a la geniva? / Amor, estel amarg / a la deriva' (BD 91, lines 9–12). Despite this, Marçal needs to reaffirm her desire for social existence. She vindicates it with the motto that opens up the book:

> Emmarco amb quatre fustes
> un pany de cel i el penjo a la paret.
> Jo tinc un nom
> i amb guix l'escric a sota.

This avowal resonates as Marçal's pledge to claim her name. This name, which refers to cultural and social recognition, becomes Marçal's concern in this second book. As the poet states:

> un nom que d'alguna manera tens consciència que està esborrat i l'has d'afirmar. [...] en el fons el nom pertany clarament al terreny de la cultura,

llavors és la meva afirmació d'existir en el món de la cultura, el fet de dir-ho és reivindicar aquest nom, perquè representa el que no hi és. (Montero 2004: 262)

The vindication of her name as a cultural representation along with her individuality socially visible through her separation, show Marçal's desire to search for a place for her individual existence. In *Bruixa de dol*, Marçal reflects this individuality in the poems: 'la dona sola: amb l'assumpció de la pròpia solitud com a condició indispensable per a l'existència com a individu autònom, com a "peix sense bicicleta..."' (Busquets i Grabulosa 1980: 217).

Thus, in *Bruixa de dol*, *poiesis* is a twofold process. On the one hand, we see solitude as a way of reappropriating her own boundaries. On the other hand, there is her condition as a woman, whose solidarity with other women poetically endeavours to open up a space for collectivity,[19] with poems dedicated to other women in 'Els núvols duien confetti a les butxaques' (BD 140–55). Alessandra Bocchetti in her article 'The indecent difference' (1991) suggests that feminism in fact carries in itself the sign of difference, since feminism links the individuality of the female subject with a claim of political performance towards 'a path of self-knowledge by women' (159). She argues that:

> the feminist movement's claim of political separatism already contained this discourse. If the old separatism-denial closed the door in the face of knowledge of the other, the separatism of political sites of today's women suggests more than anything a possible knowledge of the self in difference, but opening up the discourse of difference as affirmation. (1991: 159)

In Marçal's poetry, the beginnings of the feminist movement in Spain during the period of transition after the end of the Francoist dictatorship were very important.[20] As Bocchetti suggests above, they opened up the space for rethinking her individuality as a woman. Marçal steers towards her solidarity with other women in 'Avui les fades i les bruixes s'estimen' (136–37). This part includes other parts: 'Els núvols duien confetti a les butxaques' (140–55), 'Sense llops ni destrals' (158–66), sonnets dedicated to other women, and the last poem of the book 'Vuit de març' (168–70) includes political content on the situation of women. Her decision to take another path, as explicitly suggested in 'Tombant', was encouraged by the sense of community with these women,[21] where she found freedom and not only a personal but also a social and political force that enhanced her gendered position: 'el fet de la reivindicació o presa de posició com a dona' (Montero 2004: 262). This is reflected in the poem 'Cel negre' in which the 'I' is transformed into 'we' (BD 162):

> Sabrem refer camins pel riu de l'ordi?
> si no, no hi ha terme per al llagut
> que encén tardors amb mots de llibertat
> La lluna nova, saps?, diu que et recordi
> que el NO d'avui du un SÍ a l'altre costat. (lines 10–14)

This political vindication, along with the personal experience of her divorce, propitiously foregrounded her poetical intentions and delimited the structure of *Bruixa de dol*. The first part of the book, 'Foc de pales', describes the pain she feels when her marriage is over, despite the fact that it is she herself who chose to divorce, as the poem shows:

> la nit em clava
> el seu ullal
> i el coll em sagna.
> Sota les pedres
> l'escorpit
> balla que balla.
> La pluja, lenta,
> fa camí
> fins a la cambra.
> L'escala fosca
> del desig
> no té barana. (BD 87)

Consequently, in the second part of the book 'Tombant', the saying 'Una dona sense un home / és com un peix sense bicicleta' reflects her aim of searching for new meanings through the exploration of the boundaries of her own self. These become available only through the celebration of her solitude: 'M'he emborratxat de solitud' (BD 97, line 5), as disclosed in poem IX:

> Les hores dansen
> sobre la meua pell
> i ve la solitud
> de peus menuts,
> sense sabates ... (BD 103)

The strong sense of individuality in Marçal highlights the problem of defining woman as fixed and ahistorical. According to Marçal, the female subject cannot be constructed upon the premises of totality, unity, and universality. Rather, this subject is dynamic, diverse, and sexually different from other embodied subjectivities. In poem VI, included in 'Tombant', she expresses this idea by using the metaphor of the forest in opposition to the holm oak: 'De primer van foradar-me les orelles / de llavors ençà duc arracades. / No prengueu aquest bosc per una alzina' (BD 100).

Within the diversity of the category of woman, Marçal celebrates her own subjectivity through the exploration of her solitude in part III of the book: 'Foguera Joana'. This part, imbued with a vocabulary of joy and pleasure includes the lines: 'Dóna'm la llengua, amor. Dóna'm la sal. I dóna'm també / aquest dolç llangardaix que em duu follia / quan s'enfila per l'herba' (BD 110, lines 3–6). She vindicates her female body through the synecdoche of the 'breasts', set in a frolicsome atmosphere and a natural space, as revealed in this poem:

> El meus pits són dos ocells engabiats
> quan els teus dits els cerquen
> per entre les fulles i les flors del vestit.
>
> Però quan fulles i flors cauen a terra
> —que el desig porta dalla!—
> Són dos peixos que et fugen de les mans
> en les crestes nevades de la mar. (BD 111)

With the sonnet 'Zodíac' (BD 121), Marçal inaugurates the next part of the book 'Bruixa de dol'. This poem displays the end of a specific form of subjectivity — the conception of woman in opposition to man — which starts in *Cau de llunes*, and also the impossibility of conceiving of a relationship between a man and a woman in non-hierarchical terms. *Bruixa de dol* and *Cau de llunes* reflect the inadequacy, the vacuum, between both categories of male and female, and the tragedy of configuring both conceptualizations separately from hierarchical structures and levels of power:

> hi ha com a Cau de llunes, potser amb una formulació més aprofundida, la desfeta, les contradiccions i l'espurna de felicitat fugaç de la relació amorosa en el nostre context social i l'antagonisme complex i ambivalent entre homes i dones. (Busquets i Grabulosa 1980: 216)

Consequently, in 'Zodíac' Marçal suggests a return to the space of poetry as the only dimension where both categories converge and coexist.[22] This will only be possible in the space of the poem via the metaphor of 'cranc' and 'escorpí', which translate as 'cancer' and 'scorpio', the two astrological signs that correspond to Marçal and Ramon respectively:

> Lligo els records i tanco la maleta:
> que engoleixi aquest llast l'avenc marí.
> Que els peixos cusin la boca d'un destí
> amarinat en aigües de desfeta.
>
> [. . .]
>
> I, conjur del mal astre, a l'endeví,
> apuntem cels, amb pinzell de poeta
> on fan la trena el cranc i l'escorpí. (BD 121, lines 1–4 and 12–14)

In 'Bruixa de dol', mourning for this situation coexists alongside the shadow of the male subject that playfully appears in the poems: 'M'ets present com un déu, com un diable' (BD 129, line 1), and brings Marçal back to uncertainty as the poem shows:

> Aquest mirall em diu que sóc ben sola
> i no hi fa res que el trenqui en mil bocins.
> He enfilat el carrer trist que va a escola
> i emmarco, amb guix, entorn, els meus confins.

> [...]
> I et prenc el cor segur amb què cabdelles
> el teu destí, per fer, amb cartes velles,
> un solitari nou sobre la duna. (BD 123, lines 1–4 and 12–14)

This alternation between the solitude of the poetic subject and the appearance of the male subject is reflected in the following antibook: 'Amic i desamic et diré ara' (BD 128, line 1). At the end of this part Marçal abandons the inclusion of the male subject and the perspective achieved hitherto with his presence, and decides to continue alone:

> Bruixa de dol, al meu cau solitari,
> he clos el llibre on l'òliba fa dia.
>
> [...]
>
> Torno el mirall al calaix de la nit
> i esborro el rastre, travessat d'agulles.
> Se'm bada als dits la tristor de les fulles. (BD 133, lines 1–2 and 12–14)

From the political and social vindication of her individuality, Marçal, in *Sal oberta* (1979–1981), 'prossegueix una mena d'autobiografia simbòlica i imaginària que havia començat amb *Cau de llunes*. Un discurs sobre mi mateixa, complex i sovint oníric' (Marçal 1995a: 196). The poetic subject returns again to the same scenario, and tries to reconstruct her subjectivity from the core of the conflict: the relationship between a man and a woman: 'La foscor dóna cobri a l'averany més fosc. / Camí d'enlloc, de tornada d'enlloc / t'estimo, exiliada al perquè dels poetes' (SO 181, lines 12–14). This is reflected poetically in the first part of the book 'Freu',[23] especially in the first section 'Festanyal de l'aigua'.[24] In the second part, 'Arc i tenebra',[25] the poetic subject is hurt and defeated, with the poetic result of the impossibility of conceiving feminine subjectivity outside of patriarchal terms. This brings an iconography of sorrow and melancholia and an acrimonious poetic tone to her lines, as shown in the first stanza of the last poem of this first part 'Al far!':[26]

> Ascla d'arbre o de barca, en esqueix d'alimària,
> he triat, a ple cel, i amb fible d'escorpit
> —imant de la tempesta i amiga de la nit—
> l'urc de cremar, tot sola: d'ofici, solitària. (SO 211)

In her own words: 'perquè l'amor entre una dona i un home sigui possible, sembla exigir una mena d'inversió de tot el context' (1995a: 196). This attempt to invert the context is displayed through the use of hyperbole in the second and third stanza of Sonnet IV (SO 208) which poetically reflects this discrepancy:

> Desabraça'm! Que l'aire torni a tenir-me viva,
> lluny de l'ulall voraç que em clava a la tenebra!
> Desabraça'm i, a sang, arrenca'm de la febre
> que ha dut la meva barca fins a la teva riba!

Encerta'm de ple, llamp que signes l'enderroc!
Desabraça'm de l'aigua! Desabraça'm del foc!
Estella'm! Sigues ara el tall de la destral! (lines 5–11)

Yet, the experience of the poetic subject precedes the act of writing and the process of *poiesis*. Marçal, an independent woman, gets pregnant and the father of her child rejects his responsibility and abandons her: 'I tu — que lluny! — esborres rastre i fulles / que fan camí fins al sorral on grana / al desconcert amb averany de festa' (SO 237, lines 12–14). In *Sal oberta*, Marçal poetically details the experience of her pregnancy. However, the lack of existing literary images leads her into starting from her own experience. As Marçal herself has stated: 'A la literatura és molt important els punts de referència, els models... i en aquest tema no hi ha antecedents' (Campabadal 1981: 10). In this way, the lack of literary references and images about the experience of pregnancy places her in a pioneering role. There is no poetic precedent to elaborate the process of pregnancy in the Catalan literary tradition. Marçal equates the need for a new poetic articulation with the idea of birth: 'faig una aposta forta per l'inici, per donar possibilitat al que és nou; la idea de néixer és això, donar curs a unes possibilitats que deixes de controlar, i que jo vaig viure com un impuls molt fort' (Sabadell 1998: 18). This idea, along with the misfortune of this relationship, is merged in *Sal oberta* as a way of reconfiguring the parameters that shape her individuality and her subsequent signification in the symbolic. This means that the poetic subject has to exceed the historical and cultural situation of women at the time. Despite social configurations in a recently inaugurated democratic Spain — and the difficulties of being a single mother — Marçal continues with her pregnancy. She says:

> Quan vaig prendre la decisió de tenir la meva filla podia semblar que tot m'havia de portar a una absorció. En canvi, es va produir un impuls d'afirmació que em va donar molta força. En donar-se aquesta situació radical i assumir una maternitat en solitari, em vaig trobar embarcada en una aventura molt forta. (Sabadell 1998: 18)

This impulse and the vicissitudes of creating a new imaginary life cause the pain and hurt which unleash an imperious desire to write poetry: 'Contra el corc que m'ensenya a viure amb la ferida / parlo: sóc l'arbre pres d'angoixa tardoral. / Desabraça'm! O abraça'm sense retorn ni brida' (SO 208, lines 12–14). Against this defeat, Marçal foresees that the feminine subject cannot be constructed either within the *law of the father* or extraneous to it.[27] In these terms, she feels like a parasite of love and distress:

> Aquest paràsit, arrencat a tall
> del cos viu que el nodria i el sustenta,
> sóc jo, arrapada a l'agonia lenta
> d'una ombra que se'm fon sense aturall.

> [. . .]
> I esdevinc, ara, quan la lluna esventa,
> fent doble jo, la pols de l'enforcall,
> paràsit de l'amor i el desamor. (SO 209, lines 1–4 and 12–14)

The image of the parasite encapsulates the need for 'the other' in order to survive. The lack of independence in Marçal shows in the despair of the lines above. However, soon in the book this despair will be transformed into a vehement sense of creativity and power, that flows from the 'parasite' into the body as a 'host' which now not only 'reproduces' a child but also produces new meanings:

> és el meu cos que et serva
> com l'herba
> serva el crit del seu verd;
> que es corba al teu creixent
> i aprèn
> el teu batec obert. (SO 255, lines 7–12)

The visual transformation of her body provoked in Marçal a sense of reaffirmation. This physical evidence acknowledges female subjectivity as an agent of production, which confers on Marçal the power of creativity: 'Veus? Ara sí que sóc mercè marçal, / d'abril, maial, de juny i juliol . . .' (SO 268, lines 1–2). Through the exaltation of the conspicuous pregnant body, the poetic subject experiences a creative force that metaphorically relates birth to the arrival of new possibilities:

> El meu ventre és el món: de fora estant
> vetllo el creixent d'amor que ara l'habita
>
> [. . .]
> I, covat per tanta aigua trasbalsada,
> del cor vell d'aquest ou naixerà, nou,
> un altre món amb la fruita badada. (SO 270, lines 1–2 and 12–14)

This is reflected in the third part of the book entitled 'Heura' (SO 235–40) and dedicated to her daughter: 'A tu, quan encara eres / un dolç paràsit del meu cos; i el meu cor, de tu' (SO 235). The body as the physical evidence of her femininity now becomes the social presence of her identity, and with this, Marçal confronts, through a deep poetic meditation, the decision to continue with her pregnancy:

> M'han fet un ventre altiu que gosa navegar
> en aigües de ningú contra llei de corrent.
> Si fongués llast d'arrels i el mossec de la dent
> que clava el meu enyor al caire de l'escar
>
> segaria el llibant que em doblega a l'ençà
> i em perdria endins, sola, ciant a nit batent. (SO 240, lines 9–12 and 13–14)[28]

Marçal's situation is underpinned by a socio-cultural context and personal experience. Her abandonment by the person she loved and her pregnancy in the socio-cultural framework of Spain in 1980 places her in a very difficult situation. She says: 'Jo hauria d'haver estat una de les moltes noies que van anar a Londres a avortar' (Sabadell 1998: 21). Although she decides to continue with the pregnancy, she faces a period of doubt. This is displayed in the poem 'Ruda', dedicated to the memory of Medea[29] and with a quotation from Edith Södergran, 'si el meu fill neix mort és seu'.[30] Ruda (rue) is a plant traditionally used by midwives and witches to cause miscarriage. Through the image of 'ruda', Marçal meditates on the potential consequences of her experience within the socio-symbolic context with which she interacts. There is an oscillation between her experience and the set of rules that determine motherhood outside the tradition of the family. Therefore, via the use of 'ruda' in relation to 'heura' (ivy), the poetic subject asserts her decision to 'anar a contrallei' and overtly challenges the effectiveness of the space of 'ruda'. Using this magic connotation, the poetic subject foresees that 'ruda' threatens 'heura', as the second stanza states:

> Perquè portes la mort escrita a la semença
> i la veig a les fulles, i ha enramat el convit,
> no donaré agonia a la saba que et defensa,
> no daré llum al sol, ni tenebra a la nit.
>
> [...]
>
> I alçaré cor i vi perquè la vida guanyi:
> el meu amor serà la ruda que t'escanyi. (SO 244, lines 5-8 and 13-14)

'Ruda', therefore, has been defeated by 'heura'. This has occurred through the unity of antagonistic forces: sun and moon, fire and water. 'Heura', which stands for 'alpha and omega', the beginning and the end, creates a new existence, the space of a new configuration, a new being within the space of poetry:

> Heura que véns de mar. Freu amb l'ona a ple brull.
> L'estrall tot just et frega la pell: la vida es bada.
> Per tu, jo seré el sol i la lluna granada
> i una casa sense urc amb celler, pou i trull. (SO 245, lines 5-8)

'Heura' *(Hedera)*, or ivy, is an evergreen plant which due to its natural characteristics is often associated with creativity and knowledge. It is perennial, and is associated with the myth of Bacchus. In ancient times the *hedera* was used to crown poets and wreath Bacchus's head.[31] Ivy thus represents poetic triumph, the celebration of poetry as the space for creativity. This creativity is displayed in the last part of the book 'Sal oberta'. The poetic subject calls universal forces to the presence of a new act of creativity via the use of 'nuncis', which translates as 'nuncios', the messengers. Using the Sapphic structure, this is displayed in the first two stanzas of the opening poem of the section:

> Conjuro els quatre regnes, i l'atzur de la nit,
> les plantes dels meus peus, els turmells i les venes
> que et serven i que ritmen el meu pas i el meu pols
>   d'ona creixent.
>
> Conjuro els daus oberts i t'abraço amb la serp
> del pou de la tendresa. Avivo tots els vents
> que s'han citat, revolts, al volt d'aquesta taula,
>   nuncis de l'hora. (SO 261, lines 1–8)

According to the poetic subject, the 'winds' are messengers of time, of the moment of 'the calling' of this poem. This calling refers to the act of creativity that starts in her body, transformed visually through the pregnancy.[32] This elucidates how the body is the point of reference for symbolic transformations and the site that mediates *poiesis* between her individuality and poetic signification. This is developed in the last poem of the book 'Triar', also dedicated to Heura. She narrates how both writing poetry and the process of pregnancy represent the act of creativity, within the limits of her experience. The poetic subject, without any precedents in the Catalan poetic tradition, depicts poetically how her 'body' alienated with nature through the image of a 'tree' becomes an allegory of the experience of pregnancy:

> *Sola, d'arrel,*
> vaig deixar que pugés
> la saba, lentament,
> a mesura que obria
> les portes i s'inflaven
> tot de veles: la mar
> que envaïa la casa.
> *Sola vaig dir-te*: creix.
> I, pas a pas, sabent
> que ens duien els meus peus,
> vaig gosar créixer amb tu.
>   1982 (SO 289, my italics)

Despite the power acquired by Marçal, *poiesis* as the process of self-representation is limited by two other spheres: the moon and shadow, which thwart the purposes of the poetic subject on different levels and in different directions. In the following section, I shall focus on how these two spheres interact with the subject and her mode of self-representation.

The Moon: Atavism and Utopia

The moon, after the botanical elements discussed above, is the second emblem involved in the process of *poiesis*. It is one of the most important symbols in Marçal's poetry. The moon appears throughout her entire poetic production and occupies a special space in this first part, where its variable meanings and connotations uphold its constant presence in the three books: *Cau de llunes*, *Bruixa de dol* and *Sal oberta*. The association of woman with the moon has limited the identity of woman to a category that does not allowed her to be considered as a subject, since the moon is always dependent on the sun. This suggests that the only images available in literature are the ones that patriarchy has produced. Violi suggests that:

> women do not have social and collective forms of self-representation which they have produced themselves, as subjects. Instead, the only representations of their gender available to them are those established by patriarchal culture. Since subjectivity requires a level of social generalisation, some social and collective representations of gender are necessary, to mediate between individual experience and more general forms of subjectivity. (1992: 162)

Marçal, aware of this situation, rejects the set of images, symbols and semiotic references available within the existing symbolic order. She attempts to subvert such a position by giving the image of the moon a central place in her work. She says:

> la lluna serà en aquest llibre i en els immediatament posteriors imatge privilegiada, recurrent i obsessiva, punt de referència lluminós alhora utòpic i atàvic, amb la subversió en pantalla del seu significat tradicionalment subordinat: 'Hi havia una vegada, quan la lluna tenia llum pròpia ...' podria ser el començament d'un conte que com tots no té una localització en el temps, sinó fora del temps. (1989a: 8)

The privileged image of the moon appears in her poetic iconography from the first book *Cau de llunes* published in 1977, which won the Carles Riba prize the previous year, and translates as the *Hiding Place of Moons*. I read Marçal's poetry as an irruption into the culture of the moment, whereby the moon, as a satellite, destabilises the prevailing structure and order: 'Llavors trencà la lluna una baula de la nit' (CLL 30, line 1). Despite Marçal's subversive attitude, there are traditional roots and cultural origins that provide the harmony and order of things: 'Les rels xuclen el cor de cada cosa' (CLL 30, line 5).

By using the image of the moon, Marçal affirms her individuality as a woman. As she states with reference to *Cau de llunes*: 'va ser important, per a mi, perquè vaig descobrir o trobar un dels símbols que després més s'ha repetit: la lluna, com a imatge de la dona' (Campabadal 1981: 10). It confronts the moon with the experience of the poetic subject. This experience, as seen previously, rejects prescriptive significations and searches for new meanings that can allow the subject to achieve social construction.

In light of this, presence and absence determine the interaction of the moon in *Bruixa de dol*. The moon dies in the second part of the book, 'Tombant', which translates as 'drop', referring to a geographical *topos* that indicates a change of direction. This image is connected poetically with a significant structural alteration displayed via the death of the moon which Marçal celebrates in the following poem:

> Com un peix sense bicicleta
> cerco el meu cor entre les ones.
> Alço la copa on mor la lluna
> en vi molt dolç.
> M'he emborratxat de solitud. (BD 97)

The moon dies when the poetic subject decides to investigate the limitations of her own individuality, her independent gendered experience:

> A *Bruixa de do*l la lluna agafa el paper de model. Es un desdoblament de jo mateixa, representa l'element al qual jo aspiro i que no té les contradiccions que jo tinc. Assumeixo el paper que té la lluna a l'hora d'assumir la solitud i d'una manera gens dramàtica. (Parer 1982: 23)

This experience along with the absence of the moon allows the poetic subject to express her own subjectivity, as the last line of the poem shows. At the end of 'Tombant' the moon returns:

> Llum al balcó
> i l'estrall a la porta.
>
> Giro la moneda
> i és la lluna. (BD 105)

Regardless of Marçal's efforts to obviate its presence 'els meus ulls són el llac / on es nega la lluna' (BD 102, lines 6–7). The moon returns in splendour in 'Foguera Joana' (107–17), the next part: 'Avui regna la lluna, amor, / i cap flor no es tanca' (BD 109, lines 3–4). Although the moon dies again it gives the cup of victory to Marçal:

> Aquest pallasso amb la ganyota amarga
> em diu que el cor té la forma d'un cranc.
> (En vi molt dolç, la lluna sense sang
> mor) i jo prenc la copa que m'allarga. (BD 122, lines 1–4)

Collective images structure the way in which subjectivity achieves complete social articulation. The alternation of the presence/absence of the moon indicates that the process of 'making the self' needs to be inscribed within the structure of collective images. Violi has highlighted the importance of this fluctuation for the construction of subjectivity:

> we inscribe our internal self-representations into existing forms of social and hence visible representations. Without this inscription and mediation, subjectivity cannot develop fully, but is forced into a partiality which for women is the partiality of the 'vestals' of feeling and of the private sphere, or,

at a different level, the partiality of woman as Nature, Mother, Original matrix and so on. (1992: 163)

The power of the moon magnifies the poetic subject who eventually, at the end of *Bruixa de dol*, obeys the moon's will:

Amb pas furtiu, per fosc itinerari,
l'aranya ha pres altre cop el casal.
Cendra d'amor assenyala el portal.
Però la lluna em dicta que despari. (BD 133, lines 5-9)

In *Sal oberta* the moon appears in 'Divisa' of the book: 'Sal que m'embranqui, en temps d'hora batuda, / pel gorg lunar on tota cosa muda!' (SO 175, lines 13-14) It is the place of transition. In the book, Marçal narrates the experience of her pregnancy and her decision to become a mother despite the absence of the father, contrary to established cultural and social rules: 'passejant un ventre altiu, que s'aventurava a navegar en aigües de ningú' (Marçal 1989c: 30).

As I have highlighted above, there are certain female experiences which have not had poetic elaboration in the tradition of Catalan literature, such as pregnancy, motherhood, maternity, and so on.[33] The poetic subject, by narrating the experience of her pregnancy in the poems, opens up a space for bringing the female body into poetic discourse 'which brings to an end the silence of women' (Bocchetti 1991: 150). This silence is displaced by the performance of the poetic subject, whose experience has been articulated in the part 'Arc i tenebra', where the moon is defeated: 'la lluna perd el peu i mor, fosa, a la rasa. / Focs de mirall s'emparen de l'aigua i de l'espasa' (SO 205, lines 11-12). As a result, the symbolic structure of the moon is altered, and therefore, redefined.

In the next part of 'Heura', the moon has a full presence with magnificent power: 'Ara mestrejo sola la marea que duu / el creixent de la lluna arrapat al seu ham, / l'estoig viu on es fon l'ombra del teu anell' (SO 239, lines 12-14). This moon has now acquired a new meaning, has transgressed beyond the inherited connotations of reflection and into a new configuration of woman who not only procreates but also creates. In 'L'hort foscant de l'atzar', Marçal equates the presence of the moon with her baby. This new moon will be born with Heura, her daughter, as she shows in the first poem of this part entitled 'Averany' (Augury):

Sents? La lluna davalla i et diu Mercè-creixent,
i se t'esmuny per sota el davantal
i, a vol, et pren pel novenari d'heura
que lliga sal i sang, a cel obert...

[...]

Sents? La lluna davalla i et crida: ¿quin mal glaç
et llastà? Vés-hi! Nega't al ple de la tendresa! (SO 243, lines 1-4 and 13-14)

The moon measures the process of the 'making' of the poetic subject. When Marçal becomes pregnant, the moon reappears but the poetic subject does not surrender to its power. The moon, which represents woman, becomes a full moon, and Marçal writes: 'L'aixada de la lluna cava el meu cos en va' (SO 211, line 7). As we have seen, the moon in Marçal works as the existing configuration of the identity of woman. In contrast to the limitations of this symbol, the poetic subject confronts her experience with the element of shadow, which points towards the unexplored 'dark side of the moon' whereby the levels of significance of the poetic subject are expanded.

The Shadow: Place of Subjection, Space of Phantoms

The shadow is the third trope that intervenes in this first part of *poiesis* as the 'llast, zona no explorada, incontrolable, fat, lloc de la subjecció i dels fantasmes paralitzadors' (Marçal 1989a: 8). This unexplored field constitutes the structure that aims to preserve traditional limitations, and paralyzes any attempt to go beyond pre-established meanings. In Marçal's poetry, the space of the shadow surrounds culturally acquired traditional conceptions in her specific context. In this sense, the shadow becomes the space where possibilities for signification can expand:

> We believe that women's silence will continue to haunt our actions and thoughts, until we manage to make some sense of it, insert it into a historical perspective of thought, fill it with knowing; until we change the perspective in which to look at it; that is, at woman's implicit wretchedness. Our hypobook is that we should take women's silence not as a sign of their poverty of language, but of the poverty of language. (Bocchetti 1991: 151)

The shadow becomes available through a varied iconography that offers a plethora of images throughout the first three books. This iconography shifts from atavist conceptions to extended meanings. The poetic search for a new identity is determined mainly by the renegotiation of the poetic subject with the shadow. As Marçal herself has elucidated:

> cal una íntima baralla amb el que seria la pròpia ombra (això és un tema que surt molt en els meus poemes, i de mica en mica he anat comprenent per què). Aquesta mena de baralla amb la pròpia ombra penso que és el motor, l'origen de la meva poesia. I en el fons és el mateix tema de la identitat. (Montero 2004: 264)

The space of the shadow will not be well defined until her second book *Bruixa de dol*. In *Cau de llunes*, Marçal merely displays her sense of uneasiness towards a specific female pattern that cannot serve as a reference for her *ser dona*. As a result, the female gender category is shown in the last part of the book 'Fregall d'espart' on three different levels: quotidian, traditional — via songs (cançó popular) and conceptual, by using the images of Greek mythology.[34] This last category allows Marçal to explore how ideological apparatus has configured the category of woman since ancient thought, and deplores patriarchy's attempts to justify such categorization. The poem entitled 'D'antologia', with the note *Iambes de Semònides*,[35] states such a position: 'Diferent va fer un déu el pensament / de la dona, al principi. En va fer una' (CLL 49, lines 1–2).

In *Bruixa de dol*, as already seen, Marçal stated 'començava el meu itinerary de dona "sola", de dona sense home. Com un peix sense bicicleta?' (1989c: 29). This personal situation, enhanced by the socio-cultural context of the post-Francoist period, plunges Marçal into: 'sinistre ve, i em veig l'ombra a la cara' (BD 128, line 4) and involves her in the arduous position of re-establishing the new spaces needed for new configurations: 'Ja no m'enartes, sol, / vaixell salvat de l'ombra, que és l'ombra qui m'ha pres' (BD 102, lines 1–3). In *Bruixa de dol*, the connotation of an independent woman, 'dona sense home', is displayed via the iconography of the 'witch' and 'fairies', both independent female figures that represent the marginal woman:

> la bruixa és un personatge reivindicatiu per part del moviment de les dones, com a individus que al llarg de la història han estat massacrades. Aleshores per a mi la bruixa és el símbol de la dona solidària amb altres bruixes. (Parer 1982: 23)

The figures of the witch and the fairy involve the vindication of a female bonding, as part of the experiences that have been kept in the shadows of symbolic signification. In the part of the book entitled 'Avui les fades i les bruixes s'estimen' Marçal suggests a love-bonding between the witch and the fairy, as the first stanza of the poem shows:

> Avui, sabeu? Les fades i les bruixes s'estimen.
> Han canviat entre elles escombres i varetes.
> I amb cucurull de nit i tarot de poetes
> endevinen l'enllà, on les ombres s'animen. (BD 137, lines 1–4)

In *Sal oberta* the shadow reveals that the poetic subject has deeply meditated on her experience and the possibilities that poetry may offer. The image of 'la sal' (salt), as the title of the book indicates, represents pain and hurt, as we can see in the 'Divisa' that opens up the book:

> Sal oberta a la nafra, que no es tanqui!
>
> [...]
>
> Sal oberta i, en reble, cel obert!
> Deixar senyal de sal on l'ona manqui
> que m'assaoni llengua, nas i orelles! (SO 175, lines 1 and 9–11)

These lines refer to the wound as the aperture that can allow a dialogue between the inner and outer boundaries of the subject, limits established between the individuality of the subject and the social position of the poetic subject. The symbol of salt preludes a deeper exploration into her personal experiences (as I shall explore in detail in Chapter Four). As a result, the conversation between both the social and symbolic order is possible. As Marçal adumbrates: 'la ferida és una obertura entre l'interior i l'exterior, que comunica dos mons. A partir d'aquí, doncs, es pot establir un diàleg' (Muñoz 1998: 176).[36]

In *Sal oberta* the shadow is equated with 'la tenebra', darkness. Following the mechanism of *poiesis* established at the beginning of the chapter, 'darkness' was born from Chaos, which indicates that the 'invisible' connects with doubt. This doubt is defined as the disconnection from light and harmony. Marçal's experience of pregnancy and abandonment by the baby's father plunges her into the difficult situation of deciding between life and death, abortion or continuing with her pregnancy and undertaking motherhood alone. The vicissitudes of this decision are narrated in 'Arc i tenebra'.

The 'darkness', as a disconnection from the light, appears at the time that the chain of actions has been altered by the experience of the poetic subject. In this way, chaos is established and the mechanism of *poiesis* starts again. The last stanza of the last poem of 'Al far!' displays the tone of absence and uncertainty that plunges Marçal into the dimension of 'tenebra':

> Solitari tenaç, damunt la terra eixorca
> penja l'amor, i els corbs obren via al demà.
> L'aixada de la lluna cava el meu cos en va.
> El glaç té el cor glaçat, a l'ombra de la forca.
>
> [...]
>
> Passo al freu i, en l'afrau de l'ona i de l'atzar,
> m'escanya amb fil de seda la tenebra i el far. (SO 211, lines 5–8 and 13–14)

The 'tenebra', as the alteration of order, bestow upon other images mystic and religious connotations:

> Cenyides per la serp de la tenebra
> la lluna i tu sou u: arbre i mirall.
> Fareu el ple quan el jorn llevi l'àncora
> i naveguen banderes sense imperi (SO 243, lines 5–8).

The 'snake' serves as the idea of life, of conception against the existing rules: *ex-situ* of the traditional core of a family. In this sense, the 'snake' as temptation alters the pre-given order, the harmony of actions: 'd'un sol cop d'ull em sedueix de veure, en el mirall dels meus versos, dels meus llibres, una serp i les seves mudes de pell: mudes que parlen i alhora resten mudes' (Marçal 1995b: 24).

Marçal thought of pregnancy, from a heterodox perspective, as a way of dislocating the maternal-feminine continuum: 'és una situació molt especial en la qual ets tu i hi ha un altre, encara que l'altre sigui més que res un ésser fantasiejat. A mi em fa l'efecte que és com una relació mística, com una mena, fins i tot, de narcisisme exagerat' (Sabadell 1998: 18). She experienced this situation as plenitude of her own being, rather than as a conflicting situation for the female subject, as some feminist academics have theorized about maternity.[37] This destabilises the binary procreation/creation, which has traditionally been attached to woman/man respectively. As she says in poem VI of the 'Sal oberta' section:

> Hi ets i no hi ets. I t'abraço, retuda.
> T'estimo com estimo aquest cos d'aigua
> que s'emmotlla al teu vidre sense tall,
> que vibra amb veu de gorga subterrània.
> Per tu l'estany escampa arreu miralls
> de doble faç: sóc jo i sóc un altra.
> I tu ets jo, petit desig obert
> al fons de tot paràsit que m'habites
> tan dolçament com el sol beu la pell
> del salobre com l'heura escala la tenebra. (SO 267, lines 1–10)

She configures pregnancy as a parallel process to love-bonding as displayed in the second line: 'T'estimo com estimo aquest cos d'aigua'. The fluid body, 'cos d'aigua', stands for existence, for life. This connects the act of creation with the living desire that is being formed in her womb: 'I tu ets jo, petit desig obert / al fons que m'habites / tan dolçament com l'heura escala la tenebra' (SO 267, lines 7–10). 'Heura', as the symbol of poetry as explored above, endorses the process of redefining, re-elaborating, restructuring 'la tenebra' through the act of poetry. Poetry triumphs over the disorder derived from the lack of any literary reference in the Catalan poetic tradition: 'Experiència difícil d'elaborar, en la mesura que hi ha pocs precedents: en aquest cas, era impossible que el meu llibre fos la síntesi de molts llibres llegits' (Marçal 1995a: 196).

Immersed in the temporal dimension the poetic subject, as the central axis and reference for *poiesis*, has established an intrinsic interaction with the moon and the shadow, 'l'esquema triangular bàsic que remet sempre, en la lluita o en el festí, a la pròpia solitud' (Marçal 1989a: 8). This has allowed Marçal not only to investigate the mechanisms of the socio-symbolic dimension but also to surpass the limits of significance. This process, underpinned by a specific iconography including 'salt', 'the witch' and 'heura', creates the space for semiotic transformations as 'baules d'una cadena que genera el rovell que l'ha de trencar' (Marçal 1989a: 8). In the next part of this section, still following a diachronic perspective, I shall examine how personal experience shattered the triangle:

poetic subject, the moon and shadow, and precipitated the transition towards a new referential point as the kernel of *poiesis*.

Engaging with the Shadow

In 1982 Marçal published *Terra de Mai*, a book of fifteen sestinas that not only marked a new stage in *poiesis* but also challenged prescriptive understandings of female sexuality by poetically narrating lesbian eroticism for the first time in the tradition of Catalan literature.[38] This book was the poetic result of personal experience, as Marçal in 1981 lived with a woman.[39] Consequently, *Terra de Mai* marked a turning point in the process of signification and semiotic reference and the subsequent production of poems. The progression of the specific iconography of the shadow that starts with *Terra de Mai* continues in *La germana, l'estrangera* and the last of her poetic collections: *Desglaç*, where *poiesis* oscillates between presence and absence. Prior to examining how the poetic subject in *La germana, l'estrangera* 'inicia un cos a cos amb l'ombra' (Marçal 1989a: 8) I shall explore how *Terra de Mai* represents the climax. It becomes the space of a complete signification: *Terra de Mai* reflects, thus, 'la crisi de l'esquema jo-lluna-ombra' (1989a: 8) that operated in the first part of *poiesis* and initiates a transition towards a dual structure: the poetic subject and the shadow.

Terra de Mai: *The 'Solstice' of* Poiesis

Using the complex lyrical structure of the sestina, Marçal in *Terra de Mai* pioneered the poetic narration of sexual interaction between two female bodies in the tradition of Catalan literature.[40] The use of the sestina allows her to surpass the intellectual activity of writing poetry and 'fa que vagi més enllà d'un pur exercici d'enginy: l'estructura recurrent, cíclica, que fa progressar el poema amb un constant retorn i replantejament del seus termes inicials' (1989b: 295). However, the image of the moon from *Terra de Mai* is *in absentia*: 'hi serà ara l'absent, només present a través de l'enyor' (1989a: 8). It is equated with the poetic subject via 'maial' as a combination of Mai and Marçal in the first sestina, as the fifth stanza shows:

> L'amor és una dansa sense espasa
> quan cap rellotge no marca cap hora.
> A l'aiguaneix del dia i de la terra
> s'alça, maial, la lluna sobre runa. (TM 297, lines 25–28)

Marçal re-aproppiates the limits of her female subjectivity by identifying the image of the moon with woman, as previously examined: 'la lluna, de cop abastable, encegadora' (1989a: 9). This occurs through the erotic iconography in the sexual bonding between Marçal and her female lover. The use of such a symbology conveys an alteration of the existing symbolic: 'som d'aquest món, però encetem un món' (TM 300, line 19). The other woman becomes the reference point for the poetic subject and opens up a new space of intersubjectivity that helps to re-establish the female symbolic:

> Lluny dels topants que defineix l'espasa
> l'ombra i l'atzar s'abracen i creix l'hora
> arrapada a l'arrel d'aquest gran arbre.
>
> [...]
>
> Renego vells confins que clou l'espasa. (TM 296, lines 6–8)

The female body in *Terra de Mai* becomes the locus of signification. Sexual attraction for the other woman posits the body as the root of significance. Through the erotic iconography, twinned with a natural imagery, Marçal places her sexual desire at the epicentre of the poetic expression. The presence of the other woman is articulated via the synecdoche of 'sexe': 'hi ha una deu fosca on em xucla l'oratge / per nodrir-te quan fem nit al meu sexe' (TM 302, lines 13–14). The body of the other woman becomes a mirror whereby the poetic subject reflects her own image, now complete and unified. The sestina 'Mai' displays this lyrically in the sixth stanza:

> Mai i mirall, vius en plata de plata,
> oferts al foc del meu desert voraç,
> trenquen als llavis i en molls de tempesta
> i rodolen pel cingle del desig
> on el teu cos i el meu fan un sol nom,
> on el meu nom i el teu fan un sol cos. (TM 307)

The surface fusion of the two bodies via sexual bonding is reminiscent of one of the points assessed by women from *Il pensiero*: the need to represent female desire through actual performance between/among women:[41] 'we have a common desire for change, a common refusal to content ourselves with what we have, an awareness of the limits of emancipation, the will to be recognized in society as we are, with our sex' (Cigarini et al. 1991: 127). This practice aims to inaugurate the symbolic space needed to disclose female desire: 'Veus de desig fan que es capgiri l'aire / i escampen tretze vents arreu del món' (TM 301, lines 26–27).

However, the space for a complete identity and full significance achieved through the embodied presence of Mai is inhibited by the abandonment by her lover and the subsequent absence of the other woman: 'Trenco el mirall i em rediu que sóc sola' (TM 313, line 29). This reveals the vacuum, the frustrated ephemeral attempt to achieve significance via the presence of the other female body. This hiatus upholds the spatial difficulties of expressing female desire in the symbolic and the subsequent need for alternative spaces. The absence of

Mai confirms the lack of semiotic reference points: 'No hi ha campana per refer el paisatge / ni verd de festa per pintar nous boscos. / Trencant la copa, almenys salvaré l'ombra?' (TM 323, lines 37–39). As a result, the poetic subject is relegated to the space of exile:

> De tota espera amor visc en exili
>
> [...]
>
> Amb sang d'exili signo el meu retorn,
> quan, dejuna de dies, em ve al coll
> la primavera, perforant l'agenda. (TM 321, lines 1 and 37–39)

Exile as a result of a lack of placement within the existing symbolic leads Marçal to force the limits of the female subject — via the cyclic sestina — within available structures. As she says: 'en els processos vitals hi ha aquesta tensió, entre la tendència al retorn i la tendència a anar cap a un altre costat, a anar endavant i trobar coses noves. Un exemple gràfic és la sextina' (Montero 2004: 265). In what follows, I shall examine the exile of the woman poet as a result of the fragmentation of female subjectivity.

The Female Poetic Subject: the Fragility of the 'I'

The sense of unity and complete significance of the poetic subject achieved in *Sal oberta*, via the period of pregnancy, and in *Terra de Mai* through the fusion of the two bodies in a sexual bonding, is transposed into a fragmented identity in *La germana, l'estrangera*: 'el trencament del miratge aboca — com en un part — a un àmbit estrany, caòtic i dolorós' (Marçal 1995a: 197). The absence of the other woman at the end of the book *Terra de Mai* and the first experience of Marçal with her baby are the main themes of this book. The unity of the poetic subject was fractured by the act of giving birth, which ended the bond established during the pregnancy between Marçal and the foetus: 'la relació concreta amb la meva filla Heura, ja nascuda, i que, per tant, deixa de ser *jo*' (1995a: 197, her italics). *La germana, l'estrangera* brings a profound meditation on the fragmented identity. This rupture is upheld by the discontinuity between her embodied being and her conceptual being, which causes a multiple, fragmented subjectivity: 'aquí la lluita s'estableix entre un jo que es vol fer i els múltiples personatges que, des del mirall li retornen una imatge múltiple' (1995a: 197). Such a multiplicity argues for the change of the symbols of *poiesis*, which since *Terra de Mai* have been transferred into the different female images that participate in the poetic narration: mother, daughter, sister, the stranger: 'Mare, filla, amant?: la germana, l'estrangera. Un tu i un jo que es confonen' (1985b: 8).

The book is divided into two parts. In the first 'En el desig cicatritzat i en l'ombra', Marçal poetically displays her early relationship with her daughter

Heura. This relationship is marked by the rupture of the delivery, 'on un part és alhora "plaer / de fletxa a trenc de sang" i despossessió absoluta' (1985b: 8). This locates the body of the poetic subject as the physical evidence of this sense of dispossession:

> mentre el món, dins del meu cos obert,
> era un cor desbocat, com si una mina
> sobtadament dinamitada
> adollés el seu riu subterrani. (LGLE 333, lines 19–22)

However, this rupture unleashes the interrelation with another subject whom she 'created', yet who is strange to her:

> jo contemplava aquell bocí de mi
> esdevingut, ja per sempre, estranger,
> i alhora imprès per sempre, a cor i a sang,
> en el desig cicatritzat i en l'ombra. (LGLE 336, lines 9–12)

The 'sang' (blood) is the image that establishes the mother-daughter connection, not only as a sign of familial bond but also as a gender communion, whereby the mother-daughter relationship is imagined from a non-hierarchical perspective. In this sense, the poetic subject addresses her daughter as 'germana' (sister), which allegorizes the mother-daughter relationship as an interaction between two female subjects:

> Heura,
>   victòria marçal,
>   germana
> estrangera, de cop feta present:
> com desxifrar el teu llenguatge bàrbar
> i violent que força els meus confins
> fins a la sang, un repte que no em deixa
> ni les cames tan sols per a fugir! (LGLE 338, lines 1–8)

Heura, the name of her baby, as we mentioned earlier, is the symbol of the triumph of poetry. The birth of her baby metaphorically brings about poetry as the space of the creation of new possibilities:

> Poema viu que no urgia resposta
> com ara aquesta que sé que no sé.
> I malgrat tot t'anomeno victòria,
> heura marçal, germana, l'estrangera. (LGLE 338, lines 21–24)

Due to its natural attributes, ivy has been associated in different cultures with strength and feminine values. For the Druids, ivy was a symbol of strength due to its capacity to grow in widely differing environments and conditions; it is also very difficult to destroy.[42] For the Celts, ivy was related to the Lunar Goddess Arianrhod, whose ritual allowed the transition to the dark side of the moon.

Women worshipped it, and Arianrhod helped them to find their own feminine power.

The complexities of the mother-daughter relationship are developed in all the poems of the section 'En el desig cicatritzant i en l'ombra', with the presence of another body, her daughter Heura: 'la carn sense paraules, / davant de mi i en mi. / I jo que havia llegit tots els llibres' (LGLE 331). The difficulty of this interaction lies in the absence of a linguistic code that can mediate between mother and daughter: 'relació que durant molt de temps vaig veure molt conflictiva, fonamentalment mentre no hi havia paraules pel mig' (Sabadell 1998: 18). This maternal love is displayed as a difficult interaction with the baby due to lack of language and complicated communication: 'com desxifrar el teu llenguatge bàrbar' (LGLE 338, line 5). This is a consequence of Marçal's experience of maternity from a heterodox perspective: 'viure aquest amor maternal no com m'imaginava que estava establert, em generava un sentiment de culpa' (Sabadell 1998: 21). She lacked iconographic and semiotic references that could help her to elaborate such a conflict. Therefore, her experience again grounds the process of *poiesis*: 'em van caldre dos anys i, en certa manera, sortir de la confusió, del caos del principi, per poder convertir tot allò — contradictori i fosc — en tèrbolament lluminós, és a dir, en poesia' (Marçal 1995a: 197).

This maternal love is equated with a sense of sisterhood, a relationship between two female subjects established equally. The poetic subject refuses and rejects the image of the mother as an authoritative figure that 'castrates', censors, and thwarts the possibilities for opening up spaces and expanding signification. In this sense, both subjectivities are blurred in a continuous flux that allows the poetic subject to change positions and alter pre-established boundaries: 'com a imatges bessones, / tu i jo, la d'una banda / i l'altra del mirall' (LGLE 390, lines 6–8).

Shadow and Blood in the Mirror

> Els poemes de tot el llibre *La germana, l'estrangera* no només reflecteixen, sinó que formen part essencial del meu cos a cos amb ells, del meu esforç permanent per conjurar-los. (Marçal 1985b: 8)

These words, from the introduction to the book *La germana, l'estrangera*, reveal that the female subject finds in the mirror the space that divides the limits between her poetic subject and the shadow. The mirror reflects: 'ball frenètic d'ombres davant d'una paret closa, d'un vidre impenetrable' (Marçal 1985b: 8). This impervious glass is represented through the icon of Hydra, 'i allò que el mirall reflecteix, com la *hydra* petrifica' (Marçal 1989a: 9, her italics). The Hydra was a multiheaded water monster, guardian of the underworld in the lake of Lerna. The Hydra protected the entrance to the underworld, whose door was situated under the waters of Lerna.[43] On the other side of this mirror, the poetic subject sees all the figures that challenge the fragility of her own subjectivity reflected: 'l'assassí, pel mirall sense fons, la infanticida pel mirall del fons, la impostora, la culpable, la pròfuga, la mare, la filla, l'amant, la germana, l'estrangera. Ombra i sang' (Marçal 1989a: 9).

The image of blood links the mother-daughter bond with the hurt caused by the absence of the female lover. In this sense, the poetic subject challenges the conception of maternity: 'el teu dolor: / la meva culpa en el mirall' (LGLE 345, 1–2). This feeling of hurt discloses the most conflicted and unexplored side of maternity in sequential images that allows Marçal to demystify the category of mother:

> Ve la infanticida
> pel mirall del fons.
> Deixeu-li que canti
> el seu fosc amor. (GE 355, lines 1–4)

In this difficult situation, the semiotic reference point has now changed. It alters from elaborating the experience with images traditionally considered as feminine in Catalan culture via the moon and the witch in her early works, to capturing the experience of maternity as a conflict. Marçal experienced maternity as problematic, as difficult, and this created a sense of guilt in Marçal expressed through the use of the symbol of blood. This conflict is revealed through the use of the image of the 'impostora': the mother who is not characterized as the traditional caring, tender, loving mother. The last poem of the first part of the book 'En el desig cicatritzat i en l'ombra', dedicated to her daughter Heura, explains who 'the impostora' is and how she is inhabited by the shadow:

> Qui parla i fa per mi? És la impostora.
> M'habitava sense que jo ho sabés
> fins que vingueres. Llavors va sorgir
> de no sé quines golfes, com una ombra,
> i em posseeix com un amant tirànic
> i em mou com la titella d'una fira.
> I sovint, al mirall, la veig a Ella
> rescatada de no sé quina cendra.
> No li facis cap cas quan Ella et parla,
> encara que m'usurpi veu i rostre.
> I si et barra la porta de sortida
> amb el seu cos amorós i brutal
> cal que la matis sense cap recança.
> Fes-ho per mi també i en el meu nom:
> jo la tinc massa endins i no sabria
> aturar-me al llindar del suïcidi. (LGLE 356)

In the second part of the book, 'Sang presa', the absence of the lover allegorizes the difficulties of expressing same-sex desire: 'on l'absència esdevé un blanc llençol on ballen només, multiplicades sense fi, ombres en sang' (Marçal 1995a: 197). The two first stanzas of the poem suggest:

> M'he mirat al mirall i et veig a tu
> — i no hi fa res que el trenqui en mil bocins —.
> Ja no sé pas on són els meus confins:
> cada esvorall de vidre ens és comú.
> I miro ara el pany de paret — nu
> de signes, de paraules, de camins —
> que resta al meu davant, feu de ningú:
> no hi ha reflex que em xucli, nit endins. (LGLE 371)

The unity of the subject is fragmented here when Marçal does not find the images and words to poetically compose the experience of her love for another woman. Dominijanni has stated that the female subject faces this fragmentation within the existing symbolic order due to the absence of collective images that can provide a reference for individuality. She says:

> From a binomial common to every human being, it is destined to become for women a split: between body and language, between female sexual difference and the symbolic order. This split reveals the absence of a symbolic mediation between women and the world, it explains the defect of liberty in which woman finds herself acting. (1991: 132)

This idea is particularly developed in the poem 'Hydra' where the opacity of the fragmented subject — in contrast with the unity and complete significance, achieved in *Terra de Mai* — finds difficulty in obtaining any other space of signification:

> Què hi ha sota el teu rostre
> que em fita amb ulls de pedra?
> ¿Quan gosaré arrencar-te
> la màscara de carn
> i fer front a l'obscur
> mirall que em petrifica? (LGLE 391)

The 'màscara de carn' (mask of flesh) allegorizes the binary surface-reflection of the body reflected in the mirror, in contrast with the depth or substance of experience as part of the self. This reveals, along with the symbol of Hydra, that the poetic subject finds a deeper level of incoherence, which goes beyond the flesh, since her identity does not exclusively refer to the absence of the lover. The image of the other reveals the opacity and obscurity of the poetic subject. In this sense, the mask refers to the being, which is reflected in the mirror. As a result, the mirror, along with the shadow, reinforces the vacuum caused by the absence of the beloved woman, an absence that creates the emptiness, the void, the pain represented through the image of blood: 'testifica l'intent inútil de traspassar el llindar cap a l'altra banda' (Marçal 1989a: 9). Hence, Marçal returns, once again to the sphere of the exile:

> Sense tornada
> veus? La sang s'exilia.
> Per l'altra porta
> fa entrada, viva, roja,
> la nova primavera. (GE 405)

With this exile, the process of *poiesis* is restarted again when the absence of the beloved is restored by the presence of the other woman. In the next part, although continuing with the binary absence/presence, I will discuss how in *Desglaç* the poetic subject and the shadow relinquish the boundaries between the individual and symbolic signification.

The Poetic Subject: from Solid to Liquid

Desglaç (1989) — the last of Marçal's poetic productions — depicts the death of Marçal's father Antoni Marçal in 1984: 'l'hora del desglaç és una hora dolorosa però oberta. Hi ha una mort. Desapareix la carcassa que immobilitza, però que també sustenta, el sòlid dóna pas al líquid, els contorns es fonen' (Marçal 1989a: 9). This death of the father 'real i/o simbòlica' will evoke the presence of the other woman: 'l'amor que fa aparèixer en el mirall, sencer o trencat, l'ombra de *'l'altra dona'* (1989a: 10).

The lack of literary references to this matter in Catalan literature leads Marçal to search for poetic references in other traditions such as the Anglo-American.[44] These references were taken from the American poets Adrienne Rich and Sylvia Plath: 'De les lectures de Plath i de Rich, encara que llegides en traducció, m'ha arribat una força — una mena de risc, en el cas de Plath, i una visió política en el de Rich — (Sabadell 1998: 16).

The influence of Plath is present in the first part of the book 'Daddy', with the quotation: 'feixuc com el marbre, un sac ple de Déu' (D 424). Marçal understands her father's death as the end of paternal laws, the end of the hierarchy imposed by patriarchy, and the limitations established with his norms, that is, the norms of the father: 'la mort enderrocava les muralles / i tot pedestal' (D 440, lines 3–4). For Marçal, this death represents the possibility for the father to return to her and be born again, as a way to start the cycle of life again 'com el no-nat lorquià de Yerma' (1989a: 10):

> Com un nen tot petit en els meus braços,
> una embosta de pols en el bressol d'unes mans,
> canto perquè dormis
> i et gronxo en la sang.

> Com si fossis el fill del teu nom que no he tingut,
> sols un bolic de carn
> cos meu endins, desig,
> aigües enllà. (D 439, lines 1–8)

The poetic subject reappropiates language and reinvents the figure of the father. The metaphorical implication of recreating her father is apparent and significant. By writing about the death of the father, Marçal aims at inventing his rebirth. With this poetic elaboration, Marçal attempts to invert the foundation of patriarchy that establishes woman's first contact with culture or the political sphere through the mediation of a man.[45] She profoundly laments the death of her father but nonetheless, she questions his *law*. Because of her rejection of the established norms, Marçal is relegated to the space of silence: 'l'ombra em té tota. No em valen els mots. / La teva cendra em colga en vell caliu. / La teva llengua em clava en el silenci' (D 429, lines 3–5).

In opposition to absence and death, we find in *Desglaç* the presence of the body of the other woman. Her love for another woman brings the poetic subject to her own rebirth: 'contra la mort, contra aquest lladre absent / que pot robar-li el preu del seu rescat, / així tornava jo al lloc de l'amor' (D 463, lines 6–8). Having overcome the frontiers represented by paternal law, Marçal configures the presence of the other woman as the necessary presence for a complete feminine significance:

> Cada tombant del teu cos m'alimenta
> d'altres paisatges que l'oblit no fon:
> el foc encén de nou cada campana
> i es clou l'enyor, en retrobar-los vius,
> fets carn en tu, i tu els dónes sentit. (D 466, lines 12–16)

The Shadow: Towards a Poetic Transgression

In *Desglaç* it is difficult to determine the boundaries between the poetic subject and the sphere of the shadow. As Marçal writes:

> la desintegració aparent és també la possibilitat de fluir. Enllà queda la rigidesa, l'encarament, els moviments d'autòmata, la repetició compulsiva i mecànica dels gestos. Camí fluid, de nou sense esquemes ni pautes. (Marçal 1989a: 10)

An incessant flux between presence and absence blurs the boundaries between both dimensions: the possibility of fluidity, as shown in the passage above, is displayed in the motto of the book:

> — un llamp de pedra fòssil
> de sobte massa viu.
> Líquid esglai:
>   Desglaç. (D 421, lines 4–6)

This poem discloses a sense of 'fear', a liquid fear, which is described as *desglaç* (thawing). In contrast with the other books, silence now precedes the creation of the poem. According to Bocchetti, 'It's a discourse which frightens us: we live this silence, this absence, as a profound and secret sign of our wretched state' (1991: 151). There is a dimension of female experience that is still invisible and inhabits chaos. This is 'el pany de l'experiència encara mut, amb tot allò d'inquietant, amenaçador que hi ha en un silenci carregat d'ombra i tesat com un arc' (Marçal 1995a: 190). The death of the real father implies a physical absence that transcends into the omnipotent presence of the symbolic father as the superior force: 'Ull-subjecte-deu ordenador que defineix on és l'harmonia i la forma' (190).

As mentioned above, the death of the father implies, as in a cyclic movement, the possibility of a rebirth: 'com habitant d'un recer que implica la innocència i com a gresol de totes les possibilitats inèdites' (Marçal 1989a: 10). Despite this positive understanding of death, the absence of the father as the eternal presence is to some extent disturbing. Taking the shape of a hawk, the real father has transformed into the presence of the symbolic father. This is displayed in all the poems of the section 'Daddy', but it is especially explicit in the following poem that echoes the Lord's Prayer:

> Pare esparver que em sotges des del cel
> i em cites en el regne del teu nom,
> em petrifica la teva voluntat
> que es fa en la terra com es fa en el cel.
> La meva sang de cada dia
> s'escola enllà de tu en el dia d'avui
> però no sé desfer-me de les velles culpes
> i m'emmirallo en els més cecs deutors.
> I em deixo caure en la temptació
> de perseguir-te en l'ombra del meu mal. (D 431)

The development of Marçal's poetical evolution that I have hitherto explored finishes with the vindication of Marçal as the agent of her own creation. In other words, the poetic subject constructs her identity by reappropriating available structures and reconfiguring pre-established limits. As Marçal says in one of her last poems: 'sóc la llavor que esclata a trenc de mort / i s'arbra cega i encesa en l'embat' (D 488, lines 5–6). The reference to the other woman underpinned by the triumph of the poetic subject over the shadow determines the success of *poiesis*: 'prenc el camí que m'ha portat a tu' (D 466, line 23). Despite the complexities encountered during *poeisis*, Marçal has expanded the space of the symbolic and has illuminated the possibilities for new meanings:

> Per tu retorno d'un exili vell
> com si tornés d'enlloc. I alhora et sé
> terra natal, antiga claror meva,
> i l'indret on la culpa es feia carn. (D 517, lines 1–4)

The poetic subject, the moon, and the shadow, as seen throughout this chapter have revealed that 'des de *Cau de llunes* a *Desglaç* aquest és el ball d'ombres i màscares que les paraules *re-presenten, juguen* i es juguen. Quasi sense entreactes. I sense treva: clOs i/o Solc' (Marçal 1989a: 7). This results as a primary and intrinsic relationship between life and experience and the subsequent concrete poetic elaboration. Thus, the process of *poiesis* harnesses a specific iconography to the redefinition of the female subjectivity. In what follows, I shall explore the conditions of the redefinition of the self, examining the possibilities for the subject within the set of norms that determine the legitimacy of this redefinition.

Delimiting *Poiesis* as Construction of the Feminine Self

Poiesis, as the place where the construction of the self takes place, raises some questions regarding the effectiveness of such performativity within the structures and semiotic references that interact within a poem. If *poiesis* takes the form of poetry and becomes available through existing codes and existing images that precede this process, to what extent is it safe to rely upon the effectiveness of such a procedure? More importantly, how can the limitations on the process of redefining identity be considered if the dialogue between the structures is orchestrated through available literary and cultural spaces?

Modes of Subjectivation

I shall start by again quoting Butler's words on the way in which she understands *poiesis*: 'There is no making of oneself (*poiesis*) outside of a mode of subjectivation (*assujettisement*) and, hence, no self-making outside of the norms that orchestrate the possible forms that a subject may take' (2005: 17). Such an assertion conveys two deleterious consequences for the process of *poiesis* in Marçal's poetic project. On the one hand, it displaces the agency of the subject in the formation of her own identity and relegates this category to a mere functionality, discarding her active participation in the processes of signification. On the other hand, such a statement upholds the set of structures as fixed, reducing the possibilities of alteration to the minimum. Prior to considering these questions, which are of a primary importance for the viability of *poiesis* and its consequent contribution to a feminist epistemology, I will firstly discuss what Butler has referred to as 'the mode of subjectivation'. By extension, I would like to ask how could one conceive *a priori* such 'possible forms that a subject may take' without engaging first with the means by which these forms can be shaped? These two questions are of vital importance for my purpose, since *poiesis* precisely implies a mode of altering the poetic codes and norms, through images and language. However, my intention is not to deny the presence of existing norms in the process of signification, since every process is shaped according to the specific positions that these codes embrace. I am, thus, suggesting the difficulties of anticipating the exact forms that this subject may take without first disentangling the mechanism that has precipitated the development of such a process. These two points, derived from Butler's statement, relegate the possibilities of significant expansion to a very limited level. Marçal, as we have seen, inhabits the space of poetry, via the use of specific iconography that represents bodily images, and reappropriates the poetic space as her 'mode of subjectivation', in other words, as the 'making' of herself, as *poiesis*.

In confirmation of this, and deploying the theoretical position of *differenza sessuale*, whereby I have suggested that the body provides a specific position within the symbolic, I would like to start by highlighting that the mechanisms that delineate the process of subjectivation have not operated equitably for both sexed subjectivities.[46] In this sense, the question that Butler addresses as a form of recognition: 'Who are you?' (2005: 30) does not imply the same response from both sexed identities. However, in highlighting the ostensible neutrality and universality of the subject and its different and possible forms of articulation, I am not suggesting the existence of two exclusive forms of subjectivation. Rather, my intention is to instigate a discussion about the construction of the self in Marçal's poetry.

The interaction between norm and agency in the poems points out that biological difference should be taken into consideration when we start reconsidering writing as Marçal's mode of subjectivation, since morphology has traditionally foregrounded their categorisation from very different perspectives and from a disparity of positions. Consequently, both male and female categories have been hierarchically established, positioning the male subject as the only possible form of subjectivity, which subsequently transcended into the universal and neutral form. In common with this, patriarchy has established a relevant set of codes in order to determine the place and space of each different engendered subject. As a result, the condition of the subject as such has been specifically nominated as masculine, this being understood as 'the one' in opposition to 'the other', since this other becomes the locus of reflection of the one; in other words, 'the other' works as a reflexive subject who gives to 'the one' a sense of address (2005: 15). 'The other' enhances thus the position of 'the one' in the patriarchal hierarchy.[47]

This is precisely the starting point of *poiesis* as a socio-symbolic practice: to invert the correlation between 'the one' and 'the other' and dismantle universal and neutral stipulations about the self, subject and identity. In this sense, in *poiesis* Marçal emerges with a concrete position from the particularities of her own condition, hence, not a universal but a specific one. The fact of considering *poiesis* as praxis has allowed Marçal to encode the act of writing poetry as her mode of subjectivation, moving thus beyond theoretical contentions and monolithic categories.

If we assume that the complete process of subjectivity requires the representation of oneself in relation to available collective references, we are confirming that there is an alternation from internal stipulations to existing representations. In fact, it engages intimately with the position of the female subject and her specific process of signification,[48] and has established huge theoretical conflicts among academics and theorists of feminism. The idea that has caused major controversy in feminism is the concept of the embodied gender subject. This acknowledgment of the female body as a source of an epistemology of the self creates a certain sense of anxiety derived precisely from patriarchal considerations of the body towards a 'valid' reconstruction of subjectivity. Such a statement highly complicates the participation of the female subject within the existing norm. It also upholds a situation whereby the positions from which both sexed subjects start their process of subjectivation are disparate.

Conditions of Emergence

The complexities involved in feminine subject include a web of power relations that subjugates the existence of the self to hierarchical positions. It is true that the engagement of the female subject with the structures of power has been inevitable and necessary in order to perpetuate a specific discourse of normativity. As a result, the conditions whereby the subject 'I' comes into being are disparate. The 'I' inhabits different positions according to the rules that have set up this category, and in light of this I suggest that it is necessary to specify the conditions whereby a subject emerges and elaborates a narration of the self. The emergence of Marçal as a poet and her subsequent project of *poiesis* are not above socio-historical specificities. The oppressive political system of a dictatorship reinforced the unity of the monolithic category of woman, embedded in a tradition that encouraged a sense of discontinuity between a particular perspective and a social one. This historical period, shaped by specific religious and social discourses, generated a sense of incoherence that precipitated her emergence as a poetic subject and her willingness to surpass this 'pre-given' condition. According to this, one may agree with Butler when she suggests that the temporality of the norms in a concrete structure differs from the particular temporality of the subject. As Butler puts it:

> Because norms emerge, transform, and persist according to a temporality that is not the same as the temporality of my life, and because they also sustain my life, and because they also in some ways sustain my life in its intelligibility, the temporality of norms interrupts the time of my living. (2005: 35)

Following this statement, the temporality of normativity overshadows the temporality of the female subject in her own emergence. But if we accept that there is some kind of power that limits the conditions of the emerging subject, then, no emergence would be possible, as the temporality of the norms precedes the time of the subject, and therefore, the female subject will never be able to create and demonstrate the individuality of her own self. Yet, does the subject not take the active role in the dynamics established between subject and norm? Therefore, is Marçal not, as a writer who is in possession of the set of linguistic forms available, able to perform an act of creativity? This is crucial for Marçal, since her emergence conveys her function as a poet, and as an agent when she as a subject disregards the norms of her time and instead invades the existing temporality by reappropriating the discourse of normativity and adapting it to the particularities of her own reconfiguration. Hence, the process of *poiesis* not only relies upon the structures whereby the self emerges but also draws upon the agency of the subject as a figure of authority in the concrete temporality of her own self.

Desire and Recognition

The tension between the particularities of Marçal and the power of poetic norms determine the existence of the latter prior to the emergence of the embodied subject. It is symptomatic of the existing normativity that the female subject, in her emergence, experiences a void. This is due to the lack of spaces in the existing set of codes that permit the female subject, and particularly Marçal, to express her desire, her specific femininity. This is what *il pensiero della differenza sessuale* has denominated as *collocazione simbolica* (symbolic placement). Marçal, as a subject, does not emerge simply to offer an account of her existence. She irrupts in the diachrony of patriarchy in order to elaborate a process of self-representation whereby she, as a specific entity, embraces this position and reconstitutes the paradigms of her own specificity. In other words, *poiesis* as 'making' of the self empowers Marçal's agency as a woman poet and moves towards the redefinition of epistemology and the discourse of ethics.

In establishing *poiesis* as a methodology Marçal seeks not only to speak of her desire but also of her desire to speak. She endeavours to give voice to her desire, to become the subject of her own experience, and as a result produce, through an oscillation between the self and normativity, a narration of the 'I'. If Lacan addresses the issue of desire from a psychoanalytic perspective, Butler deploys Hegelian parameters that link desire to recognition as a sense of self-affirmation:[49] 'the desire to be, the desire to persist in one's own being' (Butler 2005: 43). This persistence is defined as the aim of *poiesis*; the making of herself is foregrounded in the desire to become a subject of her own being, followed thus by an act of recognition as the ultimate result of representing desire.

One of the challenges of the poetic subject is precisely to relate her specific desire in terms of symbolic recognition. Marçal seeks to find literary references that can function as a sense of address when she is poetically elaborating her experience. Nevertheless, what she finds is a semiotic vacuum that impedes the relationship of image and meaning and prevents recognition. There is no such space because there are no semiotic, linguistic or symbolic references that can provide the female subject with a sense of address. This is an impediment to participating within the dynamics of the symbolic, foregrounded in the uneasiness about expressing female desire, hence femininity.

Relational Being

Desire not only brings the subject into being through external recognition, via normativity as the regime that decides the validity of her specific experience. It also relates the subject to 'the other' for the purposes of self-recognition:

> Perquè en la pregunta davant del mirall no hi ha només una recerca d'una identitat subjectiva, diguem-ne narrativa: un subjecte preguntant-se per si mateix, intentant de dotar-se d'un discurs sobre si mateix. En el mirall es busca, també, i potser sobretot, la mirada anticipada dels altres, de l'Altre, d'aquell que té poder de judici sobre la nostra actuació. (Marçal 1995a: 189)

This is what Butler has referred to as a relational being, that is, a subject who by being in contact with others seeks recognition (2005: 20). According to her, this relational being frustrates the transparency and clarity of the self. As a consequence, the multiplicity and opacity of the subject causes anxiety in her self-perception. As she says: 'moments of unknowingness about oneself tend to emerge in the context of relations to others' (2005: 20). How can, thus, a subject who has never held such a capacity develop such 'moments'? We can equate unknowingness with lack of recognition. In this sense, lack of recognition evolves into unknowingness, finally resulting in a desire to tackle the question 'Who are you?', 'Without any expectation of a full or final answer' (Butler 2005: 43).

Marçal, at the point when she decides to narrate herself, suffers a discontinuity between her position as a woman and her desire to give significance to her subjectivity, which evolves into a sense of displacement and the consequent codification of her desire. In this sense, it is legitimate to assert that the opacity of the self is a consequence of her relational position towards the others. However, it is important here to return to the point I have analysed earlier, which suggested that the processes of signification for both sexed beings does not follow the same route. Consequently, this also affects the way in which the female subject is positioned in relation to others. The problem seems to be built around woman always being 'the other' herself. Although it would be interesting to analyse such a perspective, I will merely suggest that given that woman has never been 'the one', the interaction between oneself and others raises myriad questions that need to be taken into account prior to analysing the interaction of the self with others as a relational being. This is precisely the starting point of *poiesis*. For Marçal, the inadequacy experienced between the conceptual category of woman and the actual materialization of *ser dona* evolved into a sense of 'no ser prou jo' (Busquets i Grabulosa 1980: 217) and led her to investigate alternative poetical forms of self-narration. Marçal, as a female poet, has a problematic position in relation to tradition. The fact that Marçal through *poiesis* attempts to question certain parameters of her femininity posits her own position in conflict with the normativity she has been interacting with, and where she has been looking for recognition: 'posar en qüestió uns arquetipus comporta entrar en conflicte amb una tradició' (Nadal 1989: 27).

This connects with what *il pensiero della differenza sessuale* has established as one of the main goals for women: to achieve signification. Therefore, there is a need to bring the female subject to the centre of her own redefinition. In this sense, *poiesis* as a methodology enacts experience and poetry and allows the poetic subject to expand the spaces for redefinition, thus recognition. Marçal places herself in relation to other female images that serve as a part of the symbolic placement (*collocazione simbolica*). This is what the theorists of *il pensiero* have called entrustment, as discussed in Chapter One. The presence of a female link between mother-daughter, sister-sister, woman-woman in the poems permits Marçal to develop a methodology to overcome this sense of unknowingness which is nuanced by lyric self- recognition.

My reading of Marçal's project as her mode with which to reconstruct herself suggests that the interaction between experience and poetry confirms *poiesis* as a method of the socio-symbolic practice of sexual difference. The diachronic perspective is essential to inscribe the 'making' of oneself within a specific historical context, which becomes possible through the intervention of a recurrent iconography and extended metaphors. As a result, *poiesis* is a methodology that attempts to open up spaces of *collocazione simbolica*. Such spaces are established through the creation of vincula: mother-daughter and woman-woman. Praxis prevails over theory. By foregrounding *poiesis* in a dialectical and dialogic interaction of the structure, I have attempted to provide an account of the limitations that the poetic subject may encounter in her performance. Butler's conceptualization of the subject has allowed me to put *poiesis* in dialogue with the structures that govern the laws of signification, further questioning the legitimacy of Marçal, as a woman, to be an agent of her own discourse.

As seen, the space of poetry and lyric formation is the dynamic space that allows her to rewrite her self. This redefinition conflates form and content into the space of poetry, which provides Maria-Mercè Marçal with the necessary arena in which to redefine, remake, re-inscribe, and reread herself, configuring the poetic genre as a dynamic web of structures whereby the action of the poetic subject can be negotiated. Throughout her poetic evolution, we can find several conceptual paradigms about her mode of *ser dona* and her particular way of interacting with language and writing in the process of creativity. These paradigms, relevant to my purpose and this research, are the spatial conditions of poetry, the action of the poetic subject, and, finally, her interaction with 'the other' in the poems. Through various arguments and methodological approaches I will enquire into these topics in the following chapters. Considering thus that Marçal uses poetry in order to undertake her literary project, the next chapter will further elucidate the possibilities that the space of poetry offers to Marçal.

Notes to Chapter 2

1. By 'poetic historiography' I do not intend to suggest the theory of writing history, which to some extent is implied in this meaning. With this term, I refer instead to Marçal's poetic biography.
2. Unless otherwise stated, all quotations are taken from Ross 1924.
3. Aristotle considered poetry as an art, as he states in the first lines of the *Poetica* treatise: 'Our subject being Poetry, I propose to speak not only of the art in general but also of its species and their respective capacities' (Ross 1924: 1). For a relevant account of the matter, see Yanal 1982.
4. As stated in Chapter One, these groups are Libreria delle donne di Milano and Diotima.
5. The Diotima group of women philosophers comprised: Adriana Cavarero, Cristiana Fisher, Elvia Franco, Giannina Longobardi, Verónica Mariaux, Luisa Muraro, Anna Maria Piussi, Wanda Tommasi, Anita Sanvitto, Betty Zamarchi, Chiara Zamboni and Gloria Zanardo.
6. The theoretical contentions of *il pensiero* have been discussed in Chapter One.
7. See Chapter One.
8. This understanding of poetry as a way of being has been also discussed by American poet Adrienne Rich in her book *On Lies, Secrets and Silence* (1979b). She writes: 'she goes to poetry or fiction looking for *her* way of being in the world' (39). The theoretical implications of *ser dona* have been explored in detailed in Chapter One.
9. The association of darkness with the female body was discussed by Sigmund Freud, who in 1926 wrote: 'after all the sexual life of adult women is a dark continent' ('The Question of Lay Analysis' in *The Essentials of Psycho-Analysis: By Sigmund Freud* (1991: 32).
10. Hesiod's *Theogony* narrates the history of the creation of the world. This poem explains the origins of the world and the gods who will rule over human beings on Earth, establishing the place and space of each being in the order of nature. For a full account of this text, see Hesiod (2006).
11. The etymology of the word existence *ex-sistere* conveys this transition from dark to light. *Ex-sistere* means 'to be out of', 'to bring into light', 'to be in the world'.
12. Julia Kristeva determined the existence of such a pre-linguistic space: the Semiotic. This space corresponded to the pre-Oedipal stage, prior to the linguistic development of the human being. The Semiotic precedes the Symbolic, the place of linguistic configurations, which is post-Oedipal. For a detailed account, see Kristeva 1984.
13. Marçal refers to the legend of Saint George. This legend connects the image of woman,

'la donzella', with literature. In Catalonia, Saint George's day is celebrated with a festival of literature: women receive red roses and a book.

14. Unless otherwise stated, in this chapter I always refer to the date of composition of the poems rather than to the date of publication. The date of composition appears in every book collected in *Llengua abolida (1973-1989)*, where all the quotes are taken from. See Marçal 1989b.
15. Marçal met Ramon Balasch (Ramon Pinyol as *nom de plume*) whilst at university in Barcelona. At that time she established contact with other young Catalan poets such Miquel Desclot, Jaume Medina and Xavier Bru de Sala.
16. 'Atzeituní' establishes a reference to Spanish poet Federico García Lorca. Among Marçal's manuscripts written during the poetic process of *Cau de llunes*, notes were found surrounding Lorca's words: 'maledicciones gitanes, lluna gitana'. This part of the book is dedicated to reflecting poetically upon the political and socio-historical situation of Spain at the end of the dictatorship. We can find poems dedicated to Francesc Layret (executed in 1920) and Salvador Seguí (executed in 1923), both Catalan republicans who formed the Ateneu Enciclopèdic Popular. This was a cultural association whose aim was to provide culture to every citizen regardless of political and ideological affiliation or social status. It was closed by Francoist troops in 1939. Also there is a poem entitled 'Traduït d'Alceu', a direct translation from an ancient Greek poet, used by Marçal to celebrate the death of Francisco Franco. The manuscripts also reveal that this part 'Atzeituní' was first entitled 'L'esgambi de la mort' (Barcelona BC, FMMM, 3/4 Sheet 13). This leads us to consider the political concerns of this first book.
17. Xera is a fierce flame that lasts for a very short time. It is a word used specifically in the region of Pla d'Urgell in Lleida where Marçal was born.
18. The title is a homage to Catalan poet J.V. Foix from his book of sonnets *Sol i de dol* (1991, first published in 1947).
19. In 1976, Marçal frequently started going to the bar LaSal (La Riereta de Carme Cases). This was a space where various communities such as ecologists, women, gays and lesbians had their meetings.
20. She participated in 1976 in the 'I Jornades catalanes de la dona' in Barcelona. In 1977, she also participated in the feminist meetings in Paris. Intellectually, she created in 1979 the section of feminist studies at the Universitat Catalana d'Estiu de Prada de Coflent, where she was a director until 1985. She published poems in the feminist magazines 'Escrivim a les parets' and 'Dones en lluita'.
21. This solidarity went beyond literary purposes. She collaborated in the foundation of the feminist publishing house LaSal. The aim of this publishing house was to recover literary texts written by Catalan women writers.
22. The fact that Marçal started the section 'Bruixa de dol' with the sonnet 'Zodíac' is perhaps much more important than hinted at here. Astrology offers Marçal an extended space in which to explore new significations. Astrology is a sphere where physical laws converge with a magical world distant from rationality and the symbolic.
23. 'Freu', which translates as 'strait', is a narrow passage connecting two seas or two mountains.
24. This collection was a finalist in the Ausiàs March Poetry Prize in 1979, and was later included in *Sal oberta*.
25. Some of these poems were published previously in the poetic journal *Reduccions* under the title 'La tenebra i el far' (1982b).
26. This poem ends with a date: Hivern 1979–Primavera 1980, which suggests the duration of the romantic relationship.
27. I recall here Lacan's Law of the Father. According to Lacan, to accept the Law of the Father means to become part of the symbolic order, the space where subjectivity finds its place,

which is determined by language. Marçal will consider this perspective in her last book, *Desglaç* (1989d), where she attempts to challenge this Law.
28. This poem is signed with the date of her pregnancy: Primavera-tardor, 1980.
29. Medea was the goddess of both earth and moon. She married Jason and had two children. They settled in Corinth but soon after their arrival Jason left Medea and married the princess of Corinth. As revenge, Medea killed her two children and had to flee in a serpent-drawn chariot. For more details, see Graves 1960: 253–58.
30. Edith Södergran was a Swedish-Finnish poet, who wrote in Swedish. Her work was crucial for the development of Modernism in Finland.
31. 'Dicen que Baco dio al niño Ciseo como regalo los arbustos de hiedra, que no se secan nunca. Errante, desenfrenada, amarilla por sus racimos de oro, verde por fuera, tiene pálidos los enveses de las hojas. Por eso ciñen sus sienes los poetas con guirnaldas suyas: palidecen a causa de sus afanes, pero su Gloria verdea eternamente', Sebastián 1985: 247. For a detailed account of the association of *hedera* with the myth of Osiris and Bacchus, see Frazer 1911.
32. I recall here the creation of the World in the pre-Hellenic culture of 'Pelasgian'. In this culture a woman as a universal god emerges from Chaos and, not having a stable place to be, creates the universe: 'In the beginning, Eurynome, the Goddess of All Things, rose naked from Chaos, but found nothing substantial for her feet to rest upon, and therefore divided the sea from the sky, dancing lonely upon its waves. She danced towards the south, and the wind set in motion behind her seemed something new and apart with which to begin a work of creation. Wheeling about, she caught hold of this north wind, rubbed it between her hands, and behold! The great serpent Ophion. Eurynome danced to warm herself, wildly and more wildly, until Ophion, grown lustful, coiled about those divine limbs and was moved to couple with her' (Graves 1960: 27).
33. On this matter is relevant to highlight the works of Caterina Albert and Mercè Rodoreda in fiction.
34. This section was dedicated to Pepa Llopis, wife of Catalan poet Joan Brossa.
35. Semònides was a classic poet from the VIII century who wrote the poem 'Women's pedigree', where he expresses his terrible hostility against women whom he compared with animals. It was written in iambic lyric form, commonly used in religious cults, and was imbued with an acrimonious and ironic tone. See Simonides 1975.
36. Kristeva has studied this interaction between the inner self and the social self in *Strangers to Ourselves*, tr. Leon S. Roudiez (New York: Columbia UP, 1991).
37. Some feminist academics have explored the possibilities of maternity as a disruptive condition for the processes of subjectivity and the configuration of a gender identity. Examples of these include Butler, who examines maternity in *Gender Trouble* (1990) and Grosz in *Volatile Bodies* (1994). Other feminists have dealt with the maternal condition of women and its interaction with the identity of the subject, such as Rich in *Of Woman Born: Motherhood as Experience and Institution* (1976), Kristeva in *Tales of Love* (1989) and *Desire in Language: A Semiotic Approach to Literature and Art* (1980), Italian feminists such as Muraro in *L'ordine simbolico della madre*, or French feminist Hélène Cixous in *The Newly Born Woman* (1986), to mention just a few.
38. This is explored in detailed in Chapter Four.
39. Marçal travelled to Ibiza (the Balearic Islands) in 1981 with Mai Cobos, the woman with whom she had a love affair.
40. *Terra de Mai* was, in Marçal's words, 'especialment desafortunat en molts aspectes, i, en concret, en la seva difusió', Introduction to the book *La germana, l'estrangera* (1985b) where she again reprinted this collection of sestinas 'que li fan de pòrtic'.
41. This relates to 'entrustment' as examined in Chapter One, and which I shall return to in Chapter Four. See Libreria 1990.

42. This connects with what Marçal said about the name Heura. In a radio interview, 'Al cap dels anys' conducted by Guillermina Mota in Catalunya Ràdio (26 October 1997), Marçal said: 'Li vaig dir Heura per una sensació molt forta que vaig tenir al principi de l'embaràs és a dir, l'Heura és una mica filla de l'atzar i en certa manera prodriem dir que segons les lleis del món jo el que hauria d'haver fet és agafar la maleta i anar-me'n a Londres que en aquella època aquí no es podia avortar i que vaig estar plantejant-m'ho per la situació, doncs, d'alguna manera hi va haver alguna sensació que m'agafava i no em deixava i jo vaig visualitzar com l'heura i va ser el nom que vaig pensar molt al principi, de fet vaig estar fent poemes sobre l'heura, com l'heura que s'enfila i s'agafa a la paret, i que en certa manera és una planta paràsita, és una abraçada que potser una mica ambivalent. Va ser una decisió visceral que no pas racional i d'aquí va sortir el nom. No sabia que era una nena, però jo veia una nena' (Fundació Maria-Mercè Marçal, access on-line http://www.fmmm.cat/autora.html, accessed on 5 July 2008).
43. This myth is also associated with the Danaids, who were the water-priestess of Lerna. See Graves 1960: 107–110.
44. I refer to the death of the father from a symbolic point of view and from a daughter's perspective. Like Marçal, Plath also composed poems on the death of the father.
45. Marçal explains the birth of the woman writer into patriarchy with the myth of Athena. She elaborated such understanding in various texts, 'Més enllà i més ençà del mirall de la Medusa' (1996a) and 'Meditacions sobre la fúria' (1993) both reprinted in Ibarz 2004. For a full account of the myth of Athena and Marçal's interpretation of the woman writer, see Chapters One and Three.
46. Subjectivation is a Foucauldian concept that refers to the construction of the individual, and is used by Butler in her rereading of Foucault in *Giving an Account of Oneself* (2005).
47. The position of 'the One' in relation to 'the Other' for the different modes of subjectivation has been of primary importance within the elaboration of feminist studies, especially for the feminism of sexual difference, and also for *differenza sessuale*, whose claim for the need of a sexed thought lies precisely in the need to go beyond the place allocated by patriarchy to the female subject as 'the Other', as the object, in relation to the subject. Irigaray, as an influential figure of *il pensiero della differenza sessuale*, has dedicated all her feminist corpus to investigating the interaction between 'the One' and 'the Other', and providing a philosophic method to overcome the exclusion of the female subject from patriarchal discourses, and surpass the condition of 'other'. A specific account of this is her first book, *Speculum of the Other Woman* (1985a). I shall return to an examination of this point in Chapter Four.
48. For a full account of the theoretical premises that thwart the free position of the female subject within the symbolic, see Chapter One.
49. The relationship between desire and recognition is of primary importance for *poiesis*, since recognition is the ultimate goal of *poiesis* as the redefinition of the self. In this sense, the act of writing, as the medium, connects desire and recognition.

CHAPTER 3

∼

The Poetics of Space: Reconfiguring Reality

Through a detailed analysis of Marçal's poetic evolution in the previous chapter, I have examined the conceptual and iconic frameworks that allow the poet to re-elaborate her experience around the concept of being, particularly of her *ser dona*. As a result, the dynamic poetic space and form shapes this remaking, rewriting and rereading of the self. Furthermore, it highlights the system of structures (linguistic and semiotic) that merge in the process of poetically re-inscribing female identity. In this third chapter, I consider how the literary space of poetry harnesses the possibility of becoming a subject, formed and conceptualized in alternative terms.

I will distinguish between Marçal's poetic texts and her theoretical reflections in this chapter. The theoretical writings result from the exercise of poetic creativity, as it is through poetry that Marçal establishes her literary norms. The theoretical works are of paramount importance as these writings reveal her literary aims, which I shall proceed to indentify in the poetic texts. This *modus operandi* will serve to demonstrate the extent to which Marçal's poetic horizons are indeed achieved. The poetic results can either go beyond the poet's aims or simply not fulfil the poet's expectations. Thus, following this inverted heuristic process from previous investigations, the linearity of the chapter oscillates between the space of the poetry (images, symbols, metaphors, and so forth) and the position of the subject. In highlighting this methodology, I am seeking to convey that poetry provides Marçal with fertile ground from which to reconfigure reality.

From her theoretical reflections, written in essay form, to her poetic creations, Marçal's literary horizons are determined by her consideration of literature as a space that not only opens up towards a myriad of possibilities for creating novel poetic forms but also brings a subsequent feminine historical inscription. Significantly, Marçal owes the originality of her work to the development of a discourse that is not only based on her own literary experience but also on the theoretical reflections she writes.[1] In this sense, she pioneers the elaboration of a feminist poetics in the Catalan literary tradition. Her lyrics, all in all, are influenced by a specific objective, as she declared in 1978, one year after the publication of her first book of poems *Cau de llunes*:

> Cal restituir l'altra cara de la història, la veu de les dones. I aquesta la tenim tan emmascarada per allò que 'ens han dit que som!' Prendre consciència d'això ha estat molt important i té moltes repercussions a nivell literari. ¿T'has fixat per exemple que tota la simbologia literària sobre l'amor i el sexe l'han creat els homes? Tot això t'obliga a crear noves formes. (Alzueta 1978: 7)

As this passage shows, one of Marçal's literary preoccupations is with recovering 'the voice of women', a voice that Marçal herself conceives as 'masked' by a literary imagery created by male writers which has disempowered the feminine self, providing poetic images and symbols that have alienated women as producers from tradition and idealize them as objects to be poetically admired, loved, desired, and so on.[2]

This disempowerment, as I have already explored theoretically in Chapter One, finds its basis in the patriarchal understanding of corpo-reality, which acknowledges sexual difference in terms of a denial of the body. Having seen in previous chapters that embodied experience becomes the cornerstone of Marçal's lyric universe, in this chapter I shall deploy the understanding of corpo-reality, which illuminates not only how the body affects the notion of reality but also how reality is perceived from a position of sexual difference. For Marçal, the body determines the place from which the feminine self interacts with reality: 'A partir de la situació que trobes des del dia que naixes, com a dona, en el món, vius la realitat d'una forma marcada per aquest fet' (Barcelona BC, FMMM, Dona i poesia, 16/6, fol. 1).

This reality is at the same time reconfigured poetically for the purpose of altering its pre-existing values. That is, in order to give a new meaning to reality, Marçal engages in a dialectic between the body ('corpus') and its poetic signification through words in such a way that the space where this interaction occurs is transformed. There is, of course, in this dialogue a sense of action that requires an alteration from a pre-given form of reality to a newly configured one via the corresponding literary elaboration. In her manuscripts, Marçal refers to the function of literature as a practice that reveals to some extent the 'physical' engagement of the female self with reality: 'La literatura d'una banda "penetra" el sentit intern de la realitat. D'altra banda crea substituts de la realitat, interessos tangencials respecte als masculins' (Barcelona BC, FMMM, 5/7, notebook, fol. 107). In relation to the above quotation, I argue that Marçal's poetry alters the dimension of reality by figuring the female body through words that involve the literary subject with poetic action. In order to pursue this matter further, I refer to some aspects of the theory *mettere al mondo il mondo* elaborated by Diotima.[3]

Developed as a response to the need for a sexed thought, *mettere al mondo il mondo* aims to provide a socio-symbolic signification for the feminine self. This theory illustrates most acutely the difficulty encountered by the female body within reality in relation to language. In their own words, *mettere al mondo il mondo* entails 'poner el mundo en la luz de la experiencia femenina' (Diotima 1996a: 17).[4] What this theory suggests is that the instability suffered by the feminine subject in relation to reality should be surmounted through the offering of a reformulation of her specific experiences through words and language. If in the previous chapter I examined *poiesis* as a methodology that opens up the space for a *collocazione simbolica* (symbolic placement) here I propose that writing carries out the action of reformulating these experiences literarily. Hence, to discuss Marçal's work in light of the theory of *mettere al mondo il mondo* is to suggest that her work 'és més la idea de feminitzar el món que no en la igualtat en termes masculins dins del món' (Alzueta 1979: 23). By applying this theoretical framework to Marçal's poetry, I aim to highlight the feminist characteristic of her poetics, and the importance of this in the development of Catalan literary tradition at the end of the last century.

Marçal's commentary on her poetic aim to 'feminize' the world is related to the etymological meaning of *ex-sistere*. As I have previously asserted in Chapter Two, the mechanism of *poiesis* allows Marçal to transgress from chaos into light.[5] In the introduction to Diotima's book *Traer al mundo el mundo: objeto y objetividad a la luz de la diferencia sexual* (1996a), María Milagros Rivera Garretas states that this theory adumbrates 'un orden a punto de ser dado a la luz desde la necesidad en el presente de separar del caos la experiencia femenina' (14). This statement suggests that reality is therefore a chaotic dimension for the female subject, because her existence is limited to supporting the reality of 'the other': 'Aquesta manera d'estar al món, omplint de qualsevol manera el lloc de l'Altre, nosaltres la coneixem en primera persona' (Barcelona BC, FMMM, Pensament-Diòtima, 16/7, fol. 1). This specifically demonstrates that the engagement of the female subject with the body leads to further action, action that aims to provide a socio-symbolic correspondence between female existence and reality. Significantly, in Marçal's writings, the set of norms, norms that dictate which experiences can be circumscribed and defined as real, are in fact in crisis. Despite this crisis, to assume a total randomness in terms of the formation of the subject through the available symbolic significances would be to discard the possibilities of the structure that underlies its formation. This is particularly important, since the female subject is herself a specific reality — chaotic — regardless of the consequences of this statement. In particular, the claim I shall put forward throughout this chapter concerns the poetic structure that contains the formation, the becoming, of the subject in the specificity of her sexed identity, that is to say, the becoming of her *ser dona*. Therefore, this leads me to ask to what extent can the poetic space contain possibilities of reconfiguring new significations?

To explore an existing space for the benefit of the female subject is a risky project, since its exploration can yield ambivalent results. In the section that follows, I shall consider the agency of the poetic subject, whose position emanates from a space that already precedes its need for emergence. This statement raises the following questions: firstly, to what extent is Marçal subjected to the already established norms that govern the existing space of poetry? Secondly, do these norms operate similarly from the position of 'otherness'? And finally, and most importantly, is it viable to assume that poetry can underpin the reconfiguration of reality? The discussion of these questions will provide me with the necessary background to critically evaluate the limitations of Marçal's literary aims. Based upon the action of the subject in the space of poetry, I divide this chapter into three different sections: the subject; the action; and the socio-cultural function of poetry. Given the complexities of the terms I use in this chapter, I shall start by contextualizing the notion of reality and its possibilities in the poetic space for reconfiguring the horizons of subjectivity.

On Reality

In this part of the chapter, I will critically examine the concept of reality, also offering its contextualization from Marçal's poetic perspective. I start by re-iterating Marçal's words on the function of literature in relation to the understanding of reality. She says: 'La literatura d'una banda "penetra" el sentit intern de la realitat. D'altra banda crea substituts de la realitat, interessos tangencials respecte als masculins' (Barcelona BC, FMMM, 5/7, notebook, fol. 107). These words reveal that, according to Marçal, literature needs to be regarded as a space which has a specific functionality in relation to reality. This assertion leads me to consider here how the notion of reality is approached in Marçal's poems, and also from what perspective literature, specifically poetry, is related to reality. Furthermore, to claim that poetry can be a space that 'reconfigures reality' suggests firstly the existence of a pre-given reality, an existence that needs to be questioned. Secondly, there is also a need to identify exactly what must be reconsidered in relation to the real in the poems in order to understand Marçal's work fully.

Reality has been one of the central themes of discussion among the theorists of *mettere al mondo il mondo*.[6] The void between embodied experiences and the symbolic order identified by women from *il pensiero* has evolved into the need to rethink the position of the feminine subject in relation to the real. Adriana Cavarero, in her essay 'Decir el nacimiento', offers the following definition of reality:

> lo real no es el ámbito de los hechos 'desnudos y crudos' sino más bien el orden simbólico que el pensamiento (el lenguaje, la cultura, el código social) le atribuye al mundo. Como es sabido, este orden simbólico es de marca

> patriarcal; es decir, asume que el hombre — en su esencia masculina y en su pretendida valencia neutra/universal — es el único sujeto. (1996: 115)

In Cavarero's definition, reality is the signification that the world acquires through the use of specific codes, such as linguistic or cultural ones. *Mettere al mondo il mondo* attempts to reformulate the capacity of the symbolic to allow the feminine self to relocate her subjectivity. *Ser dona* is, for Marçal, the site where cultural significations are produced. However, these significations, as seen in the previous chapter, have a problematic correspondence with the existing symbolic order. If the parameters that provide meaning to individuals are conceptually delimited by the male/universal perspective, how can the feminine subject possibly find a point of reference from which to define her own being?

I have mentioned the connection between body and reality via the term corporeality. Based on this term, I shall start by considering that the conditions of existence need, thus, to be extrapolated to the limits of subjectivity. The act of writing poetry in itself contains the filter of the subject, whereby the world displayed in the text is reconfigured. Hence, it is necessary to clearly establish the boundaries that surround the self, in order to demarcate the space that is to come into being. This is especially important for the exercise of literature and for the perspective of sexual difference, since without having clearly defined the position that the subject inhabits the condition of *ex-sistere* cannot become conceivable. I have explored this poetically in the previous chapter; however, in terms of scrutinizing Marçal's poetic universe, I seek to convey that the sexual position confines her perspective within the condition of 'the other' in reference to 'the one'.[7]

In this sense, this division has been determined by the paradigm of corporeality. Consequently, this paradigm endows the female subject with the position of 'otherness'. This postural 'otherness' serves to sustain the battle between Marçal's own experiences and an external reality, already structured, that provides the individual with social signification. Marçal contrasts her position as 'the other' in her poems with patriarchal conventions of poetry (as analysed in the previous chapter, when the imagery that compounds the structure of *poiesis* — the moon, the shadow, the witch — was semiotically altered to allow the reconstruction of her identity). Marçal's rejection of male-oriented conventions of the feminine instigated her need to move beyond the limits of this established iconography. In these terms, the reality she experiences is determined in relation to the existing one. Her critique of the reality of the 'one' — culture — is based on a sense of exclusion:

> En certa manera és parlar d'una realitat que ha tingut una traducció cultural petita i que si, a més a més et planteges què vol dir tenir una identitat, per força has de tenir una actitud crítica respecte a la cultura tal com l'han baratada. I això, per força determina una relació teva amb la literatura com a forma de creació i d'expressió diferent. (Montero 2004: 264)

This demonstrates that Marçal's concrete experiences do not participate in the realm of reality, since the symbolic structure does not offer Marçal a reference point from which to seek signification. This limitation provokes in Marçal a contradiction poetically 'entre allò que havia anat fent i el model que se'm presentava' (Batista 1979: 12).

The project of self-construction, as seen earlier within the space of poetry, suggests that despite this conflictive position her existence is placed within *(in-stare)* not only the poetic structure but also the concept of woman: 'construir a partir de la pròpia feminitat, però considerant aquesta com a quelcom a construir, en relació conflictiva amb el model de gènere' (Barcelona BC, FMMM, Literatura-identitat, 16/7). The concreteness of this position is reaffirmed with the use of imagery that has been traditionally associated with the feminine, but which Marçal has subverted throughout her poetic evolution. In this sense, her existence is not inured in a fixed category, as it has already been within patriarchy. Rather, it is oriented towards the openness of transformation; Marçal's symbology testifies to her situation of perpetually searching for new forms, new meanings, whereby she can find recognition *(ad stare)*.[8] This limited existence propitiates the poetic action carried out by Marçal by breaking these forms and meanings and positioning herself towards the infinite:

> en tot acte de pensament o de voluntat hi ha implícita una capacitat d'infinit, penso que pensar voler fer alguna cosa, fins la més exigua, és com situar aquesta cosa, almenys implícitament en un horitzó infinit. Això és per a mi, el sentit de **tenir sentit**, que quelcom limitat se situï en un horitzó il·limitat. (Barcelona BC, FMMM, Pensament-Diòtima, 16/7, fol. 2, her bold)

Having delimited the conditions of existence from the locus of 'otherness', her subjectivity becomes 'un mero existir sin significación simbólica, y por tanto, irreal' (Cavarero 1996: 115). The critical question that ostensibly emerges from Cavarero's statement and Marçal's own position needs further attention. As I have analysed in Chapter One, the existing symbolic order does not contain adequate structures to decode the feminine embodied experience, therefore it cannot provide a space for cultural inscription. Marçal does not accept a feminine reality encoded in patriarchal terms. Rather, she assumes the following critical position towards literary models in Catalan tradition where she is inscribed *(in-stare)*:

> presa de consciència sobre la 'masculinitat' dels meus models literaris, la tradició literària en general, on m'inscrivia, per tant, una actitud crítica que fins aleshores no havia tingut — en referència sobretot a allò que la literatura majoritàriament feta per homes — ha pretés dir-nos de nosaltres i de la nostra realitat. (Barcelona BC, FMMM, Feminisme, 16/6)

Cavarero has identified this problematic position as an *atopia*.[9] As a theoretical concept *atopia* offers an acknowledgement of the situation of the feminine subject, yet this acknowledgement is not enough to claim a reconfiguration. To restructure what *has already been* configured involves the subject in a committed action, an action that results, predominantly, from a specific way of understanding reality as 'la acción con la cual cada uno irrepetiblemente manifiesta "quien es"' (Cavarero 1996: 138). This action is the movement where the poetic subject encounters herself simultaneously with space and time. These segments of time and space are specifically localised diachronically and oriented towards a set of norms that confer value upon the individual's existence. In Marçal's words:

> El pany de realitat que cada autora, cada autor, focalitza, selecciona per ser dit i salvat de l'oblit, o fins allò què és capaç d'imaginar [...] té molt a veure el lloc des del qual es parla, amb el sistema de valors compartit o discutit. (1996a: 159–60)

The reconfiguration of reality entails the ostensible presence of the structure that precedes the action of the subject. This framework confines the subject within certain cultural values that will be later questioned and reformulated. This is what constitutes the *here and now* of the action. The historical contextualization of the *here and now* influences and affects the particularities of action. Marçal's codified existence in the post-Francoist regime at the end of the twentieth century extols the particularities of the values that measure the significance of her feminine individuality in reference to the category to which she belongs. In her own words, these particularities are:

> Entre els 'valores eternos' que ens havia de transmetre, brillava la feminitat del drap de la pols i dels drapets de punt d'escapulari [...] Si el cos semblava no tenir dret a l'existència, una via s'entreobria per a la ment. A la ràdio, un 'Se'n va anar' mític encetava també, dificultosament, camins per a la llengua 'materna' que maldava per alliberar-se de la fàl·lica bota imperial. (Barcelona BC, FMMM, El punt de les dones, 16/6, fol. 1)

Moved by a sense of discomfort, she questions this reality founded upon parameters of eternity that negate any sort of embodiment. Thus, one wonders, how is it possible to overcome the patriarchal convention of 'feminine reality' and recapture it as a symbol of alternative configurations?[10] In order to go beyond this paradox, I suggest that action proceeds in a dual movement which extends on two different levels. In the first place, there must be an intention to go from the particular to the general; this covers the critique of the existing reality: 'hi ha una versió d'una determinada realitat. Intento expressar la meua realitat' (Moreno 1980). The act of questioning the structure in itself implies a first step towards the personal desire of narrating experiences and inscribing them within sequential events with the possibility of a transition towards a collective cultural history. The second step is to subject these experiences to a poetic elaboration.

In a sense, by questioning the existing cultural values surrounding the self and exposing them to a poetic elaboration Marçal stipulates what reality is for her, and how this reality is to be altered to the advantage of her identity. For Marçal, *mettere al mondo il mondo* means to put the self into existence by re-inscribing it within a lyric framework. In so doing, she is conferring upon the spatiality of the poem the privilege of being the site where female existence *can be said* through the words that demonstrate her experience, as well as extending the poetic space towards new formulations to provide 'nous discursos que no només critiquen el centralisme excloent masculí sinó que semblen obrir camins per a noves formulacions de la identitat femenina' (Marçal 1993: 141).

Opening Up the Space

The fluidity of the various fragments of time entwined in poetic action, which confers the possibility of sustaining the reconfiguration of experience upon poetry, extends the boundaries of reality. Yet can we account for the viability of this formulation within the poetic space? The boundaries of reality in Marçal's discourse correspond to several different levels of experience, which (following on from my previous discussion) refer to the various dimensions that her existence acquires. Gradually projecting from the realm of the particular towards the universal, the first level of reality is populated by Marçal's experiences in her daily life (*quotidianitat*), immersed within the social framework. The second level refers to the dimension she puts forward in expressing herself poetically. The third level corresponds to the reality she elaborates in terms of a new universe of relationships and interacting subjects. The fourth level of reality refers to her utopian vision of reform, of the transformation into a new culture, which is theoretically displayed in her prose. Do these realities expand towards a new space/new spaces?

Two positive results are derived from this fractured existence. Firstly, the idea of reality appears to be fragmented into various realities, and as such multiple meanings become possible. Secondly, the dynamism implied in such a statement incisively dispels the understanding of reality as a monolithic and unchangeable sphere.[11] Marçal reveals in one of her manuscripts how, since her first attempts at writing, her existence has presented a division between the realm of culture and her daily life:

> Una adolescent de quinze, setze anys, veia facilitada la seva trajectòria — potser inevitable a la llarga — cap a la llengua pròpia: es feia fonedissa de sobte aquella estranya clivella entre vida quotidiana i 'cultura', entre les paraules de la vida i les de la literatura. (Barcelona BC, FMMM, El punt de les dones, 16/6, fol. 1)

Her historical context has always divided Marçal's life between the cultural and the quotidian. This binary reality comes about in two different ways: firstly, linguistically, with the use of Castilian and Catalan in different situations;[12] and secondly, symbolically, as a woman Marçal realized that her experiences did not find corresponding social and symbolic representation. Therefore, her subjectivity was cloistered within the framework of a very limited existence. However, is this not the consequence of the reality that the female subject *has received*? As I have already provided a theoretical discussion that engages with the division between the domestic dimension and culture, and how both have relegated female existence to the silence of the private sphere (hence, the identity of woman appearing to be complete, definite and unified), I will not base my discussion on the binary of domestic/cultural. Rather, I will now explore how bringing the experiences of female subjectivity to lyric form implies a metamorphosis of spatiality. In these terms, Marçal's poetic discourse is of great importance within the development of Catalan poetic tradition in the late twentieth century.

Poetry for Marçal entails a specific purpose 'és com una espècie de conjur, davant de les realitats amb tot un seguit d'elements de frustració la poesia crea una il·lusió de positivar-ho' (Parer 1982: 23). The position of the subject — temporally and spatially limited — encounters simultaneously the space of her inner desires that vehemently push her towards the act of writing. When the Francoist regime ended, the culture of separate gender spheres in Spain was still dictating the social conditions of men and women and determining their place within society. Marçal as a writer, whose poetic beginnings were enclosed within this specific framework,[13] shows how poetry can contribute to the reconfiguring of new subjectivities:

> la poesia ha de jugar un paper important en la traducció en paraules de la subjectivitat nova de les dones que viuen una nova situació en el món. Un dels canvis més importants sociològics dels darrers anys no pot restar simbòlicament literàriament mut. (Barcelona BC, FMMM, Dona i poesia, 16/6, fol. 2)

As to the matter of how the experiences of everyday life develop into a poetic elaboration, that is left to the poet's own discretion: 'els o les poetes sovint converteixen les coses, els fets quotidians en obstacle simbòlic, contra el qual afirmar-se, o en mirall' (Marçal 1991: 104). If this is really so, in any given literary circumstance, why have women's experiences of the course of life never been subjected to poetic elaboration? She says: 'existeix el pla de la quotidianitat, sobre tot de les dones que mai ha tingut una elaboració poètica, que no ha sigut mai motiu de poesia, que no s'ha valorat' (Moreno 1980). It is immediately after the publication of her second book, *Bruixa de dol* (1979), that Marçal starts questioning the legitimacy of the spaces available for her creativity. In interview in 1979 she stated that poetry for her becomes a form of vindication: 'per mi reivindicar la poesia pot ser equivalent a reivindicar espais verds. És com un qüestionament dels valors masculins, hi ha un buit què és la veu de les dones'

(Batista 1979: 12). The political connotation of these words suggests that Marçal's position towards poetic space is not merely aesthetic, and consequently requires further consideration.

The construction of a new feminine identity within the existing space of poetry demands an act of metamorphosis from the space itself.[14] From its etymological origin, metamorphosis indicates transformation. I use the term metamorphosis in order to foreground the following factors: firstly, if poetry has traditionally negated the existence of female experience, Marçal in the act of writing claims this existing space for the purpose of positive construction; and secondly, in Marçal this spatial metamorphosis occurs at various levels, from the reality of daily life to the possibilities for poetic, therefore symbolic, inscription. The unfathomable locus of poetry, which has traditionally created a specific category of woman, moves now fluidly towards a place for potential prospects:

> D'entrada tot un seguit de fets extraliteraris, polítics i policials, prou coneguts, em van fer veure la meua tradició literària no pas com una dada prèvia, com un fet establert i clar per endavant, com en les cultures 'normals' — és a dir, les que posseeixen un estat propi — sinó com una conquesta, com un espai que havia de guanyar, com una revolta. (Barcelona BC, FMMM, Fira-dona i literatura, 16/6)

In Marçal's poems, the experiences of the tapestry of daily life occupy the centre of her poetic universe.[15] However, her poetry does not intend either to represent or to explain reality, but rather to transform it. The poetic space becomes 'més que transmetre, és un intent d'experimentar' (Batista 1979: 12). Regarding the instability mentioned, we must question what the poet's purpose is in submitting poetry to such transformations. Marçal attempts to find the space where her *ser dona* acquires a complete reality furnished with significance. In this sense, poems are conceived for her as a site of research.[16] The use of a variety of forms in the totality of her poetic work, such as sonnets, sestinas, and Sapphic stanzas, among others, reveals and underlines her intention of researching the poetic space. From this exact locus, she positioned herself after the publication of her first book *Cau de llunes* (1977): 'La variació de les formes i dels metres respon a una actitud de recerca i de provatures' (Pané i Sants 1977: 11). Marçal lived and wrote poetry, and in living she found the inspiration for her poems. Her writing was not just an illuminating activity, but also an act with specific objectives to achieve.

The experiences that flow from everyday life to the locus of the poem suggest new formulations of *ser dona*. As examined, the poem therefore does not offer a univocal view, rather 'insinua moltes coses i obre molts camins' (Moreno 1980). These experiences do not constitute the final aim but the beginning of the metamorphosis. Subsequently, this does not imply that poetry transforms daily life, but that the space that now is inhabited by such experiences acquires a new dimension, whose purpose is constantly leading towards one of Marçal's poetic horizons: 'replantejament total de l'escala de valors vigent, que fa que tot allò masculí sigui "universal" i tot allò tradicionalment femení sigui "d'estar per casa" (Alzueta 1978: 7).

The Emergence of the Female Poet: the Action towards Symbolic Birth

> El futur de les dones i de la poesia que escriguem, depèn fonamentalment d'allò que siguem capaces de fer nosaltres. Com deia Luisa Muraro, si l'home ens ha pres històricament alguna cosa, el cert és que no està pas en condicions de tornar-nos-la. (Barcelona BC, FMMM, Dona i poesia, 16/6, fol. 2)

These words, from a text entitled 'Dona i poesia' found among Marçal's manuscripts, are an appeal to the female writer about her responsibility towards action. The action implied in 'allò que siguem capaces de fer nosaltres' defies the position of *atopia* and questions the extent to which Marçal's agency as a poet can reconfigure the poetic space, and therefore reality. In order to pursue this point, the arguments I develop in this section reassert the fact that Marçal's poetic action brings about the discovery of the constitution of her *ser dona*, shaped by a constellation of heterogeneous factors (literary context, specific iconography and lyric structures) each of which extend symbolic signification to her existence as a poet. However, prior to considering in detail the implication of these factors, I shall start by contextualizing the specific vicissitudes that the female writer encounters within tradition.

One of the consequences of a fragmented existence, discussed in the previous section, is the ambivalent position that female writers occupy within literary tradition. Their subjectivities as writers to a certain extent come up against, in one way or another, the difficulties of being women.[17] Literary traditions are furnished with an almost exclusively male-centred perspective, with the striking absence of women writers within the canon:[18] 'la tradició i els canons han estat definits des del poder i el poder fins ara no s'ha conjugat en femení' (Barcelona BC, FMMM, Dona i poesia, 16/6, fol. 2). This point is central to understanding the specific ways in which women have been bearers of patriarchal meanings, subsequently creating a chain of significations that have shaped a distorted sense of reality for them.

Catalan poetry in this sense suffers an absolute vacuum, since the presence of female figures in the canon is virtually non-existent. Marçal as a poet felt this absence personally, and in one of her manuscripts she deplores the situation: 'no hi ha en la poesia noms indiscutits de, l'estil que, en prosa signifiquen Mercè Rodoreda o Víctor Català. I, tanmateix em sembla irreparablement incompleta una poesia que no es plantegi ni tan sols això com una mancança' (Barcelona BC, FMMM, Dona i poesia, 16/6, fol. 1). In this quotation, Marçal as a writer finds herself fluctuating between tradition and the female self. This creates a tension, an anxiety, in the female poet, caused by the fact that the foundations upon which her literary persona stands are insecure. This tension is justified by the opposition between her function as writer and her position as woman: 'qualsevol dona poeta, en el moment present, que vagi a fons en l'elaboració de l'experiència ha d'experimentar i elaborar un malestar de la identitat' (Barcelona BC, FMMM, Dona i poesia, 16/6, fol. 1).

As a Catalan woman poet, Marçal meditated theoretically upon her own writing, her experience as a woman, and the interaction of both these factors within the literary tradition.[19] The fundamental insights of the theoretical postulates she develops are central to Catalan literature and feminist theory.[20] My aim, however, is not to turn again to the matter of the exclusion that women writers suffer in relation to literary tradition.[21] My purpose here is to problematize the rather ambivalent relationship they experience with it. The action of the female writer encompasses the challenge to pre-existing forms, since 'només pel simple fet d'escriure, la dona escriptora s'ha situat històricament en contradicció amb l'arquetip social vigent' (Barcelona BC, FMMM, el mite d'Atenea, 14/3, Sheet 12, fol. 2). However, the question is not whether Marçal reformulates pre-established significations of *ser dona* in her poems. Rather I call into question the extent to which this action surpasses the given reality of the Catalan tradition. The identity of any writer is inevitably related to the literary tradition he or she inhabits 'aquesta identitat singular sempre és referida a una determinada tradició literària' (Marçal 1995a: 192).

In doing so, I turn to Marçal's use of myths and legends. The revisionist activity engaged in the use of symbols from these can be taken as her particular attempt to reformulate pre-established categories. Significantly, the use of these iconographic stories reveals the possibilities of an extended space of meaning, as the images that compound the stories allow Marçal as a writer to investigate her own position within tradition. Specifically, I shall focus upon the fact that Marçal rereads these iconographic images in order to locate her position as a poet. My contention is that in this revisionist activity, Marçal becomes the figure of the *poietes* ('the maker') of sexual difference, whose role is of paramount importance not only in order to successfully complete the process of *poiesis*, as already anticipated, but also to assert the importance of Marçal as an agent of transformation. It is the action of Marçal as a *poietes* of sexual difference that this section deals with.

This action is performed on two different levels, levels that I take from her theoretical writings. In these texts, Marçal engages her poetic subjectivity with the act of writing and tradition from two different spaces. The exploration of these divides this section into two parts, although both parts converge in Marçal's attempts to explore the basis of tradition. The first part of my examination corresponds to Marçal's emergence as a writer from the concrete space of Catalan tradition. In order to analyse this issue, I refer to the image of the dragon in the legend of Saint George. Linked to this symbology, the myth of Athena's birth assists me in arguing in the second part of my investigation that this emergence strives towards Marçal's symbolic birth as a female poet:

> Atenea apareix lligada a un relat mitològic grec tan emparentat amb la llegenda de Sant Jordi que avui rememorem que sens dubte té alguna cosa a veure amb el seu origen — ja que també Sant Jordi, com ens evidencia l'etimologia del nom, ens va venir de Grècia'. (Marçal 1996b: 35)

Prior to commencing my symbolic analysis of these mythologies, I shall briefly offer the general poetic context that initiated Marçal's role as a poet. This testifies to the importance of her discourse and the specific action she engages with.

The Poet as the Founder of Her Own Existence

It is almost impossible not to refer to the main tropes of tradition in order to delineate Marçal's identity as a poet, since language inscribes the poet within a particular literary framework: 'el llenguatge, de fet, t'arrela a una comunitat, als morts' (Nadal 1989: 27).[22] However, the location of *atopia* that the feminine subject occupies within the codes of the existing reality (as examined previously) leads women writers to emerge culturally from male-oriented poetic models and literary contexts. This is no less true for Marçal, who at the end of 1972 'covava des de la penombra de l'habitació' (Bru de Sala: 2000: 47).

Marçal forged her poetic spirit during the seventies in Barcelona within the group of young poets El Mall (consisting also of Ramon Balasch, Xavier Bru de Sala and Miquel de Palol),[23] where she was the only female member until 1977, the year that she divorced her husband Ramon Balasch, and subsequently started both her personal and poetic journey 'de dona "sola", de dona sense home. Com un peix sense bicicleta?' (Marçal 1989c: 29). The aim of El Mall was 'obrir l'espai a una generació molt jove i propiciar uns canvis d'envergadura en l'aleshores desestructurat panorama poètic català' (Bru de Sala 2000: 41). El Mall is central to understanding the development of Catalan literature at the end of the twentieth century. From its very foundation the importance of the group was clearly defined, since its principle of only publishing new poets provided a vital platform for authors such as Miquel Martí i Pol, who was unknown at this point. Their literary principles provoked a radical change in the conception of poetic postulates at the time. Against 'realisme social', poetry had a very different purpose for them: 'd'entendre's, de dibuixar-se amb l'extracte que les paraules posseeixen més enllà del que designen en un món d'una sola dimensió' (Bru de Sala 2000: 45). Their almost obsessive attitude towards language and the use of classical lyric structures such as sonnets and sestinas was decisive in pigeonholing the members as so-called formalists. They rejected poetry with socio-political purposes: 'a l'entorn social el que és de la vida col·lectiva, a l'individu singular l'experimentació poeticovital' (Bru de Sala 2000: 43).

However, like other members of El Mall, Marçal was nevertheless concerned with the role of the poet and her purpose in literature and society. This function, more inclined aesthetically towards the postulates of French poets such as Charles Baudelaire and Stéphane Mallarmé, or the American writer Ezra Pound and also Catalan poets J.V. Foix and Joan Brossa, defined the figure of the poet as 'el fundador de la pròpia existència' (Bru de Sala 2000: 44).[24] The adventurous poetic subject seeks signification of life through his investigation with words, through the intensity of images, and the possibilities of inverting the significations that poetic structures offer. For these writers, writing poetry was 'alguna cosa molt pròxima a l'autocreació' (Bru de Sala 2000: 45). The figure of the poet, thus, strived towards the role as 'investigador en poesia' (Marçal 1983: 2). This specific attitude was adopted from the Catalan poet Foix, whose literary influence on the group El Mall, and especially on Marçal, was central: 'l'impacte de l'obra de Foix va ésser decisiu' (Marçal 1983: 2) says Marçal. She continues, in the text written to commemorate his death:

> es considerava abans de res investigador en poesia. [. . .] Mots i imatges d'una modernitat rotunda i agosarada amb d'altres de clares ressonàncies medievals i rurals. El meravellós i el quotidià, el real i l'irreal, es feien costat i s'il·luminaven mútuament, habitats per una estranya força tel·lúrica. [. . .] Extraordinari mag del llenguatge, ens obria tots el camins i no ens en tancava cap. (Marçal 1983: 2)

This passage reveals that some of the most important vertices of Marçal's poetry are influenced by Foix. The merging of different poetic styles and dimensions, such as medieval and modern images or the use of magic within events of everyday life, was very important to Marçal's poetic ambition. The possibilities of expanding different levels of space and reality that she saw in Foix marked a turning point for her, and his postulates instilled in Marçal the sense of a positive action. Her poetic spirit of exploring poetry through the arbitrary connection that it offers between language and image was conceived together with an extraordinary knowledge of lyric sources. In interview she recalls how the poet, as the founder of his own existence, must reveal a complete awareness not only of the structures that compound the space of poetry but also of the tradition where the poet is inherently inscribed:

> Als voltants de 1972–73 quan un grup de gent vam començar el Mall, ens aglutinava la consciència i la necessitat d'ofici: d'una banda el coneixement de la tradició pròpia, dels poetes actuals oblidats (Foix, Brossa), d'altra el coneixement de la llengua, dels recursos literaris, de la professió: l'actitud d'investigació poètica. (Massip 1982: 8)

The influence of Foix in Marçal's poetry is so important that she even declared that 'dels meus poemes es pot dir que parteixen d'un vers de Foix o Brossa, que van tenir una gran importància per al grup de gent que vam començar El Mall, és a dir, que hi ha intertextualitats molt clares, molt palpables' (Sabadell 1998: 16). Marçal in particular assumed from Foix his sense of manipulating language and the inclusion of magic elements. In interview in 1981 she said 'de Foix me interesa mucho una especie de sentido de la lengua y del mundo mágico' (Barba 1981: 30).[25] From Brossa, on the other hand, Marçal adopted what was to become the cornerstone of her poetry: 'la valoración de muchos aspectos cotidianos, y en cierto modo, su concepción lúdica de la poesía' (Barba 1981: 30).

Despite these strong influences, Marçal separates herself from these postulates on the poetic subject when she realizes that to be the founder of her own existence involves a greater complexity as a woman poet. Her role as a poet was intrinsically determined by her *ser dona*. The contradiction she encountered was clear at the time of writing when she discovered the difficulty involved in taking her experiences as a theme for poetic composition. Consequently, the awareness of a literary tradition, the deep knowledge of poetic structures, and the consideration of the poet as the founder of existence take on a particular perspective in Marçal. Her impulses towards the act of writing are constituted from a different point of departure. Even her own subjectivity as a poet differs from her male counterparts: 'l'experiència de la pròpia relació amb la tradició i la cultura, doncs, és també marcada per una forta diferència' (Barcelona BC, FMMM, Dona i poesia, 16/6, fol. 2). Her poetic attitude as 'an investigator of poetry' can be found in her poems in the repeated use of the word 'cerco' (I search): 'com un peix sense bicicleta / cerco el meu cor entre les ones' (BD 97, lines 1–2); also 'cerco un tast de vi nou. Caço qualsevol ham' (SO 184, line 5) and 'i és aquí on jo et cerco, / no sé per què ni com, / dins la nit esmolada,' (SO 220, lines 17–19).

This subject, who is delimited by her sex, perceives her individual existence in alternative forms. Central is the question of an intense absence, the symbolic absence, that the female writer experiences internally, the void that her poetry constantly exalts. The sense of struggle in Marçal, that tinges the following words, reveals that to elaborate one's own existence poetically goes beyond a mere intellectual exercise for her: 'hi ha una gran dificultat en descobrir la pròpia forma de dir les coses des de la perspectiva de dona i avui això és tot un repte' (Parer 1982: 23).

Her agency from a position of sexual difference breaks traditional horizons for the purpose of creating an alternative imagery. It remains true that the poet demands the extreme condition of solitude at the time of writing.[26] However, in Marçal this solitude is not a necessary demand of her condition as a writer. Rather, it is a painful consequence of her exclusion as a subject, sexually delimited, which causes intense suffering in Marçal: 'de no trobar històricament i socialment les formes simbòliques que permeten *dir-se*' (Barcelona BC, FMMM, Ordre simbòlic, ordre social, 16/7, fol. 3, my italics). This suffering forces Marçal to experience the anguish of a symbolic absence with poetry. She speaks of a pain that her poetic subjectivity encounters with her *ser dona* and her subsequent desire to re-elaborate it poetically. She experiences the limits of her sexed being in the act of writing as a torment. Her manuscripts show that she meditated upon this matter, writing: 'els éssers humans troben una mesura en el simbòlic però si aquesta mesura és massa allunyada de la disposició dels seus cossos, dels seus desitjos i sentiments, en neix una condició de sofriment per a ells' (Barcelona BC, FMMM, Ordre simbòlic, ordre social, 16/7, fol. 3).

The Emergence of the Poet: Marçal and the Symbology of the Dragon

This section focuses primarily upon the specific form that Marçal's suffering acquires in relation to tradition. The form is symbolically represented in the image of the dragon in the legend of Saint George. The assertion that I will put forward is that the symbolism of the death of the dragon in the legend is a conduit that enables Marçal to emerge as a writer from the Catalan poetic tradition. The dragon symbolizes not only her actual birth, from Chinese mythology 'aquest animal mític que, si faig cas a vells oracles orientals, va vetllar també el meu naixement' (Marçal 1989a: 7), but foresees the emergence of her poetic identity. I read this emergence as a need to exceed the position of *atopia*, through the action of the *poietes*; that is, to expand the limits of poetic structures in order to *bring herself into the world*.

Saint George and the dragon are linked to the idea of literature in Catalonia, where the deeds of the knight Saint George are re-enacted each year on the 23 of April. In 1996 Marçal represented Catalan literature at this traditional event, and her poetic voice was called upon to commemorate the day at the Ateneu in Barcelona. In the speech she delivered Marçal associated literature not with Saint George, but rather with the dragon. She said:

> I he vingut a parar, ja, quasi sense adonar-me'n a la imatge que m'ocupava el centre de l'escena quan donava voltes entorn d'allò que volia dir avui, entorn de la diada de Sant Jordi, el llibre i sobretot la literatura: la imatge del drac sofrent, la passió del drac. (Marçal 1996b: 36–37)

The death of the dragon is the tragic ending of the sequence of events that constitute the legend of Saint George.[27] This legend relates how in Conca de Barberà (Montblanc) there was a dragon that threatened the peace and harmony of the village. In order to uphold the peace, the king decided to sacrifice one person to the dragon each time he threatened the village. One day the person chosen was the king's daughter, who was saved by Saint George when he killed the monster. Red roses blossomed from the blood of the dragon.[28]

In Marçal's discourse the image of the dragon does not appear as part of her poetic iconography but in her theoretical reflections. With the image of the dragon ('Sota el signe del drac') Marçal situates all her collected poems in the book entitled *Llengua abolida (1973–1988)* published in 1989. Remarkably, in the introduction to this book she writes: 'tinc la sensació, en donar-ho, ara, tot plegat a la llum, de deixar enrere un cicle complet — on vida i poesia fan la trena, indestriables — obert i clos sota el signe del drac' (1989a: 7). The dragon for Marçal acquires a very specific function. For her it is the image of 'tot allò que és exclòs, i allò que és exclòs retorna en forma d'amenaça, de força obscura, d'enemic' (Marçal 1996b: 37). In the speech that was read to commemorate the national day of literature in Catalonia, Marçal emphasized the association between the dragon and the writer 'aquesta secreta connivència de l'escriptor amb el drac' (1996b: 38).

This association between the writer and the dragon leads me to question on what grounds this concomitance is to be understood. In order to understand Marçal's aims in revisiting the images of the legend of Saint George, it is necessary to take up again the concept of *atopia*. Cavarero introduces the condition of *atopia* as part of the problem of a double reality, in which the reality of the existing symbolic order — patriarchy — automatically excludes from its realm the reality of the *atopia*, revealing sexual difference as 'inasimilable a lo que es otro y revelándose precisamente como alteridad irreducible que resiste' (Cavarero 1996: 131). The disconnection between facts (experience) and thought (symbolic order) demonstrates that Marçal's poetic subjectivity can legitimately interrogate the foundations of patriarchy which have caused her symbolic exile.

It also shows that following inherited literary preoccupations does not constitute a guarantee of inclusion within the tradition. Even if the process of inclusion becomes ostensibly successful the feeling of *atopia* just acquires a more subtle form, and internally the woman writer suffers a struggle between her own self and the literary structures that shape this self poetically. Consequently, this emphasizes a more critical position towards the existing tradition. In this sense, the place of *atopia* as a site of resistance should not be taken to mean passivity, fear, or a voluntary exclusion. To resist from the position of *atopia* both mirrors the aims of following a specific strategy and simultaneously reveals the discontinuity, the gaps, of the male-oriented tradition whose space (language, lyric structures, images, symbols, significations, rhythm, and so forth) cannot contain the poetic needs of the female writer. The sense of exclusion that prompts the impulse to write reveals Marcal's poetic subjectivity as the *poietes* of sexual difference. If poetic language mediates between the unsaid (*no-dit*) and what it can be lyrically elaborated, it is the poet who is thus avowedly in charge of acting towards a search for signification. This is the action needed to transgress from the space of silence to the space of poetry. The woman poet as *poietes* finds herself involved in the process of verbal creation, where her experiences, which have been hitherto negated, become the centre of poetic inscription.

Furthermore, this means that Marçal's position as a feminine subject on the margins of the symbolic is the consequence of a symbolic exile. The question of exile for Catalan women writers has been examined by Kathryn A. Everly in her book *Catalan Women Writers and Artists: Revisionist Views from a Feminist Space* (2003).[29] In her introduction, Everly considers exile as a metaphor equated with silence. In this sense, she connects exile with the marginalized position that Catalan women writers occupy and relates it to the process of creativity. Although the condition of exile for the artist in literature and art in general is a rather expanded field, as Marçal herself writes in one of her poems: 't'estimo, exiliada al perquè dels poetes' (SO 181, line 14). However, my argument goes beyond this general premise and I suggest that Marçal's *atopia*, defined via the image of the dragon, delineates the contours of a symbolic exile. In other words, Marçal's exile is based upon the vacuum between the existing iconography, which has unleashed her condition of suffering, and her attempt to create new poetic forms:

> Tot procés civilitzador exclou i limita el seu domini sobre la natura, i sobre les més diverses facetes de l'experiència, el seu control sobre els impulsos primaris de vida i de mort comporta l'exili més enllà de la consciència i del llenguatge d'allò que és negat, i implica, per tant, sofriment soterrat, passió. (Marçal 1996b: 37)

Banishment (in terms of exile), as this passage shows, is related to language: 'l'experiència femenina ha restat confinada al *no-dit*, al que *no es pot dir*: *indecent*' (Barcelona BC, FMMM, Dona i poesia, 16/6). It is precisely at the border of this linguistic difficulty that Cavarero's concept of *atopia* elucidates that the death of the dragon, through the synecdoche of blood, symbolically provides Marçal with the possibilities of her birth as a woman writer.[30]

The dragon is excluded from the rest of the population because of its difference. This difference creates a sense of fear and anxiety among the people of the village, leading Saint George to kill the dragon in order to preserve the peace. Thus, the death of the dragon argues the impossibility of being assimilated within the existing structures that shape the subject's existence. However, the death of the dragon does not imply the death of the writer. On the contrary, the death of the dragon asserts the possibilities of transformation for the poet, that is, death as a transition. It is the blood of the dragon that illustrates this death as the climax of exile: 'la sang del drac que l'escriptor o l'escriptora cova dins seu, vora la font indominable de la vida, arran de la mort — com a origen de l'escriptura literària' (Marçal 1996b: 37).[31] Death is, thus, approached and understood as a positive act that indicates transformation. The blood transforms extreme negativity into absolute positive beauty through literary writing. The blood is the space where death bears upon life in a perpetual circular movement. The ritual of the death of the dragon mirrors, for Marçal, the possibility of emerging from *atopia* by extending poetically her *ser dona*. This can only be possible if Marçal engages her subjectivity with poetic action and becomes an agent of transformation.

Marçal, like the dragon, occupies a space at the margins. The dragon, as a representation of the exclusion that the writer suffers, becomes in Marçal the inner force that contains her impulse to write. She refers in the passage above to exile as the exclusion 'més enllà de la consciència i del llenguatge' (1996b: 37). Rationality, thus, limits the condition of exile, and subsequently defines it in symbolic terms. As a figure of exclusion, the dragon becomes the inner drive that pushes her towards the act of writing. This inner force constitutes the bedrock of what it means for Marçal as a poet *mettere al mondo il mondo*; to expand the limits of her being. The writer, thus, 's'hi encara, sovint de forma esbiaixada i obliqua, amb els mots i, de vegades, aconsegueix que el monstre parli, digui bocins de la seva veritat obscura, forçant i eixamplant així els límits d'allò que pot ésser dit' (Marçal 1996b: 37).

The connection between the writer and the dragon, as already anticipated, is centred upon a symbolic exile. Both figures are equally excluded from the existing order and their presence threatens it. This situation complicates Marçal's goal of accomplishing the aim of the poet, that is, to be the founder of her own existence. Exclusion corresponds to the existent difficulty in her female corpo-reality. The tension that flows from images that provide meaning to reality arises from the absence of 'tejido simbólico del propio cuerpo, a través del cual se expresa, sin tener todavía palabra, nuestra relación con el mundo' (Tommasi 1996: 95).

In this sense, the dragon symbolizes the chaos involved in any experience that cannot find its place in the existing order. The dragon is a monstrous creature whose power exceeds the expectations of the village community. If the damsel in the legend of Saint George represents the peaceful beauty of the feminine existence in patriarchal terms, the dragon, as the opposite force, mirrors the darkness of the unknown, the irrational, which is also shaped in the figure of the feminine. The dragon is a monster that represents the forces of the underworld; it is the other side of the coin, so to speak. Chaos now finds its place distant from the light that the symbolic order provides:

> Si com a escriptora sento que les meves arrels s'enfondeixen en la sang del drac, com a dona no puc oblidar que el femení més enllà de la pobra representació de la donzella salvada per l'heroi, ha quedat exclòs històricament de la nostra civilització i es troba també, a la banda del monstre. (Marçal 1996b: 37)

Cavarero, in her essay 'Decir el nacimiento', states that 'quién nace es "nuevo" en el significado real del término: es una singularidad efectiva e imprescindible que aparece en el mundo y a él pertenece' (1996: 138). Marçal, in her singularity as a writer, returns from symbolic exile by reappropriating language and manipulating poetic symbols. If death indicates the end of an existing signification within patriarchy, birth engages with the creation of a new figure through the image of the red roses. This death, a ritual that is repeated every year in Catalonia in connection with the image of literature, reveals the power of Marçal as a woman writer, a power that brings continuity to her existence through the use of images and words in the poem (*dir-se*):

> aquest seguit de figures poderoses i alhora sofrents que, com el drac, evoquen els territoris verges inexplorats de més enllà de la norma, oferts a la nostra fam de nous espais i de noves representacions. I que amb la seva mort cíclica, no fan sinó posar de relleu i donar llum la seva força un altre cop renovellada. (Marçal 1996b: 38)

It is Marçal's agency that transforms death into birth because *mettere al mondo il mondo* requires her action in the effort to create a new being (*poiesis*). Her approach of research towards the poetic structure engages her subjectivity with the aim of transformation, of expanding the territories (symbols, words, signification, lyrical structures) that she manipulates both from and towards her sexual difference. It is only in this manner that Marçal as a female writer can be 'the founder of her own existence'. For Marçal, to be a woman poet means to be able to transform the symbolic territory already delimited in poetry.

The role of the poet as *poietes* of sexual difference responds to the question regarding the issue of poetry as a space that reconfigures reality. Death acquires the meaning of transformation through the narrative of the dragon. This death transforms her attitude towards poetic creation and the way she enters into the dynamics of the poetic structure. The limits of signification are therefore disintegrated and new configurations become possible. Her birth as a woman writer from the position of *atopia* reaffirms the contention I proposed to resolve in this part of the chapter: Marçal's agency as a woman writer offers possibilities to transform the existing space of writing in order to 'be out of' (*ex-sistere*) the already limited territories, and, similarly, to extend the symbolic spaces whereby she poetically reconstructs herself (*poiesis*).

The Woman Poet: between Athena and Medusa

Here, I critically examine the implications of Marçal's emergence as a poetic subject from the place of *atopia*. For this purpose, I use Cavarero's notion of birth in order to argue that Marçal's emergence seeks to convey that her role as *poietes* of sexual difference, as explored above, aims to provide poetically the birth of her female subjectivity. I do not focus upon either the poetic elaboration of the experience of birth in Marçal's works (a topic which I will examine in Chapter Four) or the factors that have kept this theme poetically silent.[32] Although both issues are central to the development of Marçal's poetry and the tradition of Catalan literature, at this point I focus on the concept of birth itself.

My argument is that despite the limitations encountered in the position of *atopia*, I read this emergence as a symbolic birth in the light of Cavarero's definition: 'nacer es el lugar donde la singularidad de cada uno y una aparece como lo que es nuevo, impredecible e irrepetible' (1996: 136). A further aim of this section is to suggest that this birth results from an alternating internal position between the woman and the poet, inherent in her female subjectivity. Given the complexity and controversy raised by metaphorical conventions of birth, particularly in literature,[33] I shall start by offering a brief perspective on how the concept of birth connects Marçal's agency with the theoretical framework elaborated by Cavarero, as part of the theory of *mettere al mondo il mondo* which I have been examining. This will serve to explore how both points merge in Marçal's reading of the Greek myth of Athena's birth. For this purpose I shall raise the following questions: what does the concept of birth offer Marçal as a poetic subject? And on what grounds can the physical act of giving birth be linked to her symbolic emergence as a woman poet?

The Concept of Birth

In 'Decir el nacimiento', Cavarero argues that woman can only overcome the position of *atopia* she inhabits by taking the action 'fundada en el nacimiento' (1996: 121). By examining Hanna Arendt's book *Rahel Varnhagen. The Life of a Jewess* (2000, first published in 1958), Cavarero explores the interaction between individual existence and the symbolic structure that provides signification to this existence.[34] The correspondence between these two parameters has been one of the main issues that have concerned theorists of *il pensiero*, and in particular women of the group Diotima. This group had been working specifically upon this interaction in *mettere al mondo il mondo*, in order to grasp the relationship between the female subject and reality: '*Traer al mundo el mundo* sugiere ya un orden a punto de ser dado a luz desde la necesidad en el presente' (Diotima 1996a: 14). Based on these terms, Cavarero formulates the concept of birth as a possibility that engages the female subject with action in order to move beyond the position of *atopia*.

These words raise two problematic issues that I shall address here. On the one hand, they suggest that *mettere al mondo il mondo* demands the intervention of the feminine subject, whose biological condition of 'generating life' provides the ground for a reformulation, in other words: 'de ser dado a luz'.[35] If woman possesses the innate predisposition to generating life, the possibilities of regaining access to an alternative symbolic order also correspond to her. In this sense, the concept of birth remains attached naturally to women, not only because it inevitably links women with nature but also because birth engages exclusively with the female body.[36] On this point, Cavarero makes clear that 'los hombres están necesariamente excluidos de la experiencia de dar a luz, de generar, filiar: no solo porque no paren (evidentemente también muchas mujeres, por motivos diversos, no paren) sino sobre todo porque, como todo el mundo sabe, siempre se nace de mujer y nunca de hombre' (1996: 141). Despite the controversial nature of this statement, neither Cavarero nor I are interested in highlighting an essentialist and reductionist vision of this concept. Rather, my intention is to call into question the way in which patriarchy has manipulated the concept of birth for its own benefit, relegating women's bodies to mere functional objects. On the other hand, by linking the emergence of Marçal as a poetic subject to the concept of birth, I suggest that the need to generate a new order, a new sequence of events, has the aim of producing new significations. Therefore, it is not only the resignification of the concept of birth itself that I am seeking here, but also the conceptual consequences this produces in terms of the acknowledgment of Marçal's subjectivity as *poietes* of sexual difference.[37] In Marçal's discourse, the concept of birth appears as a framework, based on action, around which the critique of literary conventions (iconography, language, literary structures, and so on) coexists with her poetic proposal of 'trobar la visió específica de les dones que al llarg de la història ha quedat amagada' (Batista 1986: 2).

For Marçal, the concept of birth links her individual existence as a woman with a subsequent symbolic transcendence as a poet theoretically. In this sense, birth corresponds to the act of 'coming to the world', in which Marçal as a poet — through the action of writing — becomes part of Catalan literary tradition. This situation for Marçal as a woman writer is 'conquered': 'no és una situació donada, sinó conquerida' (Marçal 1993: 141). In this case, as a poet, to come into the world entitles her subjectivity to the specific action of writing for the purpose of 'generating' her poetic presence within the specific literary framework she inhabits. In her own words: 'les dones escriptores, en canvi, com tot aquell qui neix en el si d'una cultura oprimida, ens hem vist abocades a la tria, a l'esforç, al repte de recuperar, d'inventar-nos' (Marçal 1993: 142).

Birth corresponds to conditions embedded in the origins of the individual's existence. These origins are affected and determined by the specific space and time that anticipates birth. In this sense, Rahel's birth (Arendt 2000) serves the purpose of demonstrating that this condition coincides with the essence of her own existence. However, the fact of being born Jewish in a space and time when being Jewish was condemned, unleashed the anguish for Rahel of rejecting these origins. The lack of space for her individual existence corresponds to a symbolic invisibility that ends in the renouncement of the individual. Based on these terms, Cavarero states that to negate the fact one is born within specific conditions is the same as negating one's own existence, the consequence of which will be to fail in any attempt to find any correspondence with reality. Thus, birth assures the existence of one's own individuality, yet it does not guarantee a place within the existing symbolic order. Cavarero extrapolates the *atopia* suffered by Rahel to the perspective of sexual difference. By asserting the *atopic* position of woman within the symbolic order, she gives prominence to female individual existence as a principle that needs resignification. This resignification considers the fact that birth has the task to 'traer al mundo a quien no ha sido ni visto ni previsto por el orden patriarcal del mundo' (Cavarero 1996: 130). Thus, birth is involved in an action that bestows a new beginning. This new beginning constitutes one of Marçal's poetic aims:

> A la meva poesia faig una aposta forta per l'inici, per donar possibilitats al que és nou; la idea de néixer és això donar curs a unes possibilitats que deixes de controlar, i que jo vaig viure com un impuls molt fort. (Sabadell 1998: 18)

Far from instigating an essentialist perspective, this passage illustrates how Marçal relates her poetic aims to the idea of birth. It is tempting, though, to relate such identification with the difficulties that any physical allusion to the intellectual capacity of writing, especially for a woman writer, has involved. Women's biological capability to give birth has led to the prejudice that this process, possibly the most natural process in the world, has served to oppose the capacity of the development of any intellectual activity for women. In this sense, birth as a bodily act has upheld women's traditional roles as reproducers, whilst men as producers have appropriated what the process of giving birth metaphorically represents.[38] The period of gestation of a baby, which occurs exclusively in a woman's body, has been associated with the elaboration of a text, which in patriarchal terms can only be possible from a man's mind.[39] Creativity versus procreativity thus finds a contradictory identification between the biological act and metaphorical inscriptions in literature.

Traditionally speaking, this contradiction results from the division mind/body. As a result of it, patriarchy has not only appropriated women's bodies but also the metaphoric assumptions derived from them. The results of this contradiction are then clear. On one hand, the manipulation of women's bodies for the benefit of patriarchy is not only physical but also symbolic. On the other hand, this ambivalent position creates a feeling of anxiety in the woman writer, whose intellectual capacity and biological capability continuously fluctuate in her subjectivity. In Marçal's words: 'existeixen a més a més tot un discurs normatiu larvat o explícit que, com a mínim des del segle XIX, contraposa criatures i llibres, com dos aspectes que s'exclouen mútuament en la vida de les dones' (Marçal 1993: 146).[40] Consequently, in a significant number of cases, this anxiety has forced women to reject maternity, a personal choice made in order to maintain the intellectual activity of writing as the primary focus.[41] In contrast, for Marçal the experience of maternity and, in particular, the period of gestation is identified with a powerful force of creation as an idea 'de força i de creació, de donar possibilitats a alguna cosa nova' (Sabadell 1998: 18). Despite the narrow understanding between maternity and the act of giving birth, here I draw attention to the difference between both. My attempt is not to restore traditional understandings of maternity in Marçal. My aim is to focus upon the need to resituate the paradoxical function of the metaphor of birth and the place of women's bodies.

To consider birth as a new beginning intimately connects with the position that Marçal occupies as 'the other' (*atopia*) in reference to 'the one'. The way in which Marçal as a woman inhabits her position within the existing symbolic has been explored theoretically earlier on in this chapter. This position, as seen, anchors Marçal's individual existence and determines how she lives and experiences reality: *in-stare* (being within), *co-stare* (being with others) and *ad-stare* (being towards others). This conditions and affects her attitude towards the act of writing and her location within the tradition of Catalan poetry. In essence, the position of *atopia* is not located outside the realm of 'the one', it does not occupy an alternative space; rather *atopia* becomes the locus of Marçal's existence within a non-symbolic projection. As the poet herself has suggested, attempts to go beyond this position and deploy the emergence of new configurations. Marçal has suggested the complexity of the situation in the following words

> no es tracta d'una deformació exterior, eliminable com s'aplana un plec malfet de la roba, sinó d'alguna cosa d'essencial a la condició femenina: **un tret històric i viciat, sí, però un tret autèntic en la mesura que la seva correcció no restableix simplement una normalitat violada, sinó que dóna lloc al nou.** (Barcelona BC, FMMM, Pensament-Diòtima, 16/7, fol. 1, bold in original)

This 'other' is conceptualized in accordance with the parameters of space and time that foresee her literary emergence. This results, firstly, in Marçal's critical position as a female writer towards literary models, iconographic forms, and metaphorical significations. Secondly, this position is also underpinned theoretically by the energy of the feminist movement in Catalonia and Spain more generally at the time. Feminism contributed to shaping a vehement sense of a specific feminine existence in Marçal's works that at the same time could have a literary, therefore political, projection. The feminist movement for Marçal was not only about political revolt but also the possibility of symbolic reformulation. In Marçal's words, the feminist movement 'en mi obra ha servido para tomar conciencia de que soy una mujer que vive en una cultura masculina y que debía situarme en una postura crítica' (Segura 1987: 30). Her existence, thus, is poetically tinged with the imagery that has served to constrain and define her identity as 'other'. This position of 'other' is indicated poetically in the symbology that she uses in her poems. In her own words, feminism:

> ha determinat també el meu món simbòlic, que s'ha alimentat en gran part de símbols i imatges lligades tradicionalment a la feminitat (la lluna, la

bruixa, la mar, la sal, la sang) però que una consciència feminista ha sotmès a un procés de redefinició, n'ha forçat els límits fins a fer-los dir coses diferents, d'acord amb la meva realitat diferent. (Barcelona BC, FMMM, Fira-dona i literatura, 16/6, fol. 1)

The horizon under which birth as a new beginning connects with poetry is now limited by the socio-historical context that forged Marçal's emergence as a *poietes* of sexual difference. The literary conditions that shape her particular poetic interests cannot be disengaged from the context in which they are developed. As mentioned before, the end of the Francoist regime, along with the first steps of the feminist movement in Barcelona, initiated in Marçal the perspective from which she interacted with reality and the poetic significations that she elaborates. Not only was Marçal persuaded by the possibilities of new political action, she also became aware of the vacuum found in male-oriented literary models. In 1982, the year of publication of her third book *Sal oberta*, Marçal wrote: 'des d'uns ulls de dona, està gairebé tot per reveure, per desfer i per refer. És tot un repte!' (Massip 1982: 9).

The action involved in the process of birth makes the poetic elaboration of a new beginning possible for Marçal. The relationship of Marçal with birth, as shown in these lines, refers to a unique experience incarnated and lived exclusively by her as a woman, whose poetic elaboration implies action. In her own words: 'Tota jo sóc el part i la naixença' (Barcelona BC, FMMM, 4/29, fol. 4). Marçal here finds herself, through poetry, with the possibilities of developing 'el que és nou' in her own words. Birth acquires an important significance for the perspective of sexual difference. The beginning of her poetic corpus is marked by the consideration of the start of her writing as a birth, when in the epigram that opens up her poetic corpus (included in her first book *Cau de llunes*, 1973–1976) she refers to the sexual, social and political conditions of her birth: 'A l'atzar agraeixo tres dons: haver nascut dona, / de classe baixa i nació oprimida. / I el tèrbol atzur de ser tres voltes rebel' (Marçal 1989b: 23). Soon after the publication of her first book, 'haver nascut dona' determines the purpose of her poetic compositions.

Cavarero, as seen, defines birth itself as one of the basic activities of human existence. Regardless of the conditions under which a specific birth occurs, it is an action rooted in the female body as this is the corpo-real presence that provides the connection between the newcomer and the world, where the newcomer will appear to others. As this unpublished poem suggests: 'Sóc mar que neix del ventre de la terra / com qui muda la pell d'un nom' (Barcelona BC, FMMM, 4/29, fol. 9). In comparison to what both the biological act and its metaphorical assumptions have hitherto provided women with under patriarchy, this understanding of the concept of birth remains genuine and innovative. In reference to Catalan poetry, the relationship between corpo-reality and symbolic transcendence appears for the first time with Marçal, not only through the composition of her poems but also as a central theoretical topic to be explored in relation to the female poetic subject.

The Myth of the Birth of Athena

To return to how the concept of birth resonates with the origins of individual existence, it is necessary to explore the symbolic basis upon which these origins were built in Western thought. As I have discussed in Chapter One, the use of the ancient Greek mythology in Marçal's discourse results from her poetic attempt to reconfigure symbolic inscriptions of the category of woman.[42] I emphasized how the use of myths in Marçal's works becomes an important source of location.[43] This indicates that Marçal, in her ongoing emergence as a female poet within the Catalan literary tradition, can only interrogate the boundaries upon which her subjectivity has been defined. The yet ambivalent position she occupies as a woman writer within the Catalan poetic tradition does not leave her space for the elaboration of complete statements. This limitation conveys not only the tightrope existence, so to speak, between her female subjectivity and her function as a poet, but also the urgent need for action.

As mentioned above, patriarchy has manipulated metaphorical inscriptions of the act of giving birth. Marçal, aware of the way that male-oriented literary models have appropriated this act, integrates both the act of giving birth and its symbolic projection in her use of the myth of Athena's birth. Taking as a starting point that one enters the world through the act of being born, this myth provides Marçal with essential insights into how the woman writer symbolically enters the realm of literature:[44] 'hi ha un mite que m'és especialment grat a l'hora d'analitzar la relació que les dones hem tingut amb la literatura: és el mite grec del naixement d'Atenea' (1996a: 163). Additionally, it reveals the problematic I aim to discuss here: the extent to which Marçal's agency can subvert the logistics that have compounded the symbolic basis of Western thought — through this myth — in order to challenge traditional conventions of the relationship between the female subject and the realm of literature.

The use of mythology in women's writing in general has received a growing amount of attention from feminist scholars and critics from the beginnings of feminist studies in the seventies. Indeed, the means by which women writers and feminist theorists revisit specific mythologies — most prominently ancient Greek myths — raised particular interest among theorists during the last two decades of the twentieth century. In her book *Feminism and Poetry* (1987), Jan Montefiore highlights the importance of the use of this strategy, particularly by connecting myth with speech. Basing her argument upon the definition of the Greek-English Lexicon, she states that myth is 'after all a form of storytelling' (40). Although she does mention the psychoanalytic revival of myths — particularly by Sigmund Freud — Montefiore seems to ignore that what precisely distinguishes mythology from other sources of storytelling is the iconographic dimension, which also intrinsically connects mythology with poetry. This is the case not only because myths shape specific images, as does poetry, but also because the first source of information on written myths comes from poetry.[45] This form of storytelling, as she suggests, goes beyond speech, and the use of imagery offers expanded possibilities that connect natural events with a deeper symbolic understanding. Perhaps the disparity of positions regarding the use of mythology and its possibilities comes from the difficulty of interpreting myths themselves.[46] What constitutes a myth and the possibilities of symbolic interpretation have been the subject of a multitude of studies by anthropologists, psychoanalysts and historians in general. Within the realm of the Catalan poetic tradition, the presence of predominantly ancient Greek myths is seen in the works of Ausiàs March, Joan Roíç de Corella, Jacint Verdaguer with 'Atlàntida', Salvador Espriu, and the prolific use of mythology is also witnessed among the *noucentistes* (Josep Carner, Carles Riba, Agustí Bartra among others).[47]

The iconographic dimension of myth becomes a powerful space that Marçal uses to excavate the complexities and contradictions of the structures that underpin Western thought. She was particularly interested in revisiting the myth of the birth of Athena as a means of unravelling the threads that tradition has sewn between poetic subjectivity and the realm of culture; between the line that connects past and present. More specifically, she concentrates on the use of mythology to support the anachronism of the category of woman since its foundations of Western thought.[48] In essence, Marçal's aims with mythology did not lie in poetically reformulating myths.[49] She was not interested in rewriting the myths in her poems as other Catalan women poets have done.[50] Marçal's interest in mythology as a source for theoretical investigation was a groundbreaking approach within the realm of feminist literary studies in Catalonia. As Mercè Ibarz has suggested in her introduction to Marçal's prose writings, Marçal explored myths from 'el sentit de la presència simbòlica femenina' (2004: 13).

As mentioned, the myth of Athena's birth refers to the means by which women writers gain access to the sphere of literature and culture in general. According to Athena's priests the myth narrates as follows: Metis (in ancient Greek Metis means cunning intelligence) was a female Titan whose power was associated with wisdom and knowledge. When Metis was pregnant with Athena, the oracles announced to Zeus that if Metis would bear another son this son would dethrone him. Having heard the oracles' prediction, Zeus took immediate action and opened his mouth to swallow Metis whole. Some time after he swallowed Metis, Zeus suffered terrible headaches and felt his head was about to burst. Prometheus then split Zeus's head in half with an axe and Athena immediately emerged, fully dressed and armed. In her essay 'Més enllà i més ençà del mirall de la Medusa' Marçal describes the myth in these words:

> Atenea neix del cap de Zeus, qui, prèviament, s'havia empassat Metis, divinitat associada a una certa saviesa ancestral femenina. Menjant-se-la, Zeus n'assimila en part el seu poder ('La nostra cultura s'assenta sobre un matricidi original ...' ha afirmat Luce Irigaray: nombrosos mites ho testifiquen). D'aquest estrany part invertit — normalment és home qui neix de dona i no al contrari — Atenea en surt completament vestida i armada: sense contacte inicial amb la seva pròpia nuesa. (1996a: 163)

Ostensibly, this passage reveals how women's subjectivity (Metis) is symbolically disempowered through the intervention of the father (Zeus). The result of this action is the creation of a new woman (Athena); a new woman born from the body of the father-god Zeus, sheltered by his rules and protected with his own tools. This myth reveals in the first place that the symbolic sequence of events does not correspond with natural processes. In the second place, it also discloses important insights on how the female body, by being 'swallowed' by the *father*, remains under patriarchal control. It also shows the transposition that the female body suffers as a consequence of Zeus's action: he transforms Metis's body as a generator of life into an invisible force that merely nurtures him with her reproductive power, a power that has been now neutralized. Basing her exploration of women and literature upon this myth, Marçal highlights in her essay several points with a tone of anger, sometimes laced with irony: 'l'estrany naixement d'Atenea, la significació de la mateixa deessa i el cap de la Medusa que apareix en l'escut' (1996a: 163).

Athena's birth unveils the symbolic significations and political projection of the act of giving birth. It also provides iconography that portrays how the biological predisposition to gestation of the female body was taken by men as the basis for a fierce historical manipulation. From this strange delivery — antinatural, in Marçal's words — the woman writer emerges into the world of literature by being gestated, generated and nurtured by the body of patriarchy. The intervention of the father (Zeus) usurps an exclusively female power and only allows the entrance of the poet into his space under rules that acknowledge his supremacy. Similarly, like Athena, Marçal springs poetically from male-oriented literary models: 'No és gaire diferent l'experiència de l'escriptora: literàriament filla del Pare, de la Seva llei, de la Seva cultura — el gran part masculí contra-Natura-: del Pare que, en tot cas, ha deglutit i utilitzat la força femenina i l'ha fet invisible' (Marçal 1996a: 163).

Based on this analogy, my aim is to go further by questioning the legitimacy of patriarchy in reappropriating women's bodies and their power to generate life. As we can see, the consequences of this anti-natural birth for the conceptualization of woman are detrimental. On the one hand, the image of Athena, born of Zeus's head and fully armed, represents the success of patriarchal rules, in Marcal's words: 'la dona revestida de Dona, és a dir, de la feminitat entesa com a construcció conceptual masculina' (Marçal 1996a: 164). On the other hand, the face of Medusa on Athena's shield becomes the image that disallows the access of women to the sphere of culture as sexually different subjects: 'imatge de la nuesa negada d'Atenea, d'allò que queda exclòs de la construcció cultural, de l'ordre simbòlic del patriarcat: la no-accessibilitat des de la cultura a l'elaboració de la pròpia diferència sexual' (Marçal 1996a: 164).

Both images of females (Athena and Medusa) represent the polarized subjectivity of Marçal. However, neither of them offers complete signification. Furthermore, with Metis's invisibility, the individual existence of a woman is nullified and the experiences that compound her subjectivity are eliminated. Zeus's action of swallowing Metis's pregnant body is indicative of the deliberate intention of patriarchy to control the female body. This control reduces female bodily agency to the extreme of absolute silence and invisibility. Zeus's action also demonstrates that the structural meaning of birth can only be available via the limitations involved in its opposite: death. In this sense, birth finds its meaning in relation to its difference from death, not only as the concept that limits its signification but also as the concept that defines it. Thus, death ensures the possibilities of birth.

Moreover, it is important to note that Metis does not simply die during the process of being swallowed, she is in fact murdered by Zeus. Although both situations would end in the same result — Metis's demise — the intentions surrounding each do not indicate the same objective on the part of the father-god. Therefore, the legitimacy of this death is to be questioned. There is a deliberate purpose implicitly engaged in Zeus' action: he kills Metis so as to acquire all her knowledge and experience, increasing, in this sense, his own power. The difference, thus, between her passive death and an active murder lies in his deliberate action. With Metis's death Athena can be born from the head of the Father of Gods, and have as her gift the power of knowledge that configures her duties as the defender of his rules, not Metis's, and according to the wisdom she has inherited from him. Metis's death in the myth is necessary in order to perpetuate the order that Athena's birth seeks to convey.

One of the consequences of death is invisibility: when someone dies they cease physically appearing in our lives. Death condemns its victim to inevitable disappearance. In this sense, the female body is buried beneath the foundations of the figure of Athena, who is built upon patriarchal rules. Presumably the embodied experience, latent at the margins of the father's kingdom, remains intact without the possibility of any symbolic transcendence. Allegedly, Zeus swallowed Metis with the deliberate purpose of absorbing her whole being and retaining her power of giving birth. It seems clear, therefore, that patriarchy has been founded upon the usurpation of female anatomy in order to silence her voice, to dissolve her agency and to grant invisibility to her body. Thus, patriarchy is founded upon the law of death, upon the silence of the figure of woman, who is forced into assimilation and rebirth from a male body.[51] As

Marçal herself has stated: 'que la cultura, com Atenea, neix del cap del Pare, completament armada. Metis, en els mites és menjada: invisible. Però hi ha rere l'escut d'Atenea, el seu rastre de sang: La Medusa' (Barcelona BC, FMMM, Dona i poesia, 16/6, fol. 1). The question now is can Marcal's agency as a female writer alters the order of death established by Zeus's action?

According to the above quotation, the presence of Medusa in the myth refers to the trace of Athena's blood that is hidden behind the shield. Athena's blood reveals itself as the sign of Metis's death. Her death does not signal the ultimate end or disappearance of the female body from patriarchy; rather it refers to a transition between acts. In this sense, for Marçal 'la mort és transformació. Va lligada al final d'una situació i a la sortida cap a una altra cosa: em surt molt sovint amb aquest sentit de canvi, de trasbals' (Massip 1982: 8). This idea links with the symbol of the dragon, as already studied. If blood, as the symbol of the wound, transforms the death of the dragon into the flourishing of poetry, Athena's blood, symbolically represented through the image of Medusa, adumbrates the possibilities of a positive response to the question I raised above. Let us see how.

Medusa is the figure who, according to Sue Blundell in her illuminating book *Women in Ancient Greece* (1995), belongs to the third classification of female beings that feature in myth.[52] This third grouping, which is essentially made up of monsters, is occupied by creatures that are half-women and half-animal. Medusa is one of the three Gorgons, who have the power of turning humans into stone if they dare to look at them.[53] Their dreadful appearance is connected with their morphology: snaky hair, golden wings, and tusks. Medusa is an anomalous creature whose hybrid form aligns the female body with the forces of nature. Blundell interprets the presence of these monstrous creatures in myths as a representation of 'the fear which women inspired to men' (1995: 17). This fear, which seems to be grounded in women's capacity for generating life, is portrayed in myth through images of females as horrible, heartless beings. Medusa's dangerous, malicious and self-destructive gaze carries the dark force that has the power to petrify. Athena, as the guardian of patriarchal interests, helps Perseus to behead Medusa.[54] She guides him with her hand to Medusa and makes Medusa petrify her own self. Perseus later gives Medusa's head to Athena who puts it on the *aegis* (Zeus's shield): 'l'altra cara d'Atenea és la figura de la Medusa que apareix en el seu escut: dona monstre, el femení indomenyat, salvatge i perillós. Mirada petrificadora d'allò que és exclòs, no dit, que, encarada al mirall, s'ha petrificat a si mateixa' (Marçal 1996a: 164).

These images enact the difference in action between Athena and Medusa: the duty of the former is to perpetuate patriarchal law; the function of the latter is to destroy it. Yet Medusa and Athena are opposite sides of the same coin. Both images continuously alternate in Marçal's own internal subjectivity, whose position as a woman writer cannot be inclined in favour of either:

> la dona escriptora i singularment la dona poeta — filla també sense mare, com he dit, en el terreny cultural — no és mai del tot aquesta guardiana modèlica de l'ordre patern que Atenea pot simbolitzar. Més aviat se situaria a mig camí, sempre en un espai híbrid entre Atenea i Medusa, excavant túnels subterranis entre una i altra, sense ser capaç de triar entre totes dues encara que una o altra pugui predominar. (Marçal 1996a: 164)

Instead, Marçal's poetry is shaded with a perpetual oscillation between both in an attempt to reconcile the two. All her literary influences, the use of lyric structures and even the corresponding imitation of poems by archaic Greek poets, come from male authors. The subtle presence of Medusa in her first book can be detected in the tone of anger, anxiety, and irony in the poems. Gradually striving towards the chaotic and monstrous position of Medusa, Marçal's agency displaces any complete identification with Athena. This is the first step towards transforming the existing chain of events that form the narrative of the myth. Action engages Marçal with both the assimilated Athena and the marginalised, chaotic Medusa. Marçal's poetic agency is thus determined by continuous movement in the poems between both positions: 'movent-se entre la Llei del pare que organitza el món tot excloent-la i/o inferioritzant-la en tant que dona, i el femení inarticulat, caòtic' (1996a: 164).

The female body is the space where the connection between individual existence and the world is established. As the myth of Athena shows, this female body does not exist as it is not fully visible in any of the three possible forms given in the myth: covered with patriarchal robes (Athena), decapitated (Medusa), or assimilated (Metis). As seen, the poet's agency emphasizes the commonality between Medusa and Athena: they both lack any direct contact with their own nudity, and, more specifically, their sexual body. The connection, thus, between their existence and the world can only be possible through the intervention of Zeus. Marçal's agency, whose position encounters both Athena and Medusa, is responsible for bringing Metis's impregnated body into a rebirth via an embodied poetic re-elaboration: 'La mar és el marjal on grano, oberta / als tretze vents de la terra, amb el cos / florit de lluna (SO 265, lines 7–9).

The perspective of sexual difference brings the possibility of altering the myth of the Athena and allows the emergence of Marçal as a female poet. In Marçal's poems, not only has the female body recaptured the capacity of negotiation between individual existence and reality, it also connects the female being with 'the other'. If the female body establishes the contact between the self and the world (*ad-stare*), I can now state that, for Marçal, to be born as a poet implies an openness directed from her individual existence towards the cultural appearance of her poetic subjectivity. This confers to the female body, to Marçal, the exclusivity of the process of creativity, since it is now this woman's body, not shrouded by mysteries and divinity but natural and common place, that both men and women inhabit: 'efectivament hi ha experiències compartides per la meitat masculina i femenina de la humanitat: entre elles l'haver nascut d'un cos femení. Tots, homes i dones, com recordava Adrienne Rich en el títol d'un llibre seu "naixem de dona"' (Barcelona BC, FMMM, Dona i poesia, 16/6, fol. 1).

If Zeus's action causes the death of Metis and the subsequent birth of Athena, it is precisely from this exact position that Marçal in the poems strives towards Medusa. It is the action of writing and her agency as an author that extend the symbolic limits of poetry and becomes the 'gresol de totes les possibilitats inèdites' (Marçal 1989a: 10), even though this would mean the opening of a space that is already formed (language and lyric structure). It remains true, however, that the action of conferring meaning from the agency of the poetic subject to the body becomes the first step towards transforming the existent parameters. In Catalan poetry, Marçal pioneers this project and, therefore, her works cannot but question poetical givens and attempt the re-elaboration of a female embodied reality not configured yet.

My aim in this chapter in considering poetry as a space for reconfiguring reality has been to map out the symbolic and corporeal dimension of female creativity. To claim that poetry foregrounds such a transformation is not to assert its social function, where the term social could suggest poetry as a form of political tract. Rather, my claim has reinforced the space of poetry at the service of the poet, as a way of providing the path between her and the world. To use this understanding via the term corpo-reality has meant that in the poetic act the body is present before, during, and after writing. In this sense, *mettere il mondo al mondo* has illuminated the way in which Marçal as a female writer has become the *poietes* of sexual difference by establishing a dialogue between body and language, transforming the course of the real. In this sense, corpo-reality has shown that the body is an empiric reality significant for Marçal in order to overcome the position of *atopia* in tradition.

In this sense, *mettere il mondo al mondo* has served to anticipate that the mechanism of poetic action should be based upon the metaphorical conventions of birth. My discussion of this action, analysed through the images of the dragon, Medusa and Athena (via the legend of Saint George and the myth of the birth of Athena respectively) has sought to convey how symbols predispose the order of a specific form of reality in a particular context. The metaphorical inscriptions of these myths have been instrumental in redefining the function of poetry and the poet in order to bring into the light the gestures and meanings that remain at the margins of language, inscriptions that the agency of Marçal has appropriated and reformulated. Therefore, *mettere il mondo al mondo* contains Marçal's poetics of her own emergence as a woman writer. The next step is to disentangle the threads that make up the world that Marçal creates poetically. This is the topic that will be addressed in the following, and last, chapter of this book.

Notes to Chapter 3

1. See Ibarz 2004. Most of these texts are unpublished and can be found in the manuscripts of the archive *Fons Maria-Mercè Marçal* at Biblioteca de Catalunya.
2. See Rich 1979b and Montefiore 1987.
3. This theory is elaborated in the book originally entitled *Mettere al mondo il mondo: Oggetto e oggettività alla luce della differenza sessuale* published in 1989, and translated into Spanish by María Milagros Rivera Garretas as *Traer al mundo el mundo: Objeto y objetividad a la luz de la diferencia sexual* (1996). All quotations in this chapter are taken from this edition. This is the second book of four produced by Diotima. The other three books are *Il pensiero della differenza sessuale* (1987), *Il cielo stellato dentro di noi. L'ordine simbolico della madre* (1992) and *Oltre l'uguaglianza. Le radici femminili dell'autorità* (1995). See Chapter One for more information on Diotima. Marçal was aware of Diotima's work, as can be seen in a document entitled 'Pensament-Diòtima' (16/7) found among her manuscripts. The document contains clear references and quotations from the theory *mettere al mondo il mondo*.
4. Although 'traer al mundo el mundo' results in one of the premises of the socio-symbolic practice, I take it from a linguistic perspective. In this sense, language becomes the medium that constructs reality.
5. For a full account of the mechanism of *poiesis* and its conspicuous appreciation to Marçal's poetic universe, see Chapter Two.
6. The book is structured in relation to its concept of reality. It is divided into two parts: the first part, including essays by Chiara Zamboni, Diana Sartori, Luisa Muraro and Wanda Tommasi, is entitled 'La realidad no dada'. The second part, with essays by Adriana Cavarero, Anna Maria Piussi, Paola Azzolini, Letizia Comba and Laura Boella, is entitled 'Dar realidad'.
7. The position of women as 'other' in relation to men has been discussed widely by feminist theorists. However, an existentialist perspective related to the sphere of the real was analysed for the first time in 1949 by Simone de Beauvoir in *The Second Sex*. She sees the parameter of 'sex' as the position of 'the other' within the realm of human existence. For an excellent account of this, see Lundgren-Gothlin 1996.
8. See Chapter One.
9. I am using Cavarero's term of *atopia* that refers to the situation of the female subject in reference to the patriarchal order as a unique reality. See Cavarero 1996.
10. Research surrounding a 'feminine reality' has occupied a significant area of feminist study, for example de Beauvoir's *The Second Sex*, where she considers 'feminine reality' as part of human existence: 'there is a whole region of human experience which the male deliberately chooses to ignore because he fails to think about it: this experience woman lives' (1988: 622). For further discussion of this, see Heinämaa 2003.
11. The literary environment in which Marçal forged her poetic spirit is notoriously important in order to understand her poetic project of recreating reality from the gaze of a female poet. Marçal was part of the group of young Catalan poets El Mall, whose rejection of 'poesia del realisme social' led them to reconsider the aims of poetry. In this sense, they were labelled by literary critics as 'antirrealistes'. They thought that 'no hi ha pitjor manera d'equivocar-se de realitat que observar-li una sola cara, a sobre la més fàcil d'instrumentalitzar a favor de les pròpies idees' (Bru de Sala 2000: 42).
12. Marçal wrote in her manuscripts: 'la llengua materna (català) es feia servir a casa, el castellà (amb l'educació) donava forma a la cultura, a la forma de ser al món de la significació'.
13. As I have already mentioned in Chapter Two, Marçal's literary beginnings are very much enmeshed with her political activism against the regime and in favour of democracy and

women's rights. However, it is important here to highlight that this activism gradually evolved into a more intellectual position. As we can see, Marçal's engagement with the situation of women socially leads her to consider poetry with the purpose of engendering new possibilities.

14. Maurice Blanchot has explored the metamorphosis of time as 'afirmación de un retorno, los movimientos más íntimos de la metamorfosis del tiempo' (2005: 42).
15. The influence of the Catalan poet Joan Brossa here is especially significant. Marçal herself has said that 'els meus poemes es pot dir que parteixen d'un vers de Foix o Brossa, que van tenir una gran importància per al grup de gent que vam començar el Mall' (Sabadell 1998: 16). From Brossa she acquired 'la valoración de muchos aspectos cotidianos, y en cierto modo, su concepción lúcida de la poesía' (Barba 1981: 30).
16. The influence of Foix can be seen in the attitude of Marçal towards poetry. She said: 'l'impacte de l'obra de Foix va ésser decisiu [...] és considerava abans de res "investigador en poesia". [...] El meravellós i el quotidià, el real i l'irreal es feien costat i s'il·luminaven mútuament, habitats per una estranya força tel·lúrica [...] extraordinari mag del llenguatge, ens obria tots els camins i no ens en tancava cap' (Marçal 1983: 2).
17. This problem affects every woman writer, either in terms of a rejection or an acceptance of their position. This is regardless of the literary themes developed in their work, their position in relation to this matter, etc.
18. In some literary cultures the figure of a woman writer stands as representative of poetry. An example of this is Galician literature with Rosalía de Castro, or American poetry with Sylvia Plath. In the case of the Catalan tradition it is important to mention Mercè Rodoreda and Víctor Català. Yet despite this 'extraordinary situation', the presence of female writers in literary traditions is still precarious.
19. Marçal reflects upon her experience as a writer and her interaction with literary tradition. See, 1993: 133–54 and 1996a: 155–66, both in Ibarz 2004. She wrote other texts on this matter during the last years of her life, which remain unpublished and can be found in *Fons Maria-Mercè Marçal* at Biblioteca de Catalunya.
20. Marçal's interest in the vinculum between female writers and Catalan tradition goes beyond theoretical and practical aims. The books *Cartografies del desig. Quinze escriptores i el seu món* (1998) and the posthumous *Memòria de l'aigua. Onze escriptores i el seu món* (1999a) show her interest in celebrating and exploring women's writings and their problematic relationship with tradition. Both books were presented in Casa Elizalde, Barcelona, between 1997 and 1998.
21. The reasons for this exclusion become rather obvious in any specific culture. However, it is striking to find a rather limited amount of research on this tenuous situation for women poets in both Catalan literature and feminist theory. See the introduction to *Paisatge emergent: trenta poetes catalanes del segle XX* (Marçal 1999b).
22. The relationship between the poet and tradition is something which has also been of central importance for male poets. For example, see T.S. Eliot's 'Tradition and the Individual Talent' (1921: 42–53), and Harold Bloom and his theory of poetry as a continuous flowing of words and concepts between writers from an exclusive male-centred perspective. In opposition to this, Sandra Gilbert and Susan Gubar have highlighted that 'female poets both participated in and diverged from the literary conventions and genres established for them by their male contemporaries' (1996: 79). For an interesting account of tradition, see Ranger 1992.
23. Although not considered as part of El Mall, there was a group of poets in the Valencian Country whose literary aims coincided with those of El Mall. These poets were Josep Bonet, Joan Navarro i Salvador Jàfer. Bru de Sala considered that they formed 'la primera generació literària catalanovalenciana en molts segles' (2000: 46).
24. In the words of Bru de Sala: 'El mateix Mall, palíndrom conceptual de llamp, abreviatura

de magall, Mal de Baudelaire i Mall de Mallarmé, de malarmats i mallarmats, era un monosíl·lab amb ressonàncies talismàniques' (2000: 44).
25. Marçal is referring here to Foix's book of poems *Les irreals omegues* (1987), which had a strong impact on her. In another interview she refers to her literary influences from Foix 'rebo, sobretot, el vessant terral de Foix. Més el de *Les irreals omegues* que el de *Sol i de dol*' (Nadal 1989: 26).
26. For an in-depth analysis concerning the author's solitude, see Blanchot 1989.
27. The legend of Saint George also represents England's national day.
28. It was in 1926 that the 23 of April was selected to mark the opening of the Book Fair, in order to commemorate the death of Miguel de Cervantes and, in the English tradition, the birth of William Shakespeare. Marçal added Catalan writer Josep Pla who died 23 April 1981 to this date of the death of celebrated writers. Marçal emphasised in her speech in 1996 at the Ateneu the consequences of this day for the woman writer.
29. In Catalan literature, the question of exile determined the majority of literary production of the twentieth century. The historical event of the Civil War caused writers to live and write in political, social and geographic exile.
30. The theme of death, along with that of love, is common in Marçal's poetic universe. In *Desglaç* (1989d) she poetically reconfigures death as an absence of both the real and the symbolic father.
31. The image of blood works as a synecdoche of death in Marçal. Blood remains at the threshold between life and death and symbolizes both processes in different works. Here I am only interested in highlighting how this image illustrates the transformation of the death of the dragon into the birth of Marçal as a woman poet. For an interesting account of images of death in poetry see Blanchot's 'The Work and Death's Space' (1989: 85–162).
32. The theme of birth, along with pregnancy and motherhood, has not received much attention in poetic composition, including in Catalan literature. The few examples of poems about these themes can only be found in works written by male writers. In the seventies women writers started questioning this situation. On this subject, see Stanford Friedman 1987. The absence of this theme in Catalan poetry left Marçal to pioneer this field.
33. The association of birth with creativity has been the subject of much debate among feminist theorists and women writers. Some have celebrated birth as a metaphor that extols the creative potentialities of women. An important example of this is seen with the French feminists of *l'écriture féminine*, in particular Hélène Cixous, who in her essay 'The Laugh of Medusa' establishes an intimate relationship between the body and language and what she calls the 'gestation drive': 'just like the desire to write: a desire to live self from within, a desire for a swollen belly, for language, for blood' (1976: 891). Some other feminists and writers are opposed to such an association and have rejected any anatomic implications in the act of writing, arguing against the essentialist, deterministic and excluding position that any biological assumption may bring to their position as writers. For example, see Jong 1979, Showalter 1981, Simó 1995 and Woolf 1994.
34. The question of birth is of much interest currently both philosophically and literarily among women scholars and writers. However, the concept of birth in reference to political action has been elaborated by female philosophers such as Arendt in *The Human Condition* (1958), María Zambrano in *Delirio y destino* (1997) and Cavarero. See also an interesting account of the concept of birth in Luce Irigaray's 'Plato's Hystera' (1985a: 243–353).
35. 'Dar a luz' refers to the etymology of the word *nascĕre*. This Latin-rooted word and its meaning of 'coming out', 'starting to', foregrounds my concept of birth as the action of generating new meaning. In Catalan 'nàixer' translates into 'donar a llum' o 'fillar'. Taking the meaning of 'coming out', I link the poetic action of giving 'birth' in Marçal's poetry with her literary purpose of *ex-sistere*.

36. My purpose in linking the act of giving birth with nature is far beyond any identification with traditional understandings of the duality of nature/culture, whose deleterious consequences for female subjectivity are apparent and often discussed by feminist theorists and writers. Nor is it my intention here to instigate such a debate. What I am seeking to convey is that this act exceeds the interference of the human hand and proof of this is the animal world, where reproduction is the basic instinct to perpetuate the species. A different but related issue is also seen in the ways in which this natural process has been institutionalized for the benefit of patriarchal power. Much research has already been done by feminist scholars and writers upon this matter. The most important and groundbreaking, related to literature, is Adrienne Rich's *Of Woman Born: Motherhood as Experience and Institution* (1976).
37. One of the most important consequences is to destabilize the binary mind/body, since my concept of birth bridges the physicality of a bodily process with the symbolic projection of this act through creativity.
38. For a full account of this, see Stanford Friedman 1987.
39. Male poets have also dealt with creativity as a metaphorical inscription of giving birth. Examples of such poets are Percy B. Shelly or T.S. Eliot. In Catalan tradition we find Salvat-Papasseit with the poem 'Amada, amada' or Marc Granell with poems such as 'Maternitat'.
40. Virginia Woolf also found a contradiction between the activities of writing and mothering. In her essay 'Women and Fiction' she notes: 'of the four great women novelists — Jane Austen, Emily Bronte, Charlotte Bronte and George Eliot — not one had a child and two were unmarried' (1966: 143).
41. This was the case with some Catalan Women writers such as Maria Aurèlia Capmany, Maria Antònia Salvà, Caterina Albert and Aurora Bertrana. From an international perspective, we find Virginia Woolf, Emily Dickinson and Simone de Beauvoir.
42. Ancient Greek myths developed over a prolonged period of several thousand years. This resulted in various versions of the myths, which have been altered in accordance with the socio-historical events of several periods. In this sense, the myth of the birth of Athena is central to the transition between matriarchal times and patriarchy. The etymology of the name Athena denotes the non-Greek origins of the word. It is thus highly probable that Athena existed as a deity in pre-Greek civilization. Greece was probably invaded around 2000 BC and Athena was incorporated to its mythology as the daughter of Zeus. Therefore, in this sense her power appears subordinated to her father's. The transition of Athena's position as deity is evidenced in a Mycenaean tablet that shows a "Lady of Atana" dated to 1400 BC, see Hurwitt 1999.
43. The use of myth is not a strategy exclusive to Marçal. Montefiore, in her book *Feminism and Poetry* (1987) argues that the use of mythology is not limited to women poets and novelists but also is also important to theorists such as Irigaray, Cavarero, Monique Wittig, and others.
44. For an excellent account of this myth, see Graves 1960: 44–47.
45. I refer to Hesiod's *Theogony* and Homer's *Iliad*. For an excellent study of myth and poetry in Catalan literature, see Bartra 1980.
46. One of the main problems that Robert Graves points out in his book is the complexities that are involved in the interpretation of myths and the several variants that can be found of the same myth. This is important, since the variants can lead to different meanings. In the introduction to his book he deplores the frequent misinterpretation of myths, which has subsequently led to a misunderstanding of the purposes of the myth and what it represents. Against a Jungian analysis of myths as part of the collective identity, Graves sets up the study of myth from a geo-historical and political point of view. See Graves 1960.
47. See Terry 2003, Magué 2007 and Anglada 1988.

48. In relation to this point, see de Beauvoir's *The Second Sex* (1988), particularly the chapter on myth.
49. The presence of mythology in Marçal's poems is often insinuated. Specific examples include a reference to Medea as a quotation in the poem 'Ruda' in *Sal oberta* (1982a). In *La germana, l'estrangera* (1985a), we find 'Hydra' and 'D'Artemis a Diana'.
50. For example Maria Àngels Anglada and Rosa Leveroni.
51. Cavarero, based on Arendt's writing, asserts that the basis of philosophic thought has been traditionally founded upon death. The innovation of Arendt's argument in *The Human Condition* lies in her introducing the concept of birth in opposition to death. In her essay 'Decir el nacimiento' Cavarero considers Arendt as 'una filósofa del nacimiento frente a la metafísica de la muerte sobre la que crece el pensamiento de occidente' (1996: 135).
52. The other two classifications are, firstly, the divine, comprised of the six goddesses (Hera, Athena, Artemis, Aphrodite, Demeter, Hestia); and, secondly, the human, as certain women of royalty can intervene in myth, such as Helena or Electra. For a full account of these three female possibilities, see Blundell 1995.
53. The other two Gorgon sisters were Stheno and Euryale. Medusa was the only mortal of the three.
54. Perseus (which should be spelled *Pterseus*) means the destroyer and, according to Graves, 'represented the patriarchal Hellenes who invaded Greece and Asia Minor early in the second millennium B.C., and challenged the power of the Triple-goddess' (1960: 17). Graves states that Medusa was in ancient times the goddess who hid behind the Gorgon mask in order to protect her mysterious powers. Perseus invaded her shrines and destroyed the Medusan calendar.

CHAPTER 4

~

Love and Passion: Towards the Process of Self-Transcendence

In maintaining the character of Marçal's poetry as praxis, in Chapter Three I examined poetry as the space where the process of the reconfiguration of reality takes place. Moving from myth to the various levels of reality, I have shown that Marçal concentrated her agency as a writer upon the action of *mettere al mondo il mondo*. The results attestes to her emergence as a woman poet, and reveals the prevalence of poetic action upon the theme of birth as Marçal's specific form of creating a novel iconographic female universe. As a writer, she reappropriates the female body and repositions not only its biological ability to generate but also the metaphorical signification of mediating her interaction within the space of poetry via the dialectics of corpo-reality.

Hence, considering that in the previous chapter I analysed Marçal's poetic subjectivity as *generator* of new symbolic universes (*poietes*), in this chapter I focus on the way in which Marçal, by poetically expressing her love for the other as the same (resemblance), not only expands, and therefore transforms, the limitations of herself but also displaces any patriarchal convention on love and the position of woman as the Other.[1] In order to pursue my point, I formulate the following question: can the action of writing poetry, based on the reiteration of the theme of love for the other as the same, *generate* new possible meanings? The complexities of *generating* signification through the exploration of love entails a perilous project, since, as Marçal specifically wrote — probably between 1986 and 1988 — in an untitled paper found among her manuscripts: 'amor, amistat són categories definides històricament per la cultura i la societat patriarcal, i a més a més han estat definides des d'una òptica masculina i heterosexista' (Barcelona BC, FMMM, 16/4, Sheet 8, fol. 1).

To explore the poet's existence through her poems inevitably entails an engagement with writing as the action that drives her, as a writer, towards the other. In this sense, the poetic subject lives, acts and writes towards the other. If in the preceding chapter the focus of my exploration was the interaction of the poet with the space of poetry (*in-stare*), in this chapter I concentrate on Marçal's problematic encounter with the other (*co-stare*). Her poetry reflects the difficulties involved in this interaction, as she states: 'crec que la poesia sempre ha reflectit el meu intent de transformar les relacions personals' (Macià 1987: 5).

In this sense, the poetic subject is never isolated, either from the world she belongs to or from the world has she constructed symbolically in her poems. Since Marçal's poetry reflects this encounter, the act of writing becomes an act of communication. In her own words: 'sempre un poema implica si més no un receptor... ço que vol dir que transmet' (Batista 1979: 12). The question of the ways in which this other is involved and the extent to which this involvement affects the composition of the poems can only be answered by each poet individually. In Marçal, this relational dialectic is constituted by the theme of love. Through expressing love poetically, Marçal explores her position in relation to the person she loves. In the poems, she invokes this person in such a way that the quest for herself turns into a quest for the other. In this sense, to write about this love redefines the limits that shape her own self. As a result, the poems display both love and solitude as the constituents of a process that culminates in the search for her identity.[2] In her own words:

> Tots dos estan lligats al tema de la identitat; la solitud és quan reprens els teus límits. L'amor quan fas l'intent, en certa manera, de trencar-los un intent de travessar les parets que t'envolten com a individu. Aleshores, en trencar aquests límits, et mesures amb un altre. (Montero 2004: 265)

Marçal's six volumes of poetry written between 1973 and 1989 convey the poet's efforts to seek her identity poetically. The development of this process reveals her attempt to examine the expression of love in relation to this particular mission. In reference to this, her lyrics of love become an act of communication, where the limits between 'I' and 'you' are put into question. Hence, the way in which this communication takes place and what it can tell us about the female poetic subject as an agent of this act is a matter that will be examined in this chapter. This is particularly important since traditionally women have not generally been considered as producers, but merely reproducers of patterns of signification already created for them. Among these patterns, the configuration of love reveals the specific position that women have occupied within the structure of patriarchy. As Marçal has lamented: 'en general sembla que els homes hagin parlat sobre l'amor o l'hagin "fet" i les dones l'hagin encarnat, l'hagin "estat" (1994a: 175).[3]

Gradually evolving from a heterosexual perspective to a lesbian one, Marçal's poetic expression of love is explored from several positions: wife, girlfriend, lover, mother, daughter of her father, and same-sex lover, positions that progress throughout her corpus in this order and correspond to the different literary steps and concerns she follows in her journey to overcome the fragmentation of her subjectivity. This significant progression disallows any possibility of pigeonholing her corpus in a specific category (lesbian, heterosexual, romantic, and so on) since the movement involved from her first book *Cau de llunes* (1977) to the last one *Desglaç* (1989d) reveals a more complex interaction with the other. In accordance with this, I suggest that this dynamic refers to her particular poetic quest to go beyond the symbolic boundaries that shape the self. The importance of the theme of love in Marçal's poetry extends, therefore, beyond the limits of a merely poetic exercise, since the action of writing clearly shapes the need to redefine, through the love for the other, the borders of her personal and lyric voice. As she states: 'hi ha la voluntat de lligar la vivència eròtica i/o amorosa — presa fins ara en una dinàmica masculina, en una "economia" sexual masculina per dir-ho com Irigaray — a una autovaloració, a una veu en primera persona' (1994a: 176).

In order to pursue this aim, I shall turn theoretically to women from *il pensiero* and their specific approach based upon the means of socio-symbolic practice. This theory, which finds its realm within the practice of *affidamento* (entrustment) as formulated in detail by Libreria delle donne di Milano in their book *Sexual Difference: A Theory of Social-Symbolic Practice* (1990),[4] will shed light on the way in which Marçal's purpose of self-definition is expressed poetically and transmitted symbolically through the expression of love for the other as the same (resemblance). With this theory I intend to bridge the problematic divisions of the fragmented female self within patriarchy and emphasize the importance of points of reference for women when seeking cultural signification of their experiences. *Affidamento* focuses mainly upon the presence of another woman who functions as a referential point (*affidataria*) to the other, and whose role is to provide the required authority to visibly legitimize her desire at the time she attempts to culturally transmit it. By approaching Marçal's poems of love in these terms, I aim to demonstrate that to love the other as the same (resemblance) functions as a poetic mechanism that not only mediates her interaction with the symbolic but also legitimates the way in which socio-symbolic existence, examined in the previous chapter, functions in the world she has created in poetry. The other, who stands for the referential point in the poems, allows the self to extend and exceed the existing configurations of love and, ultimately, the self.

This is seen particularly in *Terra de Mai* (1982c), the book that will occupy my attention in this chapter. Despite the interesting poetic display that Marçal offers in her works written between 1973 and 1988, *Terra de Mai* stands out from the rest of her production. Within the complex and rigid lyric structure of the sestina, the self and the other are entangled in such passionate dialogue that the poems offer the joy of an intense series of bodily images. These images pioneer female same-sex eroticism in the tradition of Catalan poetry. In Marçal's words, *Terra de Mai* 'significa, per part meva, una primera incursió amb les paraules en el territori silenciat de l'amor entre dones: l'estructura recurrent i laberíntica de la sextina hi engega i dóna marges a una experiència obscura com tot procés iniciàtic' (Barcelona BC, FMMM, Qüestionari Dotze més una, 17/5, Sheet 19, fol. 5).

Taking this distinctive form in which love is expressed poetically in the sestinas, and the important position of the other in these poems, I shall divide this chapter into three main sections. Firstly, I examine passion, as the specific mode of love, whose action emphasizes the aim of overcoming patriarchal conventions of the female self as 'the object of love' poetically. I claim that this results in a process of poetic transcendence. This action, which connects the body with writing through the dialogue between both, is visible poetically in the erotic iconography of the poems, which will occupy my analysis in the next section. Here, I analyse the symbolic consequences of the same-sex erotic imagery and pleasure in the sestinas. I argue that this particular iconography reinforces the existence of a specific energy, namely desire, which inspires, through writing, the transgression of the female self through excess, also displacing previous formulations of the female subject as a carrier of lack and loss. I also draw on the effects of repetition derived from the sestina, in particular, how the words and images used in Marçal's poems contest the possibilities of language to explore this particular interaction, also confirming that the exercise of writing as an act constantly directs the poet towards the other. In order to seek a theoretical framework on this matter, I use Maurice Blanchot's understanding of the act of writing and the function of the symbol to approach this process. In the last section of this chapter, I focus upon the characteristics of desire, which I analyse as the dynamic primitive force of Eros which conducts the process of self-transcendence. Given the complex and innovative treatment of the theme of love and its aims towards a gradual poetic self-transcendence that Marçal offers in her poems, I shall start by briefly defining its modes and nature, providing the specific theoretical framework whereby the love for the other as the same is based upon resemblance and provides possibilities of self-creation.

The Concept of Love in Marçal's Poetry

We have seen in Chapter Three that Marçal's purpose with poetry was *mettere il mondo al mondo*. Yet, this poetic project cannot be fully accomplished until the structure that connects this new world with the previous one is established. The world that Marçal creates through writing cannot be either determined or created without a point of reference, since language and the poetic iconography (moon, witch, blood, salt, sun, and so forth, as discussed) inform us of the presence of a previous symbolic system of relations that she attempts to reconfigure. In this sense, there is no possible form of *ex-sistere* if the poetic subject is not aware of the other.[5]

A turn towards the other in relation to the new symbolic world that is constructed is achieved in the poems through love. Here, I shall critically examine the ways in which Marçal's specific poetic treatment of love functions as a powerful source of both displacement and reassurance; a displacement of the existing structural relations based on contrasts, and a reassurance of new possibilities of symbolic mediation based on resemblance. I perceive this process in the particularities of the expression of the love for the other as the same (resemblance) explicit in *Terra de Mai*.

The use of the sestina is also central to the poetic effects that Marçal attempted to achieve with this book. The sestina is a highly complex lyric structure that finds its origins during the twelfth and thirteenth century with Arnaut Daniel. This troubadouresque form was written in the languages of Provençal and Occitan (*koiné*), linguistic ancestors of the modern Catalan language. The sestina follows a precise scheme and rigorous rules of composition, which did not allow the troubadours (*trobar ric*) to improvise. Although Marçal's use of the sestina was influenced by the Catalan poet Joan Brossa, she also acknowledges Daniel in the book: 'Aquestes sextines són més deutores de l'esperit amb què Joan Brossa s'ha llançat a la investigació sobre les possibilitats de l'estrofa, que no pas del mateix Arnaut Daniel, a qui, tanmateix, vull retre homenatge' (Marçal 1989b: 295).

Prior to engaging with this point theoretically, it is necessary to define the context of love and its connection to identity. In order to heuristically aim at this, I consider the following questions: firstly, what does the action of loving involve in Marçal's poems? And secondly, to what extent does this action forge an expansion of the self? I will begin by giving Marçal's own words on the ways in which love is articulated in her poems:

> tots dos (l'amor i la solitud) estan lligats al tema de la identitat; la solitud és quan reprens els teus límits. L'amor quan fas l'intent, en certa manera, de trencar-los, un intent de travessar les parets que t'envolten com a individu. Aleshores, en trencar aquests límits, et mesures amb un altre. (Montero 2004: 265)

These words disclose not only a highly distinctive and potentially poetic relationship to love, but also a very problematic one. Love comes to be understood in her discourse by the word 'limits'. Two important points are revealed here. Firstly, in Marçal love is not conceived as universal, ethereal or often subject to the weakness of the soul, as has been suggested throughout the history of philosophy, theology and poetry. Secondly, this love is limited by the other in as much as the other occupies a specific time and space in the poems. In this sense, Marçal delegates part of the responsibility of her poetic project of *ex-sistere* to the position of the other, who actively partakes in its conception. The question here is whether it is possible to legitimate the conception of love in these terms, since, as I have been highlighting throughout this research, Marçal as a female subject inevitably occupies the place of the other in patriarchal terms.[6] Is, therefore, this transposition viable for an alternative resolution through poetry? More accurately, is it safe to reconfigure the interaction between subjects from an inverted perspective? The line that may lead this perspective into a mere inversion of the problem is narrow and, therefore, deserves special attention.

As psychoanalysis has informed us, the position of the female individual in the symbolic has been specifically that of the Other; that is to say, an object of exchange.[7] In Marçal's poems, the consideration of the poetic subject in inverted terms is due to a change of position in regard to the duality of subject/object, which in poetic compositions of love has established the dynamics of this motion. Even though one may refer to this poetic experience as simply a particular, personal one, related exclusively to the individual choice of the poet, it is important to explore in what respects this change of perspective benefits the poet as a female subject.

Marçal envisaged potential opportunity for her own aims in the dynamics of the expression of love. This dynamism links the poetic expression of love with the symbolic search for her identity.[8] I consider this possibility by conceptualizing its nature as a motion; a movement that extends the boundaries established in patriarchal culture and mediates the distance from the one to the other. The way in which love as a motion connects the poet with the other is through the impulse of creativity. In her own words: 'per aquesta meva experiència subjectiva he estat força suspicaç i escèptica enfront de les crítiques massa absolutes de l'amor, de la passió amorosa. No puc de deixar de veure-hi la seva cara forta, la seva cara creativa' (Marçal 1994a: 172). She refers here to 'passion' as the specific characteristic of love that has initiated her need for poetry. I shall specifically deal with passion in the first section of this chapter. My purpose in this part is not to examine the typology of love in Marçal's corpus but to critically analyse the way in which love becomes the drive that connects the self with the other as the same (resemblance) through the act of writing, providing the effect of an extension of the boundaries of signification.

In the long and prolific history of poetry in Western tradition, women as objects of desire have provoked the most intense and varied manifestations of love (passion, idolatry, desperation, death, madness, to give but a few examples), resulting in some of the most brilliant masterpieces of literature. The presence of women in this plethora of poetic composition has been positioned as indirect, circumstantial and purely objectified. However love, in all its ambivalence, has engaged women with writing for centuries. The history of literature does not solely reflect upon the ruins of an incongruous feminine subject, it is also the site of the archaeological vestiges of a subjectivity that has found, throughout the years, in the expression of love 'una palanca per expressar el seu desig, la seva subjectivitat, i, en un cert sentit, la seva llibertat' (Marçal 1994a: 175). An important example of this are the epistles of love, which show the commitment of women to communicate their feelings with the other — the reader. Is it, thus, love that women seek to convey in their writings? In her paper 'La passió amorosa' (1994a), Marçal suggests a possible answer to this question: 'en el fons, a través de l'amor es busca potser una altra cosa que l'amor. Potser és un Desig sense objecte precís, sense termes, un Significat sense significat' (1994a: 176). Love has connected Marçal with language, with the desire to express in words the complexities of her personal experience.

In light of this, the expression of love for another woman provides a more specific poetic effect, to the extent that her book *Terra de Mai* becomes a turning point in her creative production. Her love for another woman brings forth important insights that I shall proceed to analyse here. In order to seek theoretical support, I shall turn to the way in which women from *il pensiero* have also grasped the opportunities involved in the dynamism between the self and the other in their theory of *affidamento*.[9] This theory sheds light on the way in which the self finds her point of reference in the other as the same (resemblance) in the composition of Marçal's poems. In this sense, the function of the other woman (*affidataria*) is to legitimate the female concrete manifestation of her actions already rooted at the threshold of sexual difference. In other words, when the female self seeks to express her desire in society and refuses to be assimilated in the current symbolic, she entrusts herself to another woman, whose presence assures the potentialities of cultural signification. This is precisely the poetic structure of the poems in *Terra de Mai*. The constant duality between the poet with 'jo' and the other as 'tu' discloses that the presence of 'Mai' as the other is necessary to display the poet's desire. In particular, the other is present through the image of the body: 'M'endinso pel paisatge del teu cos / i em trobo quan l'amor et fa de plata' (TM 306, lines 1–2).

Although the theory of *affidamento* has been formulated for the purposes of social visibility and consistency in political performance, it also provides important insights concerning the mechanics of an alternative structure for achieving this symbolic signification in literature without the intervention of the *father*.[10] As we have seen above, in *Terra de Mai*, this is of a primary importance. The dialogue between the 'I' and 'you', framed in the lyric structure of the sestina, engages two women with the poetic experience of their sexual encounter. The poet exploits the poetic repetition of the sestina whereby the six ending words are repeated in a fixed pattern. These recurring words, different in each of the fifteen sestinas, refer mainly to the body of the other woman (sexe, boca, brida, ventre, cintura, cos). The image of the other as the same not only provokes in Marçal a passionate desire towards her own body but also refers poetically to this desire as the source to conduct her own. Some years after she wrote *Terra de Mai*, and influenced by the theories of *il pensiero*, Marçal, meditated upon the possibilities of this mechanism. In the manuscript entitled 'Ordre simbòlic, ordre social', Marçal suggests entrustment as a possible system to convey her desire:

> segons una idea de disparitat reconeguda entre dues dones, sempre a partir d'aquella riquesa que es té: el desig. Es desitja alguna cosa i l'altra és sentida com aquella que pot obrir la via a la realització del propi desig. (Barcelona BC, FMMM, 16/7, fol. 4)

As the passage suggests, there is another, further aspect in the possibilities of loving the other as the same that needs examining here. This is the issue of disparity. In *Terra de Mai*, the other, represented by Mai, functions as the *affidataria*. However, the presence in the poems of this *affidataria* is not based on the idea of 'disparitat' as Marçal has pointed out above. Rather, the function of the other in the sestinas is based precisely upon disparity's opposite: resemblance. Disparity is in fact a very important matter for the success of entrustment, as it acknowledges differences, that is, diversity of thought and performance, between women. This is central to achieving social visibility. Therefore in the theory of *affidamento* the aim is to remove any possibilities of commonality among women in order to emphasize the singularity of, and difference in, each female individual. In these terms, the role of the *affidataria* in the process of entrustment is to acknowledge the specificity of the female subject's desire. In the poems, Mai acts as a mirror for the self, since the love between both subjects is based on images of the resemblance between their bodies. Marçal says: 'hi ha, altre cop, l'experiència del mirall: em reconec a través teu, m'estimo en tu, m'odio en tu' (Barcelona BC, FMMM, 16/4, Sheet 1, fol. 2). This is specifically how the movement from the self towards the other is shaped in terms of resemblance. I deliberately use the term resemblance in order to raise the point of similarity and surface. The fact that the other is physically another woman conveys some significant poetic effects. The imagery of the poems gives the effect of a mirror whereby the poet finds a sense of the unity and completeness of the self.

In this sense, to love the other — most significantly, to poetically forge passionate love towards the other as the same — provides Marçal with the possibility of expanding the limits of her own symbols. In this way, Marçal as the *affidataria* functions as a mirror for the self, whereby the self can be recognized. The natural and feminine iconography of the book serves as a referential point to mediate her desire. This movement from the self towards the other does not go only in one direction. When Marçal writes about her desire and uses specific symbols (carboncle, sexe, molsa, cingles, poma, cos, plata, amongst others) she redefines their function and meaning. In this sense, when she writes about the other she consequently rewrites herself.

The theory of entrustment supports Marçal's treatment of love in her poems with the mechanics of a structure that presents itself as an alternative form of symbolic possibility. Its application to poetry represents not only an attempt to challenge traditional forms of poetic performance but also frames the constituents of the new poetic world that Marçal is bringing forth through writing.[11] In *Terra de Mai* Marçal finds the necessary authority to acknowledge her desire via the other as the same. This is only possible in poetry through a complete and defined image, as the mirror reflects. The iconographic chain of poetic images that she offers opens up the door to a symbolic expansion.

The innovative structure that entrustment suggests displaces the current symbolic order as the sole system available with which to channel female desire. The actual and particular functioning of this system in Marçal's poems will be discussed in detail later (where I focus upon the term passion as the specific mode of love in *Terra de Mai*). However, before moving into the realms of passion, it is necessary to trace the evolution of love from Marçal's early compositions in order to put forward the contingencies of passion as a movement of transgression that places desire at the zenith of symbolic transformation.

The Evolution of Love in Marçal's Early Poems

The influence of the other in the development of Marçal's poetry is present from her first poems, yet in such a way that it divides her poetic historiography into two parts. In her early poetry, written in the years between 1973 and 1981, the other is a man. His experience of love, as displayed in *Cau de llunes* in the part entitled 'Núvols amb corc', reveals the way in which this love is conceived. Marçal writes:

> si hom ateny en una introspecció psicològica, s'adona sense gaire esforç d'una triple opressió que actua, com és clar, sobre les relacions amoroses: una opressió nacional. Una opressió social. Una opressió sexista. La triple força tenyeix les coses, totes les coses i és així que l'amor esdevé un 'núvol amb corc'. (Pané i Sants 1977: 11)

As this passage suggests, if love is a cloud 'núvol', the cloud has a warm 'corc'. In her early works love is fundamentally conceived of in terms of defeat, as an impossibility of communicating with the other. Her poetic attempt at reconciliation is frustrated by the void in structural mediation. From her first book *Cau de llunes* (1977) to the third one *Sal oberta* (1982a), love becomes the axis around which she enters into the quest for her identity poetically. The interaction between the 'I' and the 'you' occurs within the available space provided by the 'you', who is incarnated as a man. Marçal symbolically explores, through imagery, the mediation between herself and the other. Particularly in *Cau de llunes*, which is dedicated to her husband Ramon Pinyol, the experience of love bleeds ('fa sang'), as this line shows: 'ai, amic, l'amor fa sang' (CLL 69, line 3).

The failure to accomplish this love is explicit in the following lines: 'desfem l'amor a l'hora bruna: / al cap del llit ens reflecteix la runa' (CLL 28, lines 2–3).

The second book *Bruixa de dol* still reflects, like *Cau de llunes*, this defeat. In her words, 'potser amb una formulació més aprofundida, la desfeta, les contradiccions i l'espurna de felicitat fugaç de la relació amorosa en el nostre context social i l'antagonisme complex i ambivalent entre homes i dones' (Busquets i Grabulosa 1980: 216). The intensity of the failure of this love is displayed by the use of adjectives that refer to bitterness and agony, as in 'amor, estel amarg / a la deriva' (BD 91, lines 11–12), as well as with destructive images of love 'i t'abraço amb l'angoixa vegetal / d'un bosc d'amor ofert a la destral' (BD 130, lines 13–14) or in 'barques d'amor incendien la platja' (BD 131, line 9). The destruction of this love precedes the conception of a new one. In *Bruixa de dol*, Marçal encounters the love for other women, displayed as affection and solidarity and present in the images of the witch and the fairies. The poetic composition concerning the interaction between two women is challenged by the love that emerges between them. This is explicit in the part 'Avui les fades i les bruixes s'estimen', where Marçal opens the poem with this line: 'Avui, sabeu? les fades i les bruixes s'estimen' (BD 137, line 1). The connotation of blasphemy and sin implicit here is reaffirmed in the third stanza where Marçal uses Biblical images to describe temptation:[12] 'davallen a la plaça en revessa processó, / com la serp cargolada entorn de la pomera, / i enceten una dansa, de punta i de taló' (BD 137, lines 9–11).

In *Sal oberta*, the last book of this first poetic stage, the gap between the 'I' and the 'you' nullifies any possibility of reconciliation: 'Ja ni sabem on s'han trobat amor, / les nostres mans de la mateixa mida' (SO 182, lines 13–14). In this sense, love has lost any possible configuration for Marçal: 'l'avenc fosc entre arbredes, l'amor ha perdut el pas' (SO 201, line 11). Love, relegated to the margins of any possible fulfilment is, all in all of her early works, furnished with images of defeat, destruction and ultimately loss. They show that the structures available in language to encounter the other, as man, obstruct the fluidity of this emotion. As Marçal laments 'perquè l'amor entre una dona i un home sigui possible, sembla exigir una mena d'inversió de tot el context' (1995a: 196). This inversion is displayed poetically in *Terra de Mai*, where the iconography of love and poetic diction in the form of dialogue bring the possibilities of poetry to the extreme. In the next section I shall deal with this issue.

Love is a Dance without a Sword . . .[13]

This first section examines passion as the specific mode and nature of love.[14] As the title suggests, passion in its intensity configures love in the poems as 'una dansa sense espasa'. The image of the sword ('espasa') reveals the specificity of the dance that Marçal is referring to, and shows not only a deliberate position of the other as female but also the absence of any discrepancy between the 'I' and the 'you'. This same-sex dancing furnishes the poems with a specific corporeal imagery and populates *Terra de Mai* with the most joyful and pleasurable atmosphere of action. The passionate love displayed in the book becomes the *topos* where the poetic action itself takes place. This action, particularly specific and guided by the bodily images in the poems, finds its ultimate purpose in transcendence.[15]

Striving for an alternative space-time that can poetically contain the specificity of Marçal's desire, here I will demonstrate how the impulse of passion provides a poetic transcendence of the symbolic implications of the self. This is a transcendence that aims to find the object of love in the other as the same (resemblance), thus blurring the boundaries between the 'I' and the 'you': 'Et dic, amor, que a res no poses fita / i del teu mateix urc et meravelles' (TM 311, lines 35–36). Following the reverberations of these lines, the other in this section does not limit the self in the way in which we have seen throughout the first three books, *Cau de llunes, Bruixa de dol* and *Sal oberta*. Marçal here exceeds the limits between the 'I' and the 'you' to the extent that the sovereign power of the other is dissolved and love becomes a celebration: 'entre foscants a l'areny del teu sexe / l'amor és una dansa sense espasa' (TM 297, lines 29–30). This is possible through the fusion of both subjectivities. The other becomes the self in a complete identification, as the following lines suggest: 's'alça, maial, la lluna sobre la runa / a l'aiguaneix del dia i de la terra' (TM 297, lines 33–34). The word 'maial', composed by 'ma' from Mai and 'al' from Marçal, and reconciled through the conjunction 'i', becomes the beginning and the end of this ritual.

In this sense, the other as the object of love becomes also the subject when the boundaries that delineate both merge into a sexual communion. This sexual union is fundamentally a commitment to fulfilment. Both female subjects, immersed in and often identified with a natural setting 'quan fem l'amor se'ns assembla la terra' (TM 301, line 31), find in their physical bonding a mutual satisfaction of their own desire. This is the poetic and feminist importance of *Terra de Mai*. The pattern of the other as a restriction of the self is not repeated here. Rather, the other as the same (resemblance) celebrates the poetic possibilities of achievement, challenging not only previous poetic interactions with the other but also pre-existing patterns of achieving transcendence. In this sense, Marçal rethinks and redefines patriarchal forms of alterity and transcendence.[16] In Marçal's words: 'la no-diferència de gènere suscita en un primer moment, la fal·laç utopia d'una fusió absoluta, d'una sola identitat' (1995a: 197).

Written in 1981, *Terra de Mai* harnesses the utopian vision of the self as creator of the other. The iconography of the poems reveals that the intensity of the images that refer to both subjectivities is forged in order to accomplish Marçal's particular process of poetic creation. However, on what grounds can the fragmented female subject find in the other as the same the means to achieve a complete identity? The following lines disclose how self-identification, marked by 'tu' and 'jo' and at times by 'som', is constantly poetically displayed in reference specifically to their sex. An example of this is the poem entitled 'Sextina-mirall': 'Tu i jo i la terra que anomenem sexe / colguem la runa i corferim l'espasa. / Triomfa l'hora entre la sal de l'arbre' (TM 297, lines 37–39). Also, in the poem 'Solstice' the sestina that narrates the zenith of this process is determined by the verb 'som', which translates as 'we are':

> Som on l'hora i l'atzar perden la brida,
> on a cavall de la marea viva,
> llisquen sense velam, pels solcs de molsa,
> el meu sexe i la teva boca: sexes
> al mig del rostre i a l'entrecuix, boques.
> Tot és un daltabaix de sal oberta. (TM 298, lines 19–24)

A further example is the first stanza of the sestina 'La festa de la sal':

> Tu i jo som aire que estalona el foc.
> Som aigua oberta que esmola la terra.
> Som terra espessa que s'allera en l'aire.
> Som foc que imanta amb arrels noves l'aigua.
> Tu i jo, amor, avui som tot el món
> congriat en la festa de la sal. (TM 300 lines 1–6)

This passionate love brings forth specific consequences for poetic composition. This can be seen in the constant dialogue established between the 'I' and the 'you' throughout the book. By assembling the one and the other in the poems not only does Marçal achieve absolute communion between both subjects, she also provides the basis from which her own poetic horizon of communication is brought about. As Marçal herself has stated, the purpose of *Terra de Mai* is 'transcendir, anar més enllà, d'aquest ser objecte, passar-hi per sobre. En certa manera desdoblar-se, com la narcisista, en un objecte- l'estimada- i l'amant- la que estima-, i retrobar-se per mediació de l'ésser estimat. Autovaloritzar-se a través de l'altre' (Marçal 1994a: 180). It is the mechanics of this process that this section will examine. Prior to entering into details on the device of passion, I shall briefly introduce the importance of *Terra de Mai* in Marçal's poetic corpus and its possibilities not only for the tradition of Catalan literature but also for the poetics of an alternative feminist configuration.

'Terra de Mai': *The Grounds of Same-Sex Poetics*

Terra de Mai was published in 1982, appearing in the most precarious of literary circumstances. Its reception, as even declared by Marçal herself, was unfortunate.[17] However, the poet's truly rebellious nature and her essential literary principle of bringing into light as yet chaotic experiences (*poiesis*), led her to persist in the idea of gaining recognition for *Terra de Mai* as part of her *oeuvre*. Therefore, Marçal included the sestinas in her book, *La germana, l'estrangera* (1985a). This rather peculiar literary journey of *Terra de Mai* was lamented by the poet in the prologue:

> ha estat especialment desafortunat en molts aspectes, i, en concret, en la seva difusió. Així i tot, no m'hauria decidit a incloure'l en la present edició si cregués que fer-ho restaria coherència o unitat al conjunt. Ben al contrari, a hores d'ara, *La germana, l'estrangera* em semblaria incomplet sense les sextines que li fan de pòrtic. (Marçal 1985b: 7)

Not only unfortunate in terms of its lack of circulation and public visibility, the fact that *Terra de Mai* remained isolated from the rest of Marçal's publications highlights a deliberate disregard of it by critics. This disinterest may be due to linguistic and poetic factors. There is not a single word throughout the fifteen sestinas that can inform the reader that 'the other' in the poems is, in fact, another woman. No gender markers appear in the words used that refer to the other. In a letter written 15 April 1996 to Jean-Paul Goujon,[18] Marçal says:

> C'est vrai qu'il n'y a pas de féminins pluriels ni d'autres indices grammaticaux qui explicitent le sexe de l'autre. Cela a été, d'emblée, quelque chose de spontané — voire, d'inconscient —dans presque la totalité des poèmes. [...] Ce n'est pas une question de manouflage ou d'autocensure — bien que c'était la première fois que j'ai écrit sur l'amour entre femmes — mais de quelque chose de plus profond et que je ne suis pas sûre d'être capable d'exprimer avec justesse. Je vais essayer, quand même. (Goujon 1998: 108)

There are, of course, feminine words in the poems, but none of them reveal to the reader that he or she is witnessing the first female same-sex poetic encounter in the history of Catalan literature.[19]

In the review of the book entitled 'Poemas de lírica amorosa actual' published in *La Vanguardia* (14 October 1982) Marçal is compared to Daniel, Brossa, and Ezra Pound: 'Como Arnaut Daniel, Ezra Pound y Joan Brossa, Maria-Mercè Marçal hace prodigios con la sextina' (Faulí 1982: 42). In this review, Josep Faulí does not refer to the specific content of the poems. He focuses mainly on the complexities of the structure of the sestina, and its peculiar lyric reiteration in the constant repetition of certain words. There is, however, a reference to the lover as a male by the reviewer in 'la ausencia del amante', when he notes the absence of the lover towards the end of the book. Also, Faulí indirectly engages with the sexual atmosphere of the book with a very subtle comment that makes reference to the peculiarity of the imagery, which he relates circumstantially to the use of the name Mai and 'sexe'. The author says:

> *Terra de Mai*: dos veces aparece en el libro la palabra 'Mai' con mayúscula. En el poema sexto — 'Mai' — se le define: 'al punt on Mai comença a ser el teu nom.' En el octavo 'El corb absent' — es simplemente aludido en un

vocativo: 'Et diré, Mai, com sagnes i com signes'. Es preciso advertir que el nombre, pues, no aparece hasta el sexto poema, después de que los cinco primeros han sido un 'crescendo' pasional en los que la palabra más empleada es 'sexe'. (1982: 42)

Despite Marçal's attempts to gain critical attention for the text, the prediction suggested in the title *Terra de Mai* (which would translate as never land) came to pass and the book was consigned to oblivion, separate from the rest of her corpus. Only on rare occasions have critics extolled the importance of this book both in terms of form and content.[20] Marçal was aware of the critical position towards her poetic declaration of same-sex love. The repeated presence of this poetic theme in her last three books, *Terra de Mai, La germana, l'estrangera*, and *Desglaç*, lead us to consider the fact that there has been an intentional consensus to ignore such poetic accounts. As a result of this critical stance, the importance of Marçal's texts as the first same-sex poetic expression and aesthetics in Catalan poetry has been obscured. She laments this fact in the following passage:

> Jo ja havia publicat un parell de llibres de poesia on sortia el tema lèsbic. Però el món de la poesia té un punt d'ambigüitat i les lectures que s'havien fet des de la crítica mai havien destacat el tema. Ni s'hi havia fet al·lusió [. . .] hi ha hagut com una voluntat de protegir la meva reputació, una cosa molt rara. (Galarza 1995: 20)

If the convergence between experience and literature is revealed as the vertiginous moment of writing in Marçal, in *Terra de Mai* this dialectic achieves such a culmination that the book marks a defining moment not only in Marçal's poetic works — both thematically and structurally — but also in the continuity of twentieth century Catalan literary tradition. Composed when her daughter Heura was only one year old (in 1981), form and content combine to display the intensity of the physical relationship that Marçal lived with Mai:[21]

> una sola vegada he planificat un llibre, el de les sextines, *Terra de Mai*. Potser perquè jo estava vivint un moment molt obsessiu al voltant d'un tema. Un cop vaig fer la primera, en vaig fer quinze, perquè en la col·lecció aquella em demanaven quinze poemes i em vaig posar en situació de fer-les. El que passa és que quan vaig arribar a quinze hauria pogut fer-ne vint-i-cinc. És una cosa molt viciosa això de les sextines, és una espècie de voràgine. (Montero 2004: 265)

The passage suggests, at first glance, that Marçal has surrendered entirely to the joys and sorrows of the exercise of writing in its pure state. The interstice between life and poetry has merged into this never land (*Terra de Mai*) with the force of a whirlpool. The motion involved between herself and the other, poetry and life, and image and word opens up the space to a vertiginous same-sex passion. Marçal referred metaphorically to this specific experience through the connotations suggested by the image of a 'dark room',[22] a space that, in her words, remains hidden in the city: 'incrustada a la ciutat, espargida, difosa arreu, la vasta cambra fosca, opaca, quasi sempre invisible de l'amor entre dones' (1989c: 32).[23]

I have referred several times throughout this book to the extent to which Marçal's personal experience precedes poetic composition. In *Terra de Mai* their symbiosis acquires a specific nuance. In the paper entitled 'Entre dones' (1995-96) Marçal reflects upon the experience of love between women and its subsequent elaboration in literature. In this discourse, written fourteen years after the composition of *Terra de Mai*, Marçal discloses that at the time she wrote the book she found hardly any literary references to assist the poetic elaboration of this experience. Due to her classical education, she had read poems by Sappho of Lesbos.[24] Also, she would some time later read a few poems by Adrienne Rich.[25] Regarding Catalan literature, Marçal mentions the reading of some ambiguous poems by the Mallorcan poet Maria-Antònia Salvà (1869-1958), and two short-stories, Carme Riera's (1948-) 'Te deix, amor la mar com a penyora' (1975) and Caterina Albert/Víctor Català's (1869-1996) 'Carnaval' (*Caires vius* 1902). Despite this very restricted reading and the scant references for the literary elaboration of same-sex love, Marçal took the risk of giving a literary presence to an experience that at that time was not considered suitable for public display and which changed all her previous structures of significance. In her own words, 'em vaig llançar a escriure sobre una experiència que, en un determinat moment, va trasbalsar tots els meus esquemes anteriors' (1995-96: 202).

In *Terra de Mai* Marçal offers the ground, 'la terra', where the specific tree of same-sex love can be rooted for the first time in the history of Catalan poetry: 'tu i jo i la terra que anomenem sexe' (TM 297, line 37). *Terra de Mai* thus becomes the first book of poems in Catalan where the self and the other as the same (resemblance) are fully reconciled. The female body in this book becomes the backbone of poetic action and symbolic signification. This action drives the poet towards the fruitfulness of desire complete and satisfied, whose result (utopia) is incompatible with pre-existing symbolic forms. As Marçal has confessed: 'això va ser *Terra de Mai*: la sensació de trepitjar de cop el territori de la Utopia, com una mena de retorn al paradís perdut' (1995-96: 202). In the following section, I shall examine the elements that have encouraged this book to be considered as a return to Utopia.

Voices of Desire Turn the Air Upside Down . . .

Veus de desig fan que es capgiri l'aire
i escampen tretze vents arreu del món.
Ens abracem amb les plomes del foc
i mesclem l'ona com si fóssim d'aigua.
Ens batega a la boca un cor de sal
que obre finestres noves a la terra. (TM 301, lines 25-31)

I have commenced this section by quoting the fifth stanza of the sestina 'La festa de la sal' because it sheds light on the predominant assertion that the connection between the self and the other is more than a mere physical interaction. The conjunction between the images of 'foc' and 'aigua' ('fire' and 'water') indicates the route of forthcoming victory, where the force of opposites allows the communion between the self and the other in this poem. First, this stanza pictures a natural setting 'ens abracem amb les plomes del foc', where the voice of desire discloses this passionate encounter. Passion, at the zenith of its function, broadens the space on earth and bestows upon the self significant symbolic consequences: 'ens batega a la boca un cor de sal / que obre finestres noves a la terra' (TM 301, lines 29–30). These consequences, encapsulated specifically in these lines, bring about two important insights that I would like to critically examine here. Firstly, passion, in its difference from love (as suggested at the start of this section), appears not only with an extraordinary intensity but also becomes the drive for physical bonding between the self and the other. Secondly, passion, manifested poetically through the expression of desire, is metaphorically displayed in the personification 'veus de desig'. *Terra de Mai*, in Marçal's words, is 'l'expressió més clara del desig. Els poemes anteriors potser eren més continguts, com si parlés d'un desig que no es desbordava. Tal volta siga una qüestió de passió' (Nadal 1989: 26). This is indeed a question of passion. Desire, which in this book speaks openly, drives the other towards the self through images of excess, such as those of 'biting', 'bursting' or 'burning'. This movement appeals to the violence unleashed in their bodies, bodies immersed in the turmoil that only the experience of passion can instigate, as these lines of the sestina 'Solstici' suggest: 'quin mossec amb lluors d'ametlla viva' and also 'que cremi tot en un torrent de molsa' (TM 298, lines 3 and 31). This violence instigates a rupturing of previous forms of encountering the other in Marçal's poetry, and provides, at the same time, novel lyrical means whereby desire is revealed, as the fourth stanza of the sestina 'La festa de la sal' narrates:

> Som d'aquest món, però encetem un món
> que endevinem amb els sentits de l'aigua.
> Ens creixen arbres com si fóssim terra
> i se'ns arrapen vives flors de sal.
> Cremem i alhora transformem el foc
> en energia dolça i en bleix de l'aire. (TM 300)

I consider this accomplishment as part of a rather unusual poetic way of disclosing the inner desire of the self through same-sex eroticism. The primordial sense of eroticism connects body and action in such a way that the female desire, as the title of this part suggests, 'turns the air upside down'. I endeavour here to go as far as to claim that eroticism in the poems brings into play the fascination of the self towards the other to the point that there is a complete fusion of both subjectivities. This results in successfully accomplishing one of Marçal's poetic aims, the aim of creating the other as a process of recreating the self (transcendence). The question that arises here concerns whether passionate love in its futility can be taken as the basis for achieving symbolic transcendence. To claim a poetic transcendence through approaching the other as the same (resemblance) is essentially to imply that the structure that has operated poetic signification hitherto cannot validate the contingencies of the specific same-sex passion literarily formulated here. Below, I shall address this issue.

Same-sex Passion: No One's Land that Remains in the Margins[26]

To begin my interrogation of what passion can contribute positively to the purpose of my arguments, I shall argue that the central difference between love and passion is based on two premises: the body and action.[27] At first, these two paradigms seem to be part of a rather paradoxical vision of what Western thought, from its epistemological foundation, has told us. To delineate the specificity of passion through the frameworks established of body and action reveals aspects of the poetic force in *Terra de Mai* that may account for the female poet's capability of having a profound effect on symbolic transcendence. At a deeper level, passion, as a response to the corporeal, seems not to be a limitation on the individual towards the honourable achieving of love in the poems, but rather the medium through which Marçal articulates the particularity of her desire. In the sestina that opens up *Terra de Mai*, the poet writes:

> Em vesteixo de no, contra la runa.
> Em vesteixo de sí i afirmo l'arbre.
> Renego vells confins que clou l'espasa
> i, al cor de la revolta de la terra,
> convocant tots els verds en el teu sexe,
> reafirmo l'esclat urgent de l'hora. (TM 296, lines 7–12)

Her passion for the other, as the stanza shows, is affirmed by the explosion of this moment as an intense experience of the self that emerges from nature itself. The consequences of this lie in the ending of previous ways of interacting with the other, and the beginnings of new modes of interaction. This transition is made apparent in the form of a revolt against this previous mechanism, displayed poetically in the first three books (*Cau de llunes*, *Bruixa de dol*, and *Sal oberta*). In *Terra de Mai*, Marçal gives attention to this passion and shows the urgency of acknowledging its legitimacy. This is what determines the importance of this book, and also the need for a further consideration of the validity of poetry as a site for a feminist epistemology.

Literature, particularly poetry, finds the experience of love and passion a matter of reflection for most writers, and Marçal was no exception. She explored the contingencies of these paradigms in relation to literature, to writing, and to herself. In the text entitled 'La passió amorosa' (1994a) Marçal differentiates passionate love from love itself.[28] She bases this difference mainly upon the parameter of action, an action that inherently relates the subject to literature (a topic to which I shall return later). This is not only because love, in its various modes, has been a central theme in her poetic corpus but also because love is the force that leads the writer towards writing. In this sense, the active aspect of passion encounters the subject in language in both ways.

Traditionally, love for women has suggested passivity and control cloistered in the form of abnegation. This abnegation reveals that the interaction between the self and the other is based upon power. As Marçal wrote: 'en l'amor, al contrari, hi ha abnegació' (1994a: 177). This intervention of power between both subjects results from a patriarchal configuration of love, where woman has always occupied the place of the other. To explain this, Marçal, uses a mathematical formula taken from the Danish writer Susan Brogger. She says: 'Susan Brogger, en un llibre titulat, ben significativament en la seva versió castellana *Y líbranos del amor*, venia a dir que l'amor era el mite d'una suma impossible: $1 + 1 = 1$, que en realitat només es podia fer possible si un dels uns (la dona) era un zero' (1994a: 173).[29] In contrast, passion is defined by Marçal as follows:

> té dues cares; és d'una banda un sentiment amorós molt intens, incontrolable que no denota passivitat, com indicaria etimològicament el terme, sinó que la persona que l'experimenta fa coses. La passió és font d'estímuls, i sobretot per la literatura. La passió és un sentiment religiós també, té la vessant de sofriment. (Maria i Miriam 1995: 11)

In fact, etymologically, the word passion refers to the suffering and torments of the soul, and was coined in the twelfth century in order to refer particularly to the sufferings of Christ on the cross.[30] Even though this traditional background situates passion from a contrasting perspective, both viewpoints converge in one way or another upon the body. To determine the body as a source of epistemology, as I have examined in Chapter One, is a rather problematic matter. The continuous impediments found along the way to exploring the traces of the body in philosophic and religious discourses reveal how knowledge and signification were formally achieved. In the long male-centred tradition, it is difficult for a female subject, and especially for a poet, to establish her particular *modus operandi* of signification from these perspectives.

Although it is not my intention to enter into a philosophical debate, nor is it my purpose to establish the constituents that have forced the body to oppose the mind in the quest for knowledge, I consider that it is necessary here anyway to unravel the threads whereby tradition has conferred upon philosophical discourse the sovereignty of pursuing knowledge through the exaltation of the faculties of the mind, thus relegating poetry to the level of a minor epistemological result. This is related to the concept of love and the different ways in which philosophy and poetry have approached the matter. Only by clarifying these premises, and understanding the point where this controversy began, can I then move forward in order to examine the trains of thought that make the passion proclaimed in *Terra de Mai* a legitimate source for a feminist epistemology. With this claim, I am by no means rejecting the legitimacy of philosophical discourse in its foundational purposes. Rather, I am attempting to demonstrate that Marçal finds the means whereby she pursues the contingencies of her specific form of transcendence in the impulse of passion and in its poetic display.[31]

With Plato and his heirs,[32] the body has limited the self in such a way that any possibility of transcendence is thwarted.[33] Passions, innately attached to the body, though not considered entirely negative were merely a medium through which to enter into the realm of the soul.[34] In this sense, the turbulence of the passions had to be subordinated to the perseverance, stability and control of the soul. *Terra de Mai*, however, represents a locus where passion in fact provides the development of a different purpose. The self and the other, embedded in an erotic atmosphere of pleasure and joy, 'quin ball, petites llengües sense brida!' (TM 298, line 5), celebrate the lack of control over their bodies, which in turn brings forth an entirely positive result.[35] Passion in the physical excitement of both subjects rocks the foundations of tradition by placing bodies at the centre of the text. The fact that the self and the other are in fact the same (resemblance) weakens any possible form of self-control, as Marçal herself writes in the introduction of her collected poems: 'tot límit s'esborra, tota brida cau, tot és un daltabaix de sal oberta' (1989a: 8). The iconography of *Terra de Mai* reveals to the reader that the passion between both subjectivities brings about the celebration of the body as freedom, triumph and, ultimately, communication.

My own consideration of the latent power that poetry can offer in terms of Marçal's literary possibilities for self-transcendence is not an isolated one. Other women thinkers and philosophers have seen in literature fertile ground for the quest for the self.[36] Based upon the paradigm of praxis over theory, as has been the basis of this book, the Italian thought of *il pensiero* also reflected upon this issue. One of its relevant figures, Adriana Cavarero, has devoted her thoughts to meditating upon the schism between literature and philosophy.[37] In her book *Relating Narratives: Storytelling and Selfhood* (2000), Cavarero reveals the urgent need for the female subject to turn to the literary sphere in order to find and explore the traces of her fragmented self. By using the myth of Oedipus, along with the Arendtian perspective on the implications between the *what* and the *who* of a subject, Cavarero illustrates the ways in which this myth demonstrates that women need to turn to literary discourse if their aim is to give significance to their desire. Especially in the chapter 'Oedipus errs twice', Cavarero demonstrates how Western traditions, based on a philosophical foundation, become the historiography of Man's self-representation.³⁸ She writes: 'in its classic profile, philosophy is the child of Oedipus alone, not of the Sphinx' (2000: 51). In contrast, she highlights that literature offers possibilities to project what Cavarero calls women's 'uniqueness' for the female subject, in opposition to the male-centred universality that philosophy displays. In her own words, in literature 'we are dealing with the particular, resplendent with finitude and content with existing; whose glory takes the form of uniqueness' (Cavarero 2000: 53). This uniqueness accounts for the particular, the specific theme, as a form of expression that poets, especially Marçal, have chosen to elaborate their experiences around.

Taking Plato as the basis for her argument, Cavarero has suggested that the way that philosophy has taken the path of dissociating the body and the soul in order to seek immortality and eternity 'declares a war against the art of poetry' (2000: 95). In *Terra de Mai*, poetry seems to be driven by the wounds and loss of the body. Marçal speaks of the anxieties of the flesh, of the joys and sorrows of a passionate love, as the universal history of poetry has revealed.³⁹ However, this characteristic of passion does not seem to remain solely as a misfortune of the soul. There is a positive outcome that springs from her account. If philosophy, in ancient times, needed the intervention of *catharsis* as the action to disassociate the body from the soul, women have found in passionate love the stimuli for writing, as Marçal has suggested above:⁴⁰ 'sembla que les dones haguessin trobat una palanca per expressar el seu desig, la seva subjectivitat, i, en un cert sentit, la seva llibertat' (Marçal 1994a: 175). Passion in *Terra de Mai* is the primordial force that allows poetic composition. Furthermore, this force in the sestinas not only resituates the body as the source of signification, but also provides the possibilities of transcendence from object to subject of love.

Thus, the subjective experience of poetry becomes a revelation of the deepest mysteries of herself, and discloses in *Terra de Mai*, in its specificity of space and time, the vicissitudes of a same-sex passion. The synchrony implied in this form of exploring the self is of a primary importance here. The highly limited literary references that Marçal could access in order to compose the poems affirm that the only possible source that she possessed at the time of writing about this experience was the synchrony of her body.⁴¹ In other words her experience, marked by the specific space and time in which it occurred, is the only point of reference she had. This reveals that 'l'amor-passió tal com l'han viscuda algunes dones seria al mateix temps símptoma d'un desordre simbòlic femení i de l'expressió d'una subjectivitat que busca de dotar-se d'un lloc en el món en primera persona' (Marçal 1994a: 179).

The experience of passionate love in *Terra de Mai* remains the sole source of information about how Marçal as a particular female Catalan subject lives, experiences, recounts and elaborates her passion at a time when the poetic structures available to translate the modes of living love and passion did not yet contain same-sex experiences. The expression of this same-sex passion puts an end to the fissure between desire and the lyrical framework, and also to the silenced body poetically. This silence, already deafening in terms of passion and the female subject, is further reinforced when two women are involved in sexual intercourse. This silence, which traditionally has forced women to remain at the margins of poetry since Sappho, is broken in *Terra de Mai* by the voice of this same-sex desire. This voice that emerges from the margins finds the frame where this action can be rooted in the lyric structure of the sestina. *Terra de Mai*, thus, becomes the land that speaks, the land that acts, the land that is not passively waiting to be fertilized, but rather foregrounds the space of inter-subjectivity between Marçal and Mai, revealing that the same-sex passion:

> potser hi ha de ser una font importantíssima d'energia per no deixar-nos engolir del tot per un sistema que sistemàticament ens ha negat, i, en especial ha negat i ignorat, el significant d'aquest amor entre nosaltres. (Barcelona BC, FMMM, 16/4, Sheet 8, fol. 2)

From all the aspects specified here, it is in the turmoil of passion, particularly same-sex passion, that she herself finds the sense of *ex-sistere*, because it is in the sorrow of the flesh that the female being can in fact find the possibilities of action. This existence cannot be accomplished without the presence of the other. As seen, the basic principle of *ex-sistere* connects her with the body and action. This can only be understood within the realm of passion, where the physical contact of the two bodies as the same expands a new way of being (transcendence). It is this point that next section will deal with.

Eros in *Terra de Mai*: The Return to a Sacred Space

This energy of transcendence, immanent in passion, manifests itself poetically in *Terra de Mai* through eroticism. The poems are imbued with an explicit erotic iconography. This imaginary distinguishes *Terra de Mai* from the rest of Marçal's corpus. In 'Solstice', the second sestina of the book, Marçal writes:

> El teu sexe i el meu són dues boques.
> No sents quin bes de rou sobre la molsa!
> Quin mossec amb lluors d'ametlla viva!
> Quina parla, amb rellent de gorga oberta!
> Quin ball, petites llengües sense brida!
> Quin secret de congost! Els nostres sexes. (TM 298, lines 1- 6)

The act of writing poetry is, in Marçal, an act of communication. The act of writing erotic poems brings forth a specific act of communication. The specificity lies in the purpose of the action itself. No less important than the message is what the action of writing itself discloses: putting into words experiences that have not yet been subjected to a poetic composition (*poiesis*). It is through this understanding that Marçal's literary horizons can be justified. Also, it is in this manner that the erotic trope in *Terra de Mai* finds its particular configuration. Poems are made of words, and these words are constituted by the purpose they serve. As Marçal states: 'les paraules serveixen per a dir, i allò que no es diu, <u>no existeix</u>, o passa a ésser font de terror, com tot el que és inefable' (Barcelona BC, FMMM, c. 1980, Notícies en ona violeta, 16/3, Sheet 1, fol. 2, her underline).

In this sense, eroticism engages with the corporeal theme of same-sex passionate love, and the communication displayed here emerges in connection with the bodies and their poetic inscription. In the sestina 'Solstice' that started this section, we can see that the images of 'sexes' and 'boques' confer upon the body the capacity of not only speaking: 'quina parla!'; but also listening and feeling: 'no sents quin bes de rou sobre la molsa!' Thus, this reciprocity between speaking and listening proclaims this same-sex passion as the triumph of a communicative process.[42] The message delivered by the speaker is received by the listener. In *Terra de Mai*, the 'brida' disappears and the poet engages in an adventurous bodily dialogue with the other: 'petites llengües sense brida!' No words are said between the lovers in *Terra de Mai*, there is only the interaction of two female bodies whose corporeal action discloses the secrecy that this passion has hitherto involved: 'quin secret de congost! Els nostres sexes'. Despite the particularity of this imagery, eroticism is not exclusive to this book. Erotic images have also populated Marçal's previous poems in *Cau de llunes*, *Bruixa de dol* and *Sal oberta*, but with a rather different approach. The poet referred to this matter with the following words: 'als poemes eròtics anteriors, l'erotisme hi apareix com un joc; a *Terra de Mai*, en canvi, és una mena de mar desbordat, lligat a la passió, que desapareix, en certa mesura al final de *La germana, l'estrangera*' (Nadal 1989: 26).

As seen, in *Terra de Mai*, eroticism consists of a display of corporeal images. This can be seen in the first six poems of the fifteen that make up the book: 'Sextina-mirall', 'Solstici', 'La festa de la sal', 'On s'esbalça la barca', 'Sextina dels sis sentits' and 'Mai'.[43] It starts in 'La festa de la sal' with an imperious sense of openness of the other towards the self, as these lines suggest: 'cap foc no s'arbra com tu dins la terra, / dins de l'espai atònit del meu sexe' (TM 296, lines 1–2). It ends with the poem entitled 'Mai', where the bodies of the self and the other have been reconciled: 'on el teu cos i el meu fan un sol nom, / on el meu nom i el teu fan un sol cos' (TM 307, lines 35–36). At the end of this process, the fragmented body of the feminine self has achieved a complete identity with 'un sol nom' and 'un sol cos'. Therefore, there is a corpo-real progression that follows from the metonymy of 'sex' towards the unity of the body.

On this matter, I will continue my discussion by positing the problematics that the disassociation between this poetic display of eroticism and Marçal's definition of the term seems to reveal. For Marçal, 'l'erotisme és un cert àmbit sagrat, un viatge iniciàtic a un àmbit sense fites' (Macià 1987: 4). Progression in both dimensions points in opposite directions. The mysticism evoked in her understanding of eroticism seems to rather oppose the corporeal process that the sexual interaction above has suggested. In other words, if eroticism in the poetry seems to oscillate within the realm of a physical limitation (from 'sexe' to 'cos'), in its theoretical expression Marçal appears to provide a sacred dimension that strives towards the unlimited. Therefore, the question remains how this approach affects the sense of transcendence I have proposed. This leads me to ask on what grounds is the conjunction between the sacred and the secular to occur in her portrait of female erotics. Furthermore, do these two rather opposing views undermine my arguments about transcendence or could they, on the contrary, provide the key to overcoming the binary divisions that have so detrimentally categorized the female subject as only the object of erotic desire?

On the one hand, the problem is rooted in the heart of the traditional forces of passion itself. On the other, it is also the lack of critical investigation that eroticism has received among other disciplines of thought (to the best of my knowledge). There are only two major theoretical works on the matter: *La llama doble: amor y erotismo* by Octavio Paz (1993) and George Bataille's *Erotism: Death and Sensuality* (1986). Even though both studies have attempted to explore the complex limitation of the body and the unlimited soul that craves towards the unity with God (traditionally configured as transcendence) in eroticism, the problem for the female subject seems to remain unresolved. In both accounts, women have been accorded a special locus in the discourses. Both writers have dedicated a special section of their work to the position that the woman occupies within erotic play. With rather grotesque and incongruous connotations, Bataille states that the beginnings of eroticism should refer to the presence of the object of desire, which in his own terms is reduced to the fact that 'a pretty girl stripped naked is sometimes an erotic symbol' (1986: 130). It is striking to read in Bataille's book how such a sophisticated theory on the issue of eroticism, where the writer engages with important constituents inherent to the human being such as violence, death or taboo, becomes a banal and superficial treatment when he discusses women as the object of desire.[44] In a entire subsection entitled 'Women, the privileged object of desire', included in the chapter 'Object of Desire: Prostitution', Bataille commits himself to revealing woman's body and mind, describing how she sees herself, how she values herself, even taking his statements so far as to confirm that in eroticism, using the principle of logic, women are prostitutes. He says: 'not every woman is a potential prostitute, but prostitution is the logical consequence of the feminine attitude' (1986: 131).

Focused more on literature, Paz discusses the images of woman in eroticism in terms of the lady and the saint (la dama y la santa). Paz's perspectives on the images of women in love and eroticism, covering every aspect of eroticism, are dispersed throughout his discussion. However, he dedicates a specific chapter to the role of women in *el amor cortés* as the basis of Catalan poetry, the *poesia trobadoresca* and Arnaut Daniel, the *troubadour* who used the sestina for the first time and sings of love in *llengua d'oc*.[45] Although Paz acknowledges the situation of disadvantage that these images represent in the history of the Western world, in his study he does not offer either any analysis or any solution to remedy this situation. Therefore, the puzzle of the female subject in eroticism is still unsolved, although both writers' assumptions on the matter are strongly stated and acknowledged.

Amidst this controversy women have found themselves in both cases imprisoned in their body and as instruments of the Other's desire.[46] In this sense, the position of women and their understanding is incidental to the real process of the erotic game. In *Terra de Mai*, eroticism is not merely instrumental but representative of the means and modes of a female subject whose desire does not correspond to representing a prize to be gained by the Other. Instead, eroticism reveals a myriad of possibilities that generate signification. Eroticism in the book also surpasses the realm of the simple corporeal encounter. The progression implied in both perspectives intensifies the idea that the metaphor of the journey (mentioned above) becomes in fact an integral path; a path where the inner and outer, the flesh and soul, and the limited and unlimited in the poems strive towards a complete unity.

This is possible in *Terra de Mai* because in the course of this journey the *interpersonal* encounter between the self and the other in the sestinas is not only *corpo-real* but simultaneously *meta-physic* and *meta-empiric*.[47] In other words, the fusion between the two female beings that love each other intensely results from the union of their bodies and the force that impels this union to be accomplished (passion). In this sense, the self and Mai become 'un sol nom' and 'un sol cos'. This unity evidences that the communion between the self and the other as the same is possible because they encounter each other on all possible dimensions of their *ser dona*, relegating to poetry the responsibility to be the space where all these dimensions of being *inter-act* and consequently, the holistic union is possible[48]. Prior to unravelling the threads that make up the complexities of my contention, it is necessary to offer a brief account of the poetic precedents for eroticism in the Catalan tradition. This provides the essential basis from which to later engage with the dialectics of female desire that configure *Terra de Mai* as the sacred space where Eros, as primordial force, returns to the female body in all its strength and impetuosity, illuminating the capacity of the self to disclose the enigma of her desire, anticipating that this desire is the source of an as yet unrevealed repository of meanings.

Precedents of Eroticism in Catalan Poetry

Although utilized by certain poets such as V.A. Estellés, Joan Salvat-Papasseit, or Gabriel Ferrater[49] — to name some of the most important ones — the theme of eroticism has not been fully understood in Catalan Studies nor has it been analysed in regards to poetry, with a few exceptions. The only information available about eroticism in Catalan poetry comes from the publication of some anthologies and few monographic studies.[50] In these studies, the female presence and her experience of the erotic in poetry is almost inexistent. Marçal, aware of this fact, lamented that in eroticism:

> hay cierto problema en los modelos, desde el punto de vista femenino, el cuerpo marca la diferencia a la hora de componer este tipo de poemas. Es también un esfuerzo de traducción de la vivencia y en mi caso responde a la necesidad de expresarla. (Segura 1987: 30)

In 1977, an anthology on eroticism entitled *Antologia de la poesia eròtica catalana* appeared, edited by J.M. Sala-Valldaura. In this anthology, the editor aimed to 'presentar un panorama d'actituds i tractaments de l'eròtic força complet' (41). However, his suspect sense of completeness is argued to be valid, as he indicates in the introduction, even when either excluding, or, to use his own term, 'pruning' poems written by women.[51] Only a single poem written by one woman poet is included in this anthology, which comprises in total one hundred and forty-five poems.[52] The recently published anthology on Catalan women poets and eroticism *Eròtiques i despentinades* (2008), edited by Valencian poet Encarna Sant-Celoni, saw its precedent on this anthology. This book shows that the absence of women poets in the previous anthology was not due to their non-existence. On the contrary, this book aims to suggest that a woman is 'el subjecte actiu i no sols mirall del desig de l'altre, majorment masculí, seguint la tradició establerta' (Julià 2008a: 9). This anthology comprises one hundred years of Catalan female erotic poetry as the subtitle of the book suggests: 'un recorregut de cent anys per la poesia catalana amb veu de dona'.[53] The volume is specifically dedicated to 'Maria-Mercè Marçal *in memoriam*', who pioneered with *Terra de Mai* the lyrical voice of female eroticism in Catalan poetry. Due to the lack of any model apart from the patriarchal one, Marçal's direct literary influence in this matter was the poet Salvat-Papasseit.[54] In homage to the writer in 1994, Marçal said:

> Salvat obre les portes de la poesia catalana del segle vint al Cos — aquest cos que la nostra cultura, de Plató ençà, ha tractat tan malament. I si en algun cas ha succeït que la meva sensibilitat ha discrepat de la forma concreta en què Salvat canta l'erotisme, sobretot de la seva 'fatxenderia' i el seu xovinisme 'viril', ell mateix, a través de la llibertat amb què s'expressa m'ha donat les armes per emprendre una desmitificació d'aquella mateixa 'virilitat'. (93)

In this sense, Marçal ventured to write herself the erotic encounter that she lived. These poems, thus, contain the formulae she followed in order to demystify the male imaginary. This demystification will be the focus of my discussion in the following section.

Eroticism in *Terra de Mai*: Pleasure as the Lyrical Display of an Overflowing Sea...

I have presented above a detailed overview of the treatment that poetic eroticism has received within the modern period of Catalan poetry. The results suggest that any poetic attempt on the part of Marçal in this matter must entail a demystification of the male imaginary. Thus, the question that arises from this is to what extent can this demystification be feasible, considering her lack of any poetic reference? And if it is possible, what does this demystification of eroticism consist of? In this part, I will examine the lyrical methods that create such a confrontation of this lack of symbolic and literary references in *Terra de Mai*. In so doing, I critically read eroticism as the mechanism which, initiated by passion, directs the 'I' and the 'you' towards a common aim: pleasure.[55] In order to justify my argument, I shall take as the basis of it the way that eroticism involves in its first phase a process of transgression. This transgression allows, in a second phase, the journey towards the ultimate poetic purpose: transcendence. This is a transcendence that will occur, as already pointed out, through the actions of both a *meta-physic* and *meta-empirical* encounter in the poems. In this part, I shall focus exclusively on the first phase. The second phase shall occupy my discussion in the last part of this chapter.

In order to seek substantial theoretical support with which to examine the forms in which this transgression occurs, I shall turn to texts written by women from *il pensiero*. More specifically, I will consider the work of women from *Il Centro Culturale Virginia Woolf di Roma* (The Virginia Woolf Cultural Centre of Rome) and from the group Lesbofemminismo,[56] who have theorized on the potentialities that the domain of pleasure offers to the female subject. Although this is still a not very expanded field of analysis, women from these groups have asked themselves about the imagery that has contained women's pleasure throughout tradition. Their texts, although brief and not numerous — there are only two — are theoretically relevant and introduce illuminating perspectives on this matter.

In terms of form and content, Marçal unlocks the limits of the female body, through eroticism and pleasure. Therefore, I read eroticism in *Terra de Mai* as the instrument that permits the exploration of not only the inner space of the self but also of the novel dimension that the two female bodies inaugurate. With eroticism, the silent, neglected and ephemeral body is brought to the centre of the poetic scene, where its capacity to speak and ultimately communicate female desire is at stake. An example of this is the sestina 'El corb absent'. In this poem, every stanza begins with the verb 'diré' (I will say). In the first stanza, 'diré' reveals that the body of the other woman provides the self with the necessary reference to say:

> Diré el teu cos, llibre de meravelles,
> romeva del teu nom i dels teus signes,
> analfabeta de l'enllà que em fita
> des del desig i de l'ençà que grua
> entorn de tu i de la mar en lleva,
> deixebla del neguit que fuig d'escola. (TM 310)

Marked by a rhythm of duality, eroticism in *Terra de Mai* is structured in terms of reciprocity. The self and the other on equal terms and at the same time share the experience of their bodies in a synchronized way. This fluid oscillation leaves no place for the limits imposed by a rational, dual division of subjectivities in patriarchy. As a result, neither is a hierarchy implied in intercourse nor is their movement exerted in terms of power. If reason has imposed itself in his(story) as superior in the scheme of power, the body in *Terra de Mai* reveals the possibilities of diluting such boundaries so a new space of *inter-subjectivity* can broaden in order to recover the traces of her(story). As these lines of the poem 'Solstice' suggest: 'A esglai colgat, fos l'eco la brida / que domava la dansa de la molsa, / de bat a bat tenim la platja oberta' (TM 298, lines 11–13).

Eroticism versus Sexuality

In order to resituate the body, I take the discussion that often sees eroticism as indistinct from sexuality as my starting point. The two are joined by the point where the bodies come into action, but should be distinguished by the nature of their purposes, the aims of both actions. This distinction is of a primary importance here. Not only does it concern the symbolic contingencies of the poems but also affects the development of a legitimate form of transcendence. Sexuality is primarily concerned with the act of reproduction, whereas eroticism becomes an activity with the purpose of pleasure.[57] Bataille and Paz in their respective studies on eroticism also referred to this distinction in order to begin their analyses. In *La llama doble: amor y erotismo*, Paz states that 'la metáfora sexual, a través de sus infinitas variaciones, dice siempre reproducción; la metáfora erótica, indiferente a la perpetuación de la vida, pone entre paréntesis a la reproducción' (1993: 11).

In this sense, sexuality contains the instinct of reproduction of the species; therefore, it is shared with animals. On the other hand eroticism contains a plethora of codes and bodily significations that function as signs and permit pleasure to be projected literarily. The boundaries of eroticism can vary, depending on external factors such as the context, the culture or the time when they occur.[58] In accordance with this, it should be clear that I am not denying any aspects of pleasure that subjects may experience in sexuality as the act of procreation. Rather, the claim that I will put forward is to consider that the purpose of the erotic act is the enjoyment of the body, and the possibilities that this brings in relation to poetic significance.

In sexuality, which is to say in reproduction, the position of the female body, limited to the maternal function, can lead the analysis of pleasure into dangerous terrain. This terrain is what the male imaginary, furnished as it is by images of women as mothers, has informed us about female sexuality. The indistinct use of the terms of sexuality and eroticism and the resulting lack of accuracy (in my own view) regarding their distinction, blurs the line necessary to legitimate this mechanism for increasing the poetic importance of *Terra de Mai*. Furthermore, and more importantly, the lack of distinction also increases the risk of falling into the trap of patriarchal significations. Eroticism connects the corpo-real with the symbolic, and the most intimate personal desire finds cultural codes that provide poetic significance to it. Eroticism varies and modifies its referential elements according to the culture, to the times, to discourses, but retains, regardless of all these variations, the essence of its purpose: pleasure. Eroticism is therefore understood here as a system that symbolically frames the poetic expression of a rewarding sexual encounter.

Thus, with this distinction at in mind, I aim firstly to displace any instinctive, therefore, 'natural' implications of sexuality, and concentrate mainly upon the symbolic possibilities that spring from eroticism. In this sense, I do not intend to discuss sexuality in the poems but rather sex, as an image that is often and inevitably implied in one way or another in the erotic act. Also, I shall be referring here to images of nature and the natural. In my argument, nature and the natural refer to images of the plant kingdom, such as fruits, trees, plants, or elements in natural landscapes such as waterfalls, rivers, etc. The bucolic atmosphere that this imagery provides evokes pleasure, with the possibilities of embracing a space without limits: 'Som amb el foc al centre de la terra, / brollem amb l'aigua i alenem amb l'aire. / Fem rodar el món a l'era de la sal' (TM 301, lines 37–39). Sex, like nature, becomes the locus where Man's control through reason is reduced to its least powerful. This is what Marçal has suggested with her understanding of sex:

> és el lloc de descontrol, de procés que vius de cop i no saps on et portarà, com un retorn a l'espai sense fites què és la infantesa, un viatge, i en els viatges pot sortir i passar de tot i tornar canviada. (Macià 1987: 5)

The sexual experience narrated in *Terra de Mai* is understood as a journey. A journey always brings the spatial transferring of the self, that is to say, every journey is ultimately a process of transposition. From the point of departure to the point of arrival, the journey in this never land presupposes a lyrical quest of the expression of a same-sex passion. In *Terra de Mai* this journey is specifically symbolic. The symbols used in the poems such as bodily images (sex, mouth) and those of nature (fruits, vegetables, trees) vary their connotations constantly through the precise repetitive pattern that the sestina follows.[59] In this sense, the manifold possibilities of the images multiply the significations that the different combinations of the words can provide. Marçal anticipated this poetic effect of the sestina in the introduction to the book: 'l'estímul lúdic que ofereix la combinatòria de les paraules clau en contextos diferents i, per tant, la multiplicació de les seves connotacions' (1989b: 295). This provides a sense of freedom for the self, since the recurrent combination of words expands the perspective whereby passion finds its voice. This voice communicates, speaks of a pleasure not with the articulated tone of a voice but with the flesh: 'res no calla, amb la dalla a la cintura: / tot neix i els pits donen llet a l'oratge' (TM 302, lines 11–12).[60] The attempt to find the way of poetically expressing the nature of the same-sex experience that Marçal lived is, in fact, the essential purpose of travelling through this never land.

This journey did not end with this book, but was also decisive to the last two books she wrote after *Terra de Mai*. In these books, *La germana, l'estrangera* and *Desglaç*, Marçal clearly shows a different approach to poetry. The strict lyric structure disappears and the poetic diction is subsequently more contained. The poem now acquires the function of a mirror whereby the image of Marçal as a woman reflects back a fragmented train of images that blur the sense of completeness and unity acquired in *Terra de Mai* and that the image of the mirror suggests. In this sense, the fragmented images of mother, daughter and lover coexist in a dialectical struggle in the poems: 'un gran mirall sense marcs ni límits divideix l'espai. Qui, a banda i banda? Mare, amant, filla, germana, estrangera?' (Marçal 1985b: 8). The masculine presence as the other in these last books is only determined by his absence, through the theme of the death of the father.[61]

The Pleasure of the Other: Transforming the Limits of Love and Knowledge

Hitherto, I have spoken of pleasure as the element that distinguishes eroticism from sexuality. Alessandra Bocchetti (director of the *Centro Culturale Virginia Woolf di Roma* at this time) argued in the article 'The Indecent Difference' (1991) that the issue of pleasure is for women the area of their lives that touches the most sensitive and controversial aspect of their subjectivity. Despite this, she claims that women should turn to pleasure in order to explore the elements that furnish their subjectivity in order to reconcile them with the roots of their difference. In these terms, Bocchetti asserts:

we have never considered it a worthy subject of analysis; when there have been analyses of this kind they have been cautious, hesitant or fearful; coming from the masculine imaginary they found themselves enclosed in the trap of masochism, the interpretative key which opened all doors of the feminine. And yet it seems to us that precisely this ground is most fertile for an analysis of the feminine as difference, in the effort to bring out values which have been submerged, different, other meanings which it suggests. (Bocchetti 1991: 154)

What kind of values can pleasure bring forth for the uncovering of the feminine sexual difference? What can *Terra de Mai* offer in regard to this research? Pleasure in *Terra de Mai* is not a mere account of the sexual enjoyment that occurs between the two subjects. This way of articulating eroticism and pleasure, especially in literature, has come to contribute to a common understanding of the female body as the repository of all sorts of denigrating experiences.[62] In opposition to this, the sestinas show that the poetic sense of pleasure, which starts in the joy of the bodies, goes beyond the corporeal. The bodies, immersed in the journey of their sexual relationship, not only allow the development of physical pleasure but also this pleasure echoes its presence in nature. On one side, this provides the presence of joy; on the other, it determines the capacity of the corporeal to communicate. An example of this is seen in the fifth stanza of the sestina 'On s'esbalça la barca', where the verb 'remor' (murmur), which contains the symbolism of the sound of the sea, enhances the erotic atmosphere and the movement of oscillation that is, in fact, necessary in the act of communication. The conversation has a specific locus — sex:

> Remor de bosc en les ones dels cingles,
> remor de dents on parla la cintura,
> remor de llengües en foc i en el sexe,
> remor de sègol en la nit del ventre,
> remor, follia de geniva, oratge
> quan t'endinses en mi, amb risc i barca. (TM 303, lines 25–30)

Pleasure asserts that the path to self-knowledge needs to commence in the other. The fact of loving the other, in any of its forms or intensities, is in a sense knowing the other, and in return knowledge becomes a form of love.[63] This is precisely the core of the act of communication in Marçal's poetry. It is the action whereby the self makes herself known to the other. Also, it is through this other that the subject comes to know the self. The year that Marçal published *Terra de Mai*, she suggested that 'amb la poesia es manifesta el teu jo més personal, per a estimar s'ha de conèixer i conèixer és una forma d'estimar' (Parer 1982: 23). Certainly, the experience of pleasure does not need the other in order to be achieved. In *Terra de Mai* the presence of another woman is the specific factor that prompts the pursuit of pleasure. In this sense, it is fair to say that in the sestinas one of the precepts announced in the text 'Suggestions from Irigaray' is realized:

our sexuality is detaching itself from models, it is taking shape outside of permitted rhythms and forms. We presume to experience pleasure, separating ourselves off from the values of the world. Love of self is the dynamic element which creates a new attraction between women's bodies, which creates new images. (1991: 177)

This text is considered as one of the most important theoretical points of departure announced by Lesbofemminismo. These lines state the need to explore the field of pleasure as a genuine form of 'being', of experiencing the body, of discovering the particular way of articulating female desire. Pleasure, as they state, is thus 'continually learnt and again forgotten' (1991: 179) if a theoretical exploration or a literary display is yet to be made. The unexpected irruption of Mai into Marçal's life brought serious poetic and symbolic consequences both for Marçal's own poetic development and for the tradition of Catalan poetry. For Marçal, it provided a different way of experiencing her body and raised the urgency for her of conferring upon it a poetic value. The other woman pushes the threshold of her own limits, and, with her presence, the poet enters into a new world of bodily inscriptions, thereby creating a genuine iconographic display in Catalan poetry. Marçal herself expresses this from the start in the 'Sestina-mirall', where she exalts her feeling of astonishment: 'Cap foc no s'arbra com tu dins la terra, / dins de l'espai atònit del meu sexe, / on es dreça el deler contra la runa' (TM 296, lines 1–3).

The presence of the other is the key that opens all the doors to a novel dimension, from intimacy to performance, from the private to the public. This is explicitly displayed in the sestina 'Solstici' (TM 298–99), where the combination of the ending words 'boques, molsa, viva, oberta, brida, sexes' engage in a corporeal dialogue. The image 'mouth', equated in the poem with the image 'sex', becomes the metaphor that reproduces a fluid conversation.[64] The poem starts 'El teu sexe i el meu són dues boques'. Again the first line of the second stanza reaffirms this same metaphor and strengthens the purpose 'amor, són dues boques. I dos sexes / ara ens bateguen al lloc de les boques' (lines 7–8). In the third stanza, the bodies already intensely involved in a dialogue of fluids bringing forth a whole scenery of natural display. The erotic act and pleasure in its abundance are, in this sestina, framed with images of fruits and vegetables. This association is not new in the context of what is labelled as 'lesbian erotics'.[65] The use in texts of images of trees, flowers, fruits has been connected to the experience of joy and pleasure. This is owing to the term fruit, which brings together the meanings of both a product of nature and a sense of enjoyment. 'Fruit' finds its roots in the word 'fructus', which in Latin refers to joy, often indicated as the liquid that springs from fruit when eating it.[66]

The fact that the main tropes of the erotic displayed in the poems are equated with nature is not to enforce the patriarchal condition between female sexuality and its 'natural' predisposition to give birth. The use of this natural language refers entirely to the need to find the form of expressing this hitherto unstated experience in the Catalan literary landscape. The imagery of sex and pleasure in a natural setting displaces any aspects of hetero-normative intervention and its aims of manipulating and controlling nature.

Eroticism and pleasure in *Terra de Mai* are detached from the power of 'male reason'. This is clearly stated in this sestina, where the fruit is metaphorically represented by the 'molsa' ('the pulp') of the fruits. This voluptuous image, along with 'boca, sexe, oberta, viva i brida' (mouth, sex, open, alive and bridle) encompass the scenery of joy in the sexual act. The dialogue can be seen in the use of 'your sex' and 'my mouth':

> el teu sexe i la meva boca viva,
> a doll, trenats com si fossin dos sexes,
> entremesclen licors de fruita oberta
> i esdevenen, en ple desvari, boques. (TM 298, lines 13–16)

Images of Transgression: Pleasure, Blasphemy and Birth

The viability of this dialogue entails a transgression of the female subject, from silence to speech, from secrecy to disclosure. This transgression implied in the act of communication contains specific aims when the other is the same (resemblance) as the self. Transgression can only be possible if a previous act of prohibition has been ascertained. Specifically, transgression here consists of defying the female body's prohibition from sexual pleasure. The physical encounter between two women can forcefully displace the bias of conceiving sexual interaction for reproductive purposes. In this sense, *Terra de Mai* poetically demonstrates that the female body cannot be solely categorized as a repository of reproduction as it is also a source of experience and knowledge.

Transgression is represented specifically in the poems through the idea of blasphemy. Bocchetti has in fact defined pleasure as a process of transgression. The concept of transgression inevitably has religious connotations. In Bocchetti's own words: 'women's pleasure cannot be anything but transgression within a value system which labels woman as "*mater dolorosa*"' (1991: 153). In the tone and the terms of this definition, there is an explicit reference to religion, particularly to Catholicism. This source of cultural significations has been embedded in both Spain and Italy for centuries. This long tradition has inevitably shaped the common image of woman to a large extent, based upon the symbol of the Virgin Mary as the suffering mother that has experienced the alienation of her body. Around this icon, therefore, there are images of evil and sin that test the capacity of women to remain loyal to their common duty. The female body must remain pure, and free from excessive pleasures and joys of the flesh.

Evil and sin have been symbolically represented via specific images in literature. In *Terra de Mai* 'the serpent' is the Biblical symbol that represents evil and sin.[67] The symbol of the serpent acquires in the book generally, and in the 'Sextina del sis sentits' particularly, the function of representing transgression in the form of blasphemy. In this sestina we can see the clear Biblical references with the words 'poma, geniva, molsa, carboncle, mirada, sentit'. This poem is a reconfiguration of the story narrated in *Genesis* about so-called 'Original Sin'.

There is a relevant point in this parable which questions the basis of foregrounding only disobedience in the story of original sin. There is a sensation of pleasure for Eve, when she eats the apple:[68] 'it was a delight to the eyes, and that the tree was to be desired to make one wise' (Genesis 3. 7). Not only there is a sense of joy in her eyes but in the fruit (the apple) itself, as the etymology of the word fruit has informed us earlier. Hence, is it only disobedience that we are witnessing here, or in fact the prohibition of the experience of pleasure and desire in the pursuit of knowledge?

The sestina shows from its first stanza to the last that the poem narrates the poet's efforts to make 'sense' of this experience. The two subjects are not equally active here, but rather it is the self, through an intense display of the corpo-real 'senses', who is engaged in this quest. It is clear that Marçal is playing here with the multiple meanings of the word 'sense', which integrates bodily perceptions (sight, smell, hearing, taste, and touch), with direction and coherence. Among the five senses, the other becomes the sixth sense of the self: 'tu, que ets avui el meu sisè sentit' (TM 304, line 6). It is in this sixth sense that each of the other five find a complete meaning. As the second stanza says:

> Tots els sentits avui tenen sentit
> en tu i en mi i en la pell de la poma,
> que encetem amb saliva a la mirada,
> que flairem amb orelles i geniva.
> Àvid d'avencs, l'amor és un carboncle
> vibrant sota els dits tebis de la molsa. (TM 304, lines 7–11)

In the next stanza, this quest is framed in the 'garden', in an 'extreme garden' as the poem narrates. Here, there are no binaries, no good (God)/evil (Devil), no man/woman, only the force of love which foresees the triumph of the apple: 'triomfa la veu vella de la poma' (TM 304, line 16). The wisdom inherent in their love is finally acquired. The body in the poem, represented through the image of a serpent, is the carrier of desire. It is in this temptation that blasphemy is integrated in the poem. This temptation, in its essential function, resounds with the potentialities of the female subject to overcome her given condition. Therefore, temptation becomes, in its ultimate purpose, the invitation to surmount the limits of prohibition. This is, in fact, the essence of Marçal's understanding of lyrical action. In the text 'Qui sóc i per què escric', Marçal relates the image of the serpent with both poetic action and temptation. In order to illustrate this, Marçal narrates an incident from her childhood:

> la serp potser és com aquella que la meva mare em deia que hi havia dalt d'un sostremort: la seva intenció era que m'hi enfilés per una escala de mà massa insegura. Jo pujava sigil·losament, fins que, dos o tres travessers abans d'arribar al capdamunt, la veia, veia la serp com es despertava i, de l'esglai, arrenca a córrer fins a baix de tot. Per tornar-hi, un i altre cop, sense esmena. Temptació o repte, transgressió i mancança: l'escriptura. (1995b: 24)

Marçal subverts the parameters of original sin as explained in *Genesis* in order to reconfigure it poetically. The foundations of the world are not based upon the lack of knowledge of a woman but upon the prohibiting of a woman acquiring knowledge. This prohibition has upheld the taboo of the female body on the basis of condemning pleasure. The woman in her incarnation as evil has found symbolic significance in the other as the same: another woman. The transgression has, therefore, occurred and is manifested poetically in these lines: 'Reptant, pel nus dels vents i la geniva, / dins de tu trobo i sento el meu sentit' (TM 304, lines 21–22). The new dimension that the subjects inaugurate starts through the actual quest of such a knowledge in their *ser dona*. The metaphor of the serpent asserts the victory of evil as the force that displaces the power of patriarchy over woman. This connects pleasure with wisdom as a form of birth instead of as a form of death. Marçal can now eat the apple and lyrically challenge death over life:

> I culls tot el plaer, com una poma
> assaonada. Sents? Sobre la molsa
> la mort sols és un nom sense sentit
> quan m'escoltes l'olor amb la geniva. (TM 304, lines 27–30)

As seen in the stanza, pleasure is not a path towards death, as is the suggestion that we find in Bataille's and Paz's proposals. Instead, pleasure is directed towards generation and birth, towards the construction of knowledge, which is feminine in its symbolic roots. Its continuity is assured through the communication between the subjects. The sole aim of binding pleasure with listening removes any association of eroticism with death: 'la mort sols és un nom sense sentit'. In the poetic plenitude of its characteristics, pleasure blossoms in *Terra de Mai* in a way that begins in the body of the self and ends in the body of the other woman, only to return, ultimately, to the self as a process of self-configuration. In her own words: 'el tu amb qui monologo només té ulls que li concedeixen els meus ulls, la veu que li concedeix la meva veu. Potser en el fons intento reproduir altre cop la il·lusió fallida al crear-te' (Barcelona BC, FMMM, notebook, 5/7, fol. 52).

Therefore, there is no place in the sestinas for death,[69] because poetic creation is a continuous movement of regeneration: 'brollem amb l'aigua i alenem l'aire.

Fem rodar el món a l'era de la sal' (TM 300, lines 38–39). In the female subject, continuity and generation are inherent to the liquid pleasure that they both generate.[70] Words such as 'aiguaneix, rou, platja, llacuna, marea, aigua, mar, ona' (spring, dew, beach, lake, tide, water, sea, wave), are indicative of the fluidity of their dialogue and the ongoing process of the bodies, which flow in a continuous movement like waves against the rocks, like the water of an overflowing sea.

This continuity, which I have identified through Marçal's understanding of sex as a journey, takes pleasure as the necessary common space that the self and the other create. It is the joy of their bodies that annihilates the distance between the 'I' and 'you' and exceeds the boundaries of their bodies. This excess expands the territory of signification. We encounter in the joy the space of *intersubjectivity*, the locus of the integral path, which started (as mentioned earlier) with a fragmented body represented by 'mouth', and 'sex'. Pleasure is indicative confirmation that in *Terra de Mai* eroticism does not account for a purely sexual encounter, but rather for the means of a *meta-physical* and *meta-empirical* journey. This indicates that the corpo-real excess produces meaning through language in its structural and symbolic form.[71] Bocchetti has stated the way in which pleasure is not a merely bodily function. She suggests that such a dynamic movement implies the consideration of pleasure as 'the portion of a woman's life which "power-wisdom" does not know and which simultaneously allows this "power-wisdom" to perpetuate itself: it is what exceeds it and at the same time keeps it alive' (Bocchetti 1991: 153–54). This impulse that exceeds temptation and transgresses the boundaries of the body is the issue that will occupy the focus of my discussion in the next section.

From Mercè of Salt to Mercè of Desire

Having defined passion as an active dimension that raises the need for the writing of poetry in Marçal, here, in the final section of this chapter, I examine the factual conditions of such an action and its innate characteristics as clearly displayed in *Terra de Mai*. In the preceding section I have examined the points whereby eroticism in the sestinas provides a process of transgression necessary to foreground the ultimate aim of poetic transcendence. Through the examination of some of the issues involved in eroticism, I have discussed the ways in which the dynamics of an erotic encounter do not lead the female subject towards death but towards life. In this sense, the continuity demanded of the process of creation is, therefore, accomplished. The dynamism that contains this continuity is desire, which is the cornerstone of this last section.

I have in fact been speaking of desire throughout the elaboration of my arguments on the poetic matter of love and its specificities in this chapter, without acknowledging the particularities and possibilities of the term. These, as I will show, correspond to the pure poetic action of *Terra de Mai*. In this sense, the analysis of passion and the iconographic display of eroticism come to the core of their function here with Marçal's words: '*Terra de Mai* és l'expressió més clara del desig. Els poemes anteriors potser eren més continguts, com si parlés d'un desig que no es desbordava. Tal volta sigui una qüestió de passió' (Nadal 1989: 27). The questions, thus, that remain here are, firstly, what does Marçal refer to when she declares this book as the most conspicuous poetic display of desire? Secondly, what do the sestinas in *Terra de Mai* tell us about this desire? Finally, one must also ask what can eroticism and pleasure, as examined, reveal about the specific desire in these poems? Prior to proceeding with the poetic insights on desire, I shall clarify, in the first place, the way in which I approach desire in order to do justice to the various aspects that have hitherto inhabited the domain of passion in the chapter, and which find in this last section the place of coexistence (*co-stare*).

Along with love and passion, much has been written about the theme of desire. From Plato to Jacques Lacan, the debate on the matter has filled thousands of pages and has occupied a great deal of the attention of philosophers, theologians, writers and ultimately psychoanalysts in the Western world. The motives of desire and its purposes seem to be an extraordinary fascination for thinkers on the topic of love, as its very essence connects rationality with the emotions and reveals, therefore, important insights on the way in which human nature functions. However, in all interpretations and considerations of desire, there is a common feature that asserts itself as the main characteristic of this concept. Regardless of the perspective and direction desire takes, there is always a motion, a movement that connects the subject with the world s/he inhabits through the object s/he desires. The question here is how this motion is to be understood, and which direction is taken, in the poetic demonstration of the female self.

The topic of women and desire is, in fact, studied in psychoanalysis specifically, where theories by Sigmund Freud and Lacan in particular have paid attention to this issue.[72] Their conclusions, although they have reached them from different angles, have stated that the position of woman in reference to desire is to be analysed in terms of lack and loss. In order to dismantle these arguments, most prominent feminist scholars and academics have addressed the issue of desire from a psychoanalytic perspective. Based upon the economy of need, absence and loss, feminist theorists — from different backgrounds — have devoted themselves to elaborating varying strategies to deconstruct its fundamental basis, adopting a critical response to the formulation of desire in relation to language and the justification of sexual difference.[73] In this sense, desire, conceived as a force of oppression, has determined women as incomplete beings. Also, desire has been located in the subject with no possibility for the female individual to come into existence through language. Thus, women have been objectified as the carriers of desire: 'a la societat patriarcal el desig femení és encaminat i lligat al món fent per manera que el lloc de l'Altre no sigui mai buit per a una dona, posant sempre algú, un qualsevol, en el lloc de l'Altre' (Barcelona BC, FMMM, Pensament-Diòtima, 16/7, fol. 1).

However, the consideration of desire has a specific approach in literary terms. In *Terra de Mai*, desire is articulated in a very distinctive manner. Marçal, as a woman poet and agent of creation, deposits in her desire to write the impulse of overcoming the locus of object, and therefore challenges any vestige of loss. This evidences the existence of an energy that escapes the limitations of lack and loss. This energy, which Marçal considers as 'riquesa', in her own words, 'té com a punt focal el desig' (Barcelona BC, FMMM, Ordre simbòlic, ordre social, 16/7, fol. 4). The letters, poems, fiction, and journals that we find in the history of literature inform us of this desire that traditionally has been suppressed, controlled and ultimately suffocated under patriarchal structures that cannot contain it. The woman who experiences passion and desire reveals herself as a carrier of excess. This excess opens up the possibilities of reconsidering patriarchal formulations of female identity and its pre-existent characteristics of lack and loss: 'l'excés que sovint l'ha acompanyat potser no pot ser *només* interpretat com un indici de la seva situació subordinada' (Marçal 1994a: 173).

There is, in Marçal as a writer, a deliberate poetic intentionality that follows the direction of desire. This intention is to be found in the act of desiring itself, which in *Terra de Mai* is activated by the presence of the other woman. She enhances the sphere of signification and contributes to the discarding of any parameter of absence, loss, or theoretical impediment for the construction of female identity. The presence of the other woman and the passion she felt for her provoked the need to write about this in Marçal. The expansion of this particularity demands its appearance in the shape of poems. Her renouncing of the universality hidden in male patriarchal discourse about the experience of desire impels her to write about the way in which she experiences it. The deliberateness of such a movement counts as the core of self-transcendence: 'No vull tornar salva de la tempesta / que trenca límits pel sud del teu cos, / on horitzons extrems criden desig' (TM 306, lines 7–9).

In this sense, the need to exert control over the female body is weakened and poetry becomes a fertile ground whereby these drives of oppression and imprisonment of the self are displaced. Taking into account the theoretical background of *affidamento*, I demonstrate that desire lies at the core of the ultimately poetic act that directs the self towards the other.[74] This force, activated by the presence of the other subject as the same, re-affirms that the other (*affidataria*) becomes the lyric figure of authority. Mai is not depicted within the structure of a hierarchy, quite the opposite. Equality, based on resemblance, shapes the dialogue between the 'I' and the 'you' of the sestinas. Marçal acknowledges Mai's presence when she writes about her desire for Mai; she rewrites the way in which this desire can be shaped. In other words, when the self writes about the body of the other woman, this mode of 'writing the other' returns as 'writing herself'. In this sense, the feminine authority, analysed theoretically in Chapter One as an important figure for the accomplishment of *affidamento*, verifies the theoretical understanding of loving the other as the same that I formulated at the beginning of this chapter. This authority, represented by Mai, is necessary in *Terra de Mai* in order to engage this force with a credible symbolic circulation. In this sense: 'el desig és aquell moviment que obliga interiorment a alçar contínuament la posta en joc del propi viure històric' (Barcelona BC, FMMM, Ordre simbòlic, ordre social, 16/7, fol. 4).

The Image of Salt in Terra de Mai *and the Ultimate Action of Self-Transcendence*

I begin by quoting a line from the sestina 'Mai': 'Mercè de sal a mercè del desig' (TM 306, line 19) which serves as the title of the previous section and elucidates the point I am going to discuss here. After the 'Sextina dels sis sentits', where the poet finds her 'sense' in the other woman, in 'Mai' the self achieves a physical and symbolic union: 'on el teu cos i el meu fan un sol nom, / on el meu nom i el teu fan un sol cos' (TM 307, lines 35–36). This communion occurs when both women, at the summit of their passion, move beyond the corpo-real and encounter themselves exceeding its limits in a new place where eroticism and sexual pleasure, as seen, provide the possibilities of *ser dona* as complete:

> Mai i mirall, vius en plata de plata,
> oferts al foc del meu desert voraç,
> trenquen als llavis i en molls de tempesta
> i rodolen pel cingle del desig. (TM 307, lines 31–34)

This cathartic movement, which propels the self and the other towards holistic union, occurs in the poem through 'desire'. Therefore, there is an active essential principle inherent in the term desire itself. This action is displayed poetically through the presence of verbs of transformation in the poems, such as 'fer' (do, make) as in the sestina 'La festa de la sal' (TM 300–01): 'l'urc del desig fa el ple al grat de l'aire / i torna lívides herbes i foc' (lines 15–16) and in 'veus de desig fan que es capgiri l'aire / i escampen tretze vents arreu del món' (lines 25–26). Desire shows itself in *Terra de Mai* in this active disposition also with verbs such as 'prendre, salpar,' (take, set sail) as in 'saó de lluna solca la cintura / quan el desig pren l'horitzó del ventre'/ i salpa la raó de duna i barca' (TM 303, lines 25–27) or 'exaltar' (exalt) as 'i la serp del desig, a la geniva / exalta els ulls, l'olfacte i la mirada' (TM 304, lines 17–18).

This active principle functions through the mediation of the symbol of salt, as 'Mercè de sal a mercè del desig' reveals. Salt is one of the most important images in Marçal's poetic corpus. It appears as the title of her third book, *Sal oberta*, and its presence is constant and reiterated throughout her *oeuvre*. However, in *Terra de Mai*, this icon has a particular nuance that connects the quest for poetic transcendence with passion and eroticism. This connection is linked to the initiatory journey that the poetic display of eroticism encompassed for Marçal, and not only because salt is integral to the image of sea, which, as shown, is the metaphor of pleasure ('mar desbordat'). In her own words:

> La sal en llibertat, no tant la sal domèstica, encara que també la idea de la sal com a quotidiana, necessària. En la quotidianitat tancada en un saler, en el mar l'apoteosi de la sal. L'origen de la vida des del meu punt de vista està molt associat amb la idea de l'aigua i del mar simbòlicament. La sal també té la connotació de cosa positiva. (Barcelona BC, FMMM 17/3, Sheet 11, Tarrés i Vallespí 1992: 8)

The transposition analysed in the previous section here finds its *raison d'être*, since salt is the image that informs us of the capacity of symbols to merge in poetry. This is seen especially in the third sestina of the book, entitled 'La festa de la sal', where salt appears along with the other four primordial elements: fire, earth, air and water, as well as the 'world'. The imaginary of salt, along with the four elements and the world, intensely engages the reader with a realm of power and creation:

> rebem, com a penyora, tot el món:
> fora del nostre abast, ni un pam de terra,
> ni un bri de verd, esgarriat en l'aire,
> ni un bri de blau, dissolt al clar de l'aigua. (TM 300, lines 9–12)

In the long tradition of the Western world, particularly in Mediterranean culture, salt carries a special meaning with regard to the symbolism of *alchemy*.[75] It is one of the three elements of the ancient, covert science of alchemy (the others being mercury and sulphur) and is also the material that forms the Philosopher's Stone, known as the essence of wisdom and the aim of the alchemical search.[76] It is not my purpose here to discuss the insights of alchemy, but rather the system and the aim that salt constitutes in Marçal's poems. To equate the function of desire in her poetry with the function of salt in alchemy sheds light upon the way in which Marçal's lyrics approach the quest for a feminist epistemology — as shown in the preceding chapter.[77] In Marçal's poetry and in her aim of self-transcendence, as in alchemy, there is always a principle, a primal impulse, which with Marçal underlies the composition of the poem itself. This precipitates the act of creation into the abyss of transformation, whereby the symbolic elements that participate in the poem go beyond their pre-established limits. The materiality of the two bodies and the passionate force that establishes their encounter in *Terra de Mai* is driven by the iconographic universe and the words that conduct the symbolic alteration. In the sestina 'La festa de la sal' the desire that provokes the presence of the other woman in fact results in a transformation of the world they both inhabit. This is determined by the verbs that are found in the poems such as 'cremar, transformar': 'cremem i alhora transformem el foc / en energia dolça i en bleix l'aire' (TM 300, lines 23–24).

It seems that this image of salt in Marçal's poetry acquires a rather particular function. In poetry, as in alchemy, the function of the symbol is of vital importance. In its capacity of transforming and developing the traces of an alternative world, the ancient symbolism of salt connects with Marçal's perpetual need to mark the sublime dimension of her own experience with words. At this point, Blanchot's reflections upon the function and characteristics of the symbol elucidate my argument. In the chapter 'El secreto del Golem', Blanchot considers the symbol and the symbolic experience as an opportunity for the writer to explore alternative realities, realities other than those already configured. In any expression of art, and more intensely in poetry, with the symbol there is a leap, an exhaltation, where 'el plano del que nos hace partir no es más que un trampolín para elevarnos o precipitarnos hacia una región distinta, la cual carece de todo acceso' (Blanchot 2005: 115).

There is a strong power in the symbol of salt, of both transforming and conducting transformation, which is led in the poems by the force of desire. Its alchemical function as a unifier of opposites suggests the poetic equation of the sestinas as the lyric framework in which symbolic meanings are negotiated. The symbol brings together the movement of two opposite forces: one that retains the already defined meaning, and one that seeks expansion and strives towards the infinite. In the first stanza, Marçal begins by highlighting that the self and the other personify the union of opposites:

> Tu i jo som aire que estalona el foc.
> Som aigua oberta que esmola la terra.
> Som foc que imanta amb arrels noves l'aigua.
> Tu i jo, amor, avui som tot el món
> congriat en la festa de la sal. (TM 300, lines 1- 6)

The fact that their union brings forth transformation verifies the communion of the corporeal as material, and desire as immaterial[78]. In this sense the art of alchemy, and the art of poetry, as Marçal understands it, do not differ in a great deal in their objectives.[79] The alchemical function of the symbol is not based on destruction-construction, but on the achievement of a higher level of signification (transcendence). In Blanchot's words: 'el símbolo no es destruido jamás por lo invisible o lo indecible a lo que pretende apuntar; alcanza por el contrario, con este movimiento una realidad que el mundo corriente jamás le ha brindado' (2005: 116). Just as salt functions in alchemy as the catalyst of transformation, so does desire in poetry.

The poetic intervention of salt alongside desire affirms the legitimacy of the *meta-physical* and the *meta-empirical* encounter analysed in the preceding subsection. In accordance with this, I read that the line *'Mercè de sal a mercè del desig'* discloses the fact that it is inevitably in the self — since the poet uses her own name — that the catalyst function occurs. Furthermore, it is in the impulse of this desire that Marçal expands the boundaries of herself towards the other in a movement that strives towards her final poetic aim of self-creation. Only in the exercise of writing poetry, and specifically in the poet herself, can the experience of self-transcendence be advocated, because ultimately 'el tu amb qui monologo només té ulls que li concedeixen els meus ulls, la veu que li concedeix la meva veu. Potser en el fons intento reproduir altre cop la il·lusió fallida al crear-te' (Barcelona BC, FMMM, notebook, 5/7, fol. 56).

Desire as Excess: Recapturing the Origins of Eros

Now that I have determined the way in which desire functions in *Terra de Mai* I turn to examining how poetic desire encompasses the power of concentrating and reuniting the elements of the erotic encounter, just as salt does in the alchemical process. Also, I focus here on the specificities of desire in *Terra de Mai* that propel such transformations. I have shown above that pleasure is a significant source of knowledge for the female subject, because it connects the corporeal with the poetic. In these terms, desire comes to be understood not in general terms but within the particularity of creation and in its constitution as the root of passion through eroticism and pleasure: 'passió té unes connotacions d'intensitat i desmesura. Des-mesura: sense mesura. Fora de les mesures, dels motlles unificadors dominants' (Marçal 1994a: 173).

This corresponds to the manner in which desire is displayed in the poems and desire's symbolic effects. The pulses and rhythms of the body go hand in hand with the schemic repetition of words and images in the sestina, creating a unique tempo and a multiplicity of significations. These motions are led by the force that exceeds the corpo-real in the sexual encounter. The excess is, in fact, what emerges in the poems as the source of an intellectual joy, permitting, therefore, the connection between body and action. Insofar as my investigation is concerned, desire, understood in terms of erotic excess, is rooted in the poetic motion that carries the self towards transcendence and displaces desire from its traditional attachment to lack and loss. In Marçal's words:

> el propi desig com a excés i com a mancança alhora. Podem interpretar els 'excessos' amorosos i passionals femenins com a vies de canalització d'una energia, d'un Desig que no troba la seva mesura a través dels codis culturals, de l'ordre simbòlic vigent. (1994a: 179)

In order to resituate this energy (symbolised by salt) within the specificity of poetry, and also in order to assert my claim of desire as the victory of excess over lack and life over death in *Terra de Mai*, I will refer to the etymology of eroticism and the ancient functionality of this term. This will clarify the point where desire becomes a catalyst of transformation and literary creation.

We find the etymology of the word eroticism in Eros. Eros, which has been variously translated as 'sexual passion', 'desire', 'love', 'carnal appetite', and so forth, has been studied, analysed and ultimately represented with several forms and meanings.[80] However, despite the various perspectives established in the history of ancient thought, above all Eros is the primordial force that precipitates the act of creation.[81] The first intervention of Eros in Western culture was in fact in poetry, around 700 BC with the previously mentioned Hesiod's *Theogony*. Although not considered a deity in the full sense like Gaia and Chaos, Eros is one of the three original forces that participated in the birth of the world. Eros emerged from Chaos, and with his desire provided the offspring of the subsequent parts of the world:[82]

> Chasm it was, in truth, who was the very first; she soon
> was followed by broad-breasted Earth, the eternal ground of all
> the deathless ones, who on Olympos's snowy summits dwell
> and murky Tartaros hidden deep from Earth's wide-open roads,
> and Eros, the most beautiful among the deathless gods —
> limb-loosener he is of all the gods and of all men:
> thought in the breast he overwhelms and prudent planning, then.
> (2006: 26–27)

This fragment of the *Theogony*, with the speculative action of Eros in the narration of this cosmogony, links with the arguments raised in Chapter Two where I demonstrated how Marçal's poetic historiography corresponds to the process of *poiesis* as the craft whereby she reconstructs herself. The mechanism of *poiesis* that I assert is identified through the central process of this ancient creation myth, which is based upon the transition from chaos into light. The idea that this kind of process constitutes the core of Marçal's poetic composition is furthered in the fact that it is only when the impulse of Eros is activated that the mechanism can indeed accomplish its purpose. Consequently, Eros does not emerge as an exclusive and irreducible sexual drive, whose origin is based upon the absence of the object of love, but rather as a primal impulse of attraction that foregrounds the creation of the world that sprang from Chaos (*poiesis*). Due to this power, Eros was soon declared a fierce enemy of reason in the classical world.[83] Only the excess found in the infinite and eternal space of Chaos can appreciate the offspring of Eros as a catalyst of creation. At the centre of these statements lies the idea that Eros can only be found in the realm of passion, and that Eros's main characteristic is not lack but excess: 'tot i la seva etimologia, la paraula passió sembla tenir una dimensió activa, creadora, que tendeix a expressar-se, i a expressar-se quan ho fa, fora de la mesura preestablerta, i per la qual cosa li cal dotar-se un llenguatge' (Marçal 1994a: 176).

Derived from these primordial impulses of creation, a poetic praxis and epistemology provide a strong literal and symbolic foundation to the way in which poetry, body, and action coexist in *Terra de Mai*. There is a crucial point that emanates from the mechanism of *poiesis* and the active impulse of Eros. This is the structure that the movement of desire follows in the book. The association of Eros (as Eros appears in the *Theogony*) with desire, desire being the force that underlies the poetic composition of *Terra de Mai*, does not turn the focus of this research towards the object of desire, but rather towards the subject who desires and the possibilities that this desire generates poetically. In this sense, desire always refers to *excessus*, which is to say to the 'going out' of the subject who desires and the inevitable 'referring back', where the poetic self is redirected in order to activate the original mechanism of creation. This is performed in the poems through the structural frame of the sestina. The combination of a rather limited six words, in a specific pattern and different in every sestina, charges desire with a perpetual progression:

> l'estructura recurrent, cíclica, que fa progressar el poema amb un constant retorn i replantejament dels seus termes inicials. I, d'altra banda, l'estímul lúdic que ofereix la combinatòria de les paraules clau en contextos diferents i, per tant, la multiplicació de les seves connotacions. (Marçal 1989b: 295)

These words resound like an explosion of natural pleasure and fulfilment, as examined previously. Images of nature with fruits ('molsa, poma') and vegetables ('arbre, menta, boscos, paisatge'), combined also with the body ('sexe, boca, cintura, ventre, cos, geniva') and the four fundamental elements of the cosmos (air, earth, fire, water), are subjected to the artifice of the poet in order to undergo a visible transformation through the intervention of desire. Its function, like the alchemic salt, is to activate the principle inherent in any act of creation and transcendence.

As a result, desire is not exclusively located in the self, as psychoanalysis has informed us, but instead from the feminine self towards the poetic world that is inhabited in *Terra de Mai*. This poetic world is occupied not only by herself but also by the other. Therefore, desire links the poet with the poem, the subject with the world, and the self with the other. It is the movement that informs us of the way in which the subject is connected with the world she poetically creates:[84] 'Si interrogo, de fet, un desig meu d'aquell essencials i no superflus, i vaig a la seva arrel, trobo que aquest és meu, però alhora no és meu: és una direcció del real. El desig té alguna cosa d'impersonal' (Barcelona BC, FMMM, Ordre simbòlic, ordre social, 16/7, fol. 3).[85] This is not, therefore, to delegate the responsibility of the poet to the vacuum of tradition, neither is it to present desire as a force beyond the subject's control. Rather this suggests that, in order to understand the way in which the poet's desire for the other woman can be a catalyst of poetic and therefore symbolic transcendence, it is necessary to understand the original dynamics of Eros involved in the movement of creation and the direction it acquires in *Terra de Mai*. This is central to understanding how desire transforms and fuels transformation.

Through the exploration of the theme of love, particularly passionate love, in this chapter I have shown that displaying love for the other as the same expands the boundaries of the self, bringing forth possibilities for a poetic self-transcendence. Through the theoretical framework of *affidamento* and other related concepts, I have demonstrated how *Terra de Mai* foregrounds passion as the realm where the self encounters the other (*co-stare*). Also, I have illustrated how passion links the poet with both body and action. The iconography displayed in the sestinas reveals traces of eroticism as the transgressive journey towards birth. As a result, the association of eroticism and passion with death and self-destruction, as elaborated by prominent male authors, is displaced in Marçal's poetry. The playful bodily images and the atmosphere of pleasure have depicted desire as excess over lack, and life over death. This ongoing process has provided images and symbols of self-transcendence, ultimately advocating poetic writing as an alchemy of the self.

Notes to Chapter 4

1. The Other here with capital letter refers to the patriarchal position of woman in reference to the One, as first formulated by Simone de Beauvoir and reformulated by Luce Irigaray. De Beauvoir, in her attempt to equate the intellectual capacities of both sexes, based her ideas upon refuting the identification of women as 'the other sex' with its connotations of inferiority. Irigaray, re-examined this problematic in 'the Question of the Other' (1995), and, taking a psychoanalytic perspective, in *Speculum of the Other Woman* (1985a) she discusses how otherness has been reduced and referred exclusively to the One.
2. The theme of solitude in Marçal's poetry is associated with writing. Although this is not relevant for the issues at stake here, it is important to emphasize that solitude stands in opposition to love. Solitude is, according to Marçal, an important condition that every woman writer will seek to pursue.
3. For a theoretical account of the configuration of 'being' in Marcal as *ser dona*, see Chapter One.
4. This has been previously discussed in Chapter One.
5. 'The other' in Marçal acquires a dual dimension. The first dimension is horizontally directed, and refers to the other as 'not the self'. The second dimension is vertically directed, and refers to the other in terms of language. Although this double perspective is a highly important aspect of Marçal's treatment of poetic discourse, to examine this point in detail would move this research beyond the scope of the book.
6. I have analysed woman as 'the other' in Chapter One through reference to Adriana Cavarero's essay "Towards a Theory of Sexual Difference" in Bono and Kemp 1993: 198–221. I use 'the other' in reference not to 'the one' but 'the other' as in reference of another 'other', that is to say, 'the other' as in 'not the self' as proposed and discussed by Irigaray in the article 'The Question of the Other' (1995) In order to avoid any possible confusion with the terminology I prefer to use 'the self' and 'the other'.
7. This is explained in detail by Jacques Lacan in 'A Love Letter (*une lettre d'âmour*)' in *Book XX Encore 1972–1973: On Feminine Sexuality, the Limits of Love and Knowledge* (1998).

8. The relationship of love with identity was also explored in Catalan literature by Marta Segarra and Àngels Carabí in their book *Amor e identidad* (1996).
9. The theoretical reasons for using this specific framework to analyse Marçal's poetry have already been discussed in detail in Chapter One. This theory owes its origins to Irigaray and her work on female genealogies. See *Sexes and Genealogies* (1993b).
10. This idea of female signification among women to the exclusion of the intervention of the father was also proposed by Adrienne Rich in terms of a 'lesbian continuum', in her groundbreaking essay 'Compulsory Heterosexuality and Lesbian Existence' (1980). This theory was extended from her controversial suggestion that female creativity is inherently linked to the lesbian tendency that every woman carries inside her, see Rich 1979a. For an interesting and detailed account of the lesbian metaphor and creativity, see Farwell 1988.
11. The need for women writers to seek other female references is not exclusive to Marçal. Throughout the history of literature, women writers have sought references. A few examples of these are Virginia Woolf, Emily Dickinson, Marina Tzvetàieva, Katherine Mansfield, Colette, and Anna Akhmàtova.
12. I shall examine in detail the use of Biblical images in *Terra de Mai* and their specific signification on pages 157–70.
13. The title of this section is a translation from the line 'L'amor és una dansa sense espasa', taken from the sestina that opens the book *Terra de Mai*: 'Sextina-Mirall' (first line of the fifth stanza 297, line 30) published in 1989b.
14. The term passion occupies an interestingly ambivalent place in Marçal's discourse. Whilst the word does not appear itself in her poems, it is an important term to consider when approaching her understanding of literature and the exercise of writing. The ambivalence lies in her literary and theoretical endeavour. Her theoretical reflections on 'passionate love' in the paper 'La passió amorosa' (1994a) bring about the positive side of passion as creativity. Her literary thought, however, on passion refers to the suffering and tormented soul of the writer, which she analyses through the image of the dragon. See Marçal 1996b. I have examined this second aspect of passion in the preceding chapter. Here I am interested in exploring the potential consequences of passionate love for the construction of the same-sex poetics in *Terra de Mai*. Passion is also part of the title of her only acclaimed book of fiction, *La passió segons Renée Vivien* (1994c).
15. I shall use transcendence in its general sense of 'going beyond' the existing limits. In this chapter, to 'go beyond these limits' refers to the patriarchal condition of the female subject as the 'object of love'. Nevertheless, the theological connotations of the term 'transcendence' are, to some extent, implied. As shown in the preceding chapter, any act of thought strives towards the infinite as its own way of achieving significance for Marçal: 'penso que en tot acte de pensament o de voluntat hi ha implícita una capacitat d'infinit, penso que pensar o voler alguna cosa, fins la més exigua, és com situar aquesta cosa, almenys implícitament en un horitzó infinit. Això és, per a mi, el sentit de **tenir sentit**, que quelcom limitat se situï en un horitzó il·limitat' (Barcelona BC, FMMM, Pensament-Diòtima, 16/7, fol. 2, bold in original). Here, I am interested in showing that the same-sex passion displayed in *Terra de Mai* anticipates the aim of surpassing this condition of 'object'. It is in this sense that the term transcendence should be understood here.
16. The dialectic between love and alterity in language and its effects on transcendence has been examined by Emmanuel Lévinas in *Alterity and Transcendence* (1999). Blanchot and Irigaray were influenced by his ideas.
17. *Terra de Mai* was the fourth book in a collection entitled 'Papers Erosius'. It was brought out by a small Valencian publishing house called El Cingle, which closed down the day after the publication of Marçal's book. Even when she presented the book in interview (as *Temps de Mai*, its original title) its theme was not made explicit, her interviewer

introducing the presentation thus: 'Maria-Mercè Marçal presenta hoy su cuarto libro "Temps de Mai", obra poética en la que hay un intento de encontrar una poesía erótica' (1982: 25). The interviewer, Suris, does not go into ask any questions about the contents of this specific volume. Rather, she asks Marçal about her previous books, about her understanding of poetry in general and her thoughts on her success as a poet. For further details, see Suris 1982.
18. Goujon is a French writer, and biographer of the poet Renée Vivien. Marçal and Goujon maintained correspondence until her death.
19. Marçal revealed in an interview that the passion displayed in the book was a passion for another woman. She said: '*Terra de Mai* ve donat per una relació molt intensa i nova per a mi que va ser una relació amorosa amb una dona, i en aquest sentit em va descol·locar', see Tarrés i Vallespí 1992.
20. See Julià 2000, Díaz Vicedo 2004 and Pérez Boluda 2007.
21. Mai in English translates as 'never'. Being both never and the name of the lover, the poet strategically exploits this word play in order to indicate the state of utopia which is the poem's theme.
22. The metaphor of the room as the space of poetry is fairly recurrent in Marçal's discourse. Influenced by Virginia Woolf's *A Room of One's Own*, Marçal's 'dark room' refers to woman-identified love. The influence of Woolf's works in Marçal's discourse was indeed important. Her paper 'Entre dones' begins with the following words: 'L'any 1929, en *Una cambra pròpia*, Virginia Woolf escriu sobre la necessitat d'una literatura que revelés "l'ampla cambra on ningú no ha estat". L'espai de la relació entre dones' (1995-96: 201). It also appears in the introduction of her collected poems *Llengua abolida (1973-1989)* entitled 'Sota el signe del drac' where she says: 'Què deu ser la poesia sinó el mirall que em fa retornar un i altre cop a aquest escenari i, alhora, l'intent també reiterat d'arrencar-me'n, amb els mots, i conferir-me un espai propi, *una cambra pròpia*?' (1989a: 7, my italics).
23. The city always refers to Barcelona, where she lived for most of her life.
24. Marçal completed her studies in Classical Language and Literature at the University of Barcelona, which she attended from 1969 to 1975. There is a visible poetic display of this influence in *Cau de llunes*, where we find translations of the works of archaic poets as well as poems which follow the Sapphic structure.
25. For a detailed account of the influence of Rich in Marçal, see Abelló 2000.
26. Love and passion between women was defined by Marçal as 'la terra de ningú que queda en els marges'. These words are taken from her essay 'Viratges, reminiscències' (1989c) in Ibarz (2004: 25-34)
27. The action implied in passion has traditionally been discussed by philosophers since ancient times. Starting from the etymology of the words action and passion as *poiéin* and *páschein*, philosophers have questioned from various angles and understandings what kind of effects the movement implied in both terms might have upon knowledge. Descartes in *The Passions of the Soul* defined passion and action as follows: 'a Passion with respect to the subject it happens to, and an Action with respect to what makes it happen. Thus, even though the agent and the patient are often quite different, the Action and the Passion are always a single thing, which has two names in accordance with the two different subjects it may be referred to' (1989: 19).
28. This paper was read by Marçal for the *Jornades de cinema de dones: una camera pròpia*, in Fundació 'la Caixa' and Centre d'Investigació Històrica de la Dona, which took place in Barcelona between 19 October and 22 November 1994.
29. I would like to underline here that Marçal, as an active participant in the first feminist movements in Barcelona, was firmly conditioned in a rejection of any institutionalization of love. For a full detailed account of this, see Chapter Two. This book by Brogger had a

huge impact on Catalan and Spanish feminists at the time. It is cited by Catalan writer Montserrat Roig in ¿Tiempo de mujer? (1980), and in *Hacia una crítica de la razón patriarcal* (1991) written by Spanish philosopher Celia Amorós.
30. Another important discipline besides theology and philosophy that has dealt with the connotations of passion is psychoanalysis. Although it is not the subject of this chapter, it is relevant to note that psychoanalysis, and particularly Sigmund Freud, saw in the exploration of the passions, which he denominated 'human instincts', the basic points to develop his theories, foregrounding the nature of the human being as an instinctive creature to the basis of civilization, culture and ethics.
31. The validity of poetry as a space that reconfigures reality has been already argued in Chapter Three. However, here the discussion is established in relation to philosophy, where the concepts of love and passion have predominantly been discussed throughout history.
32. Plato was the first philosopher to formulate the complexities of love and its implication for knowledge. Before Plato, poets were highly esteemed in Athens. For a detailed account of this issue, see Nussbaum 1990.
33. With the exception of Hume and Nietzsche. For a counterargument to my assertions (and a favourable analysis of patriarchal thought), see Bordo 1987.
34. Ancient Greek thought never denied the body entirely; the body was considered as the means by which to arrive at catharsis, where the soul is finally extricated from the body and free to accomplish its own aims.
35. This is what George Bataille in his study on passion and eroticism has labelled as 'transgression'. See Bataille 1986.
36. Two significant examples are Zambrano 1993b and Nussbaum 1990.
37. Although Cavarero was part of the Italian thought of *il pensiero* she distanced herself from this group and continued her career separately.
38. I deliberately use a capital letter in the word 'Man' to emphasize the hegemony implied in this term.
39. This is first specified in Plato's *Republic* (2008).
40. Marçal gives examples of this, such as Djuna Barnes or Marguerite Yourcenar, Marguerite Duras, Marina Tsvetèieva, Renée Vivien.
41. I am using here the term synchrony to justify that the particular is indeed framed in the specific space and time that marked the experience and the composition of the poems.
42. Irigaray wrote a book on the matter of love and the act of communication. See Irigaray 2004. Her linguistic and psychoanalytic approach, highly illuminating and sophisticated, tends to address the problem within the discourse of philosophy. As I have clarified earlier, what is at stake here is not within the realm of philosophy. Marçal herself confessed the difficulties she found with Irigaray's discourse examining love: 'em sento deutora de Luce Irigaray, n'he tret idees o suggeriments de cara a la meva poesia, a la meva obra literària, però en canvi, no em sento amb prou competència per instal·lar-me en el seu llenguatge que oscil·la entre la psicoanàlisi i la filosofia més especialitzada' (1994: 171).
43. This first part was entitled 'Solstici', as it appears in the manuscript of an earlier draft. It indicated the pleasure and the Utopian vision of a fusion between two female bodies. Following a different order from the existing published edition, Marçal included the following sestinas: 'Sextina-Mirall', 'Solstici', 'Sextina en festa a l'era de la sal' (published as 'La festa de la sal'), 'Crit de verema on s'esbalça la barca' (published as 'On s'esbalça la barca'), and 'Sextina dels 39 sentits' (published as 'Sextina del sis sentits').
44. This superficiality is evidenced in the mere enumeration of the acts that women undertake in their bathrooms for the purpose of their physical adornment. He says 'by the care she lavishes on her toilet, by the concern she has for her beauty set off by her adornment, a woman regards herself as an object always trying to attract men's attention. Similarly, if

she strips naked she reveals the object of a man's desire, an individual and particular object to be prized' (131). The way in which Bataille refers to the means whereby men's desire is directed towards a woman demonstrates clearly the lack of any intellectual discussion, and as a consequence, he does not engage with the realm of desire itself. The concept of desire, be it felt towards a man or a woman, clearly surpasses the frivolity described in Bataille's book.

45. See 'La dama y la santa' in Paz 1993: 75–101.
46. In this case, the Other with capital letter refers to the Other in reference to the One.
47. The basis of my argument lies in the etymology of the words 'meta-physical' and 'meta-empirical'. The prefix 'meta' in Greek means 'after' in a condition of change; 'physics', means 'natural' as in the form of 'physis' which means nature. Therefore, 'meta-physic' refers to a condition that goes beyond nature, that is to say, the bodies. For 'meta-empirical' it is the same: 'empiric' means 'experience', thus 'meta-empirical' shall refer to a meaning beyond the experience itself.
48. In this sentence I am using the etymological meaning of the word 'holistic', which in Greek means 'where all dimensions of the being are interpreted'.
49. Following J.M. Sala-Valldaura's criteria, the series of important poets who wrote about eroticism is extended to include Carles Riba, J.V.Foix, Josep Palau i Fabre and Francesc Parcerissas.
50. *Antologia de la poesia eròtica catalana*, Sala-Valldaura (1977), *Poesia eròtica de Vicent Andrés Estellés*, Perez Montaner (1985), *Poesia eròtica i pornogràfica catalana del segle XVIII*, Rossich (1985) and *El jardí de les malícies: de la poesia eròtica universal*, Desclot (2001).
51. This was the case with the poetry of Cèlia Viñas i Olivella (1915–1954). Sala-Valldaura decides not to include her poems due to the fact that 'llur obra continuava sense cap mena d'innovacions el corrent general o era endarrerida: és el cas, per exemple, de Cèlia Viñas i Olivella (1915–1954), de la qual havia elegit, primerament, dos poemes del seu llibre — una mica neolorquià — *Del foc i de la cendra* (1953)' (1977: 41). His criteria do not stop here; Sala-Valldaura later emphasizes the fact that her exclusion from the anthology was a matter of measuring the quality of the book. In his own words: 'gràcies a aquesta "poda", em sembla que els arbres no taparan el bosc, ni gaire espès ni molt agrest, de la poesia eròtica catalana del segle' (1977: 41).
52. This woman poet is Rosa Leveroni. Sala-Valldaura emphasizes that eroticism in her poetry is 'vist des de la recança i el desig d'un amor que, gràcies a la senzillesa de l'expressió, sabem patèticament real però impossible. Només l'objectivitat aparent de les glosses mallorquines o les cançons li permet d'esplaiar amb una mínima claredat eròtica, la necessitat de repòs que sent i la melangia d'amor que ha d'idealitzar a vegades, partint de la seva assumpció constant d'un paper passiu i de víctima' (1977: 30).
53. It includes one hundred and twenty-five poems written by the remarkable number of 69 women poets.
54. Often Salvat-Papasseit has been considered as the best poet in portraying eroticism in his poems. For instance, Joan Fuster states that the poem 'La rosa als llavis' (1923) by Papasseit is not only the best erotic poem in Catalan poetry but 'podem afegir-hi, sense por d'exagerar, que és un dels millors poemes eròtics de la literatura europea' (Fuster 1972: 231). Another example is Carme Arenas Noguera in the prologue to *Joan Salvat-Papasseit. Obra completa* (2006) who stated that 'l'amor despullat de retòrica, directe i desvergonyit, el poeta com a mestre d'amor i l'enamorada com a aprenenta, ingènua' (2006: 23). Dominic Keown, in his book *Sobre la poesia catalana contemporània* (1996), has linked the features of sexuality and technology in Salvat-Papasseit's poetry with a sense of reproduction and creation: 'El que havia estat, en un principi, l'exaltació gratuïta del món tecnològic adquireix una dimensió líricament més evocadora amb l'imbuïment

d'una qualitat sexual que funcionarà en la resta de l'obra de *leitmotiv* de la visió poètica salvatiana de la promesa de reproducció i de futuritat que comparteixen tots els elements de la creació en tota la seva varietat' (161-62).

55. The recurrence of eroticism and its power to reveal traces of the experience of women, and hence its suppression at the expense of rationality, is one of the main points raised by Audre Lorde's paper on eroticism 'Uses of the Erotic: The Erotic as Pleasure'. This was read at the Fourth Berkshire Conference on the History of Women, Mount Holyoke College on 25 August 1978. See Lorde 1988: 106-12.
56. The theoretical arguments of this group are not officially separated from the main feminist movement. Their theoretical proposals are strongly influenced by Irigaray, especially Irigaray's first texts based on the understanding of *écriture féminine* in contrast with other groups from *il pensiero* which reiterate a more political concern with sexual difference. The text I shall be using is entitled 'Suggestions from Irigaray' in Bono and Kemp 1991: 177-80.
57. I would like to highlight here that my understanding and use of the term 'pleasure' does not contain a specific psychoanalytic perspective. Despite acknowledging the importance of *jouissance* for both psychoanalysis and especially for French Feminist thought, I will not differentiate this state of 'excessive pleasure' from pleasure itself. The problematics I encounter in this debate are derived from my own view of equating eroticism with sexuality.
58. As Paz states: 'el erotismo cambia con los climas y las geografías, con las sociedades y la historia, con los individuos y los temperamentos. También con las ocasiones, el azar y la inspiración del momento' (1993: 15).
59. In a previous project, I have examined this point and I have specifically equated this pattern of the sestina with the art of bell ringing, whereby the variation in the rhythm provides the changes. For full details of this see Díaz Vicedo 2004: 47-48.
60. I wish to highlight here the deliberate use of the metaphor of the milk that feeds the world. In it a link is established with Hélène Cixous and her metaphor of "white ink". For the female writer, this metaphor bridges the gap between biology and the symbolic, because it connects the corporeal and the poetic rhythm, the movement of the body and the movement of the poem. It is a pulse, a fluid that runs in the body and creates the world.
61. The dialectic between Eros and Thanatos is at stake in this second part of Marçal's corpus. However, for this research, I will leave this statement as it is. The exploration of this matter here would lead me into a different field of analysis, neither relevant nor pertinent to the contingency of this chapter. All that matters here is that it is crucial to recognize the impact of *Terra de Mai* on her later poetic production.
62. Pornography, for example.
63. In order to find, from a philosophical point of view, a detailed account of how pleasure, as an emotion, can actually pursue the quest of knowledge, see Jaggar 1996.
64. I have studied elsewhere the combination of corporeal fluids and metaphorical inscriptions of the body in the poems using Irigaray framework of *l'écriture féminine*, see Díaz Vicedo 2004. Here I am more interested in demonstrating how the field of eroticism, novel in its feminist configuration in Catalan literature, in fact elucidates a symbolic impact upon the parameters of understanding of female difference through poetry.
65. See Jay 1995 and Meese 1992.
66. Gabriel Griffin, in her study on lesbian images in literature *Heavenly Love: Lesbian Images in Twentieth-Century Women's Writing*, suggests that the use of images of nature 'is one way of suggesting that lesbian sexuality is natural because of its affinities with nature. In a culture, in which the normality or otherwise of lesbian sexuality is perpetually under scrutiny, women's writing on lesbian sexuality can celebrate and affirm that sexuality by maintaining, through nature imagery, that lesbian sexuality is natural' (1993: 147).

67. The historical context of Spain plays a central role here. The strong Catholic formation of the country during Franco's dictatorship shows its symbolic consequences in Marçal's poetry. Marçal was always educated in Catholic schools for girls. When she arrived at the University of Barcelona her religiosity was avowedly known among her friends. During her first two years at university, before her marriage to Balasch, Marçal lived with the Teresian Nuns. Her ex-husband, commented about these years: 'Des del punt de vista religiós, exhibeix un catolicisme militant, que començà a virar connectat amb el Fòrum Vergés, on hi havia catòlics universitaris progressistes. Més endavant, connecta amb comunitats de base i el moviment ecumènic', p. 33. See Balasch 2007.
68. In a poem entitled 'Eva' included in Llengua abolida (1973–1988) (1989b), Marçal narrates explicitly how Eve, and more specifically her pleasure, are taken by the poet as a main trope of knowledge.
69. Cavarero, in her essay 'Eros and Narration', has also affirmed that love in any of its forms can never be a celebration of death: 'The myth is false — because it is false to celebrate existence in rites of dissolution, turning the impulse of love into a desire for death' (111). For further details see 'Eros and Narration' in Cavarero 2000: 109–18.
70. I have explored the ways in which the concept of generation is embedded in the female subject in Chapter Three.
71. A significative structural form of pleasure can be seen is Roland Barthes' book *The Pleasure of the Text* (1975), where he analyses pleasure as an important element of the text to be considered as part of any theoretical approach.
72. It is fascinating to witness how psychoanalysis came into existence through the observation of emotions and behaviour in female subject, and how these are turned against her in a patriarchal interpretation of them.
73. Among the most influential feminist theorists it is important to highlight the contributions by Irigaray, Julia Kristeva and Teresa de Lauretis.
74. It is relevant to recall here Montserrat Lunati's analysis of desire in Imma Monzó's texts. Lunati configures desire as the space of freedom between the self and the world. She examines the approach of the self to the other not in terms of love but in terms of the Irigarayan concept of *admiration*: 'L'*admiration* no contempla esborrar o fondre's amb la figura de l'Altre/l'Altra, sinó fer possible la interrelació entre el subjecte i l'objecte, també en el sentit que qui és mirat pot modificar qui mira de maneres inesperades i creatives' (425). For a detailed account, see Lunati 2005: 423–34.
75. For Homer, salt was a 'divine substance'. For Plato it was 'especially dear to the Gods'. Salt has also been the subject of study in psychoanalysis. For instance, Ernest Jones attempted to bring the symbols of superstition and folklore to a scientific investigation in order to determine their effects upon mind. See Jones 1951: 112–203. Hillman 1995: 145–79 and Jung 1963: 183–91 also dealt with the symbolism of salt as a means of investigating the effects of symbolism on humanity on a psychological level. For an account of these three interesting texts, see Marlan 1995.
76. It is interesting to note here that for Jung salt is a feminine force associated with the moon, 'lunar salt' (Marlan 1995: 106).
77. Understanding poetry as akin to alchemy is not something new. Josep Palau i Fabre (1917–2008) conceived the exercise of poetry as an alchemical process. He wrote a book of poems called *Poemes de l'alquimista* (1945) and various essays and prose writings on the act of writing poetry as an alchemical process: *Quaderns de l'alquimista* (1976), *Nous quaderns de l'alquimista* (1983) *and Quaderns inèdits de l'alquimista* (1991).
78. In Mediterranean thought, desire has been labelled as 'anima', 'blow', 'aspiration' (*spiritus* from *spirare*, which means 'wind', 'breath', 'desire'). For a detailed account of this, see Fernández Ardanaz 1987. Zambrano also relates poetry to air, as *in-spirare* is the

movement whereby the human being takes air from his or her exterior, draws it into his or her soul and reaches knowledge. For full details, see Zambrano 1993a.
79. It is significant that Jung in his essay on salt acknowledges that this power of consolidating opposite forces is innate to women, since they are closer to nature. Without taking any position on this matter, Jung assumes the ambivalent position of women, both as fragmented beings yet also extremely powerful ones. This is the reason why Jung relates salt to lunar symbolism.
80. See Graves 1960 and Frazer 1911.
81. Jung related the force of Eros, which he considers feminine owing to the ability of unifying opposites, with salt. He says 'salt represents the feminine principle of Eros, which brings everything into relationship, in an almost perfect way' (Marlan 1995: 124).
82. In ancient Greek Eros is a masculine word and Chasm (Chaos) is neutral, but interestingly enough is often referred to as a feminine word.
83. An important example in Literature is *Antigone* by Sophocles. In this play, Eros is accused of driving Antigone to her own tragic end.
84. This is the function of the theory of *mettere il mondo al mondo* that I have analysed in Chapter Three, and that in here finds the movement that activates it.
85. This brings me back again to the preceding chapter, where I have examined the way in which poetry in fact reconfigures reality. This also reveals desire as the poetic act *par excellence* in Marçal's project.

AFTERWORD

Marçal's Feminine Poetics as a Powerful Principle of Being

This book has explored, through the analysis of contested images, the convergence between language and body in Marçal's poetry and has considered the extent to which its poetic effects reveal the possibilities of theorizing the construction of a feminine poetics within the Catalan context. This research on Marçal's work is situated within the field of Catalan feminist studies in the Peninsula, which has seen the exploration of sexual difference in critical theory and literature. My contribution to the existing debate has been the consideration of the body as a point of reflection in order to redefine the boundaries of the feminine self within the space of Catalan poetry, whilst also considering the possibilities of this space in terms of the poet's particular experience of being.

The return to an embodied thought in order to examine poetry, as put forward in this book, has been motivated by a postmodern problematic vision of feminism and the identity of woman, the consequent divergence between gender performance and sexual difference, and the need to overcome the conditions of binaries, for which a novel understanding of the concept of the body is required. A cultural construction of the body does not offer a response to the demands of surmounting binaries. Rather, it provides a fierce critique of the implications of corporeality in the formation of identity and neglects the participation of physicality.

Nor have the theories of *l'écriture féminine* provided the means whereby the linguistic implications of the body can have a visible social and political projection within culture. The relevant contributions of this theoretical discourse for philosophy, feminism and critical theory are not being questioned here. Their challenging and stimulating proposals are of great importance for literary criticism and other related fields. However, regarding the concerns of Marçal's literary project, *l'écriture féminine* does not provide the necessary framework with which to sustain the dialogue between life and poetry, theory and praxis, outside of the linguistic context.

In order to re-evaluate the importance of an embodied thought in Marçal's discourse, the Italian feminism of *differenza sessuale* has been crucial. Continuing on from a personal and conceptual connection between Marçal and the group of women from *il pensiero della differenza sessuale*, I have interpreted her main aesthetic traits through the lenses of this specific approach. My intention has not been simply to provide theoretical support to my arguments. The use of this framework has allowed me to reconsider poetry from an alternative theoretical basis. This basis refers to a feminist model of poetry, which focuses not only upon the lyric factors concerned in the art of poetry but also reflects upon how these affect and are affected by a female poet. In this sense, the analysis of poetry from a gendered angle has further contributed to expanding traditional territories such as feminism and the art of poetry in Catalan literature.

Considering the fact that Marçal's poetic universe is constructed around parameters of body and language, I have pursued four different trains of thought in four chapters that have demonstrated the fluctuation between embodied experience and symbolic placement in poetry as Marçal's mode of existence (*ex-sistere*). Chapter One has conducted the hermeneutics of the body in relation to language and writing. Chapter Two explored the female body within the existing symbolic world (*ad-stare*). Taking poetic action as its centre, Chapter Three analysed this action and considered the spatial conditions of poetry (*in-stare*), also focusing upon the agency of the female writer. Finally, Chapter Four has taken the premise of contemplating poetic action as the means of self-creation, and has dealt with the display of love and passion as paradigms that position the poet in relation to the other (*co-stare*).

In reference to the conclusions drawn in each part, Chapter One focused on the concept of the body upon which my understanding of *ser dona* has been based. Continuing on from a dialogue between biological determinism and cultural construction, I put Marçal's aesthetics into a dialectic process with Italian feminist discourse and its demand for a sexed thought. This has allowed me to link the social with the symbolic and offer a formula whereby writing as an intellectual practice reveals poetry as a space for the subject's self re-creation. Therefore, the reassessment of the implications of the corporeal as the central theme of discussion does not bring about an essentialist vision of the problem. Rather, it reveals some aspects of the corporeal yet to be explored. As a consequence, I have considered the body as a dynamic, open space where the self is displayed both intellectually and socially. This presence is also in a continuous interaction with other elements such as symbols, the poetic space and language.

The acknowledgment of the body as a central issue in literary creation has been important in order to disentangle the alleged universality and neutrality of discourse. The category of the body, through the lens of *differenza sessuale*, has shed light on the way in which corpo-reality and its subsequent cultural performance overcomes the discontinuity marked by patriarchy. It has also dismantled the recognition of only one specific subject, the male, as symbolically accepted, and bridges the gap between theory and praxis, culture and nature and, ultimately, private and public.

Having delineated a new concept of body and its possibilities for *ser dona*, Chapter Two has traced the mechanism of *poiesis* that instigates Marçal's need to write poetry. Assuming the meaning of *poiesis* proposed by Aristotle in his poetics as the 'making' of poetry, this chapter has revealed the extent to which Marçal's approach to poetry connects her embodied experience with the poetic construction of her identity. Judith Butler's reappropriation of the term *poiesis* has been vital in order to critically examine the conditions of this process. This has been done by exploring how the mechanism of *poiesis* works as an act of creation and how it is represented and manifested in Marçal's creativity. Following thus a chronological course and an inductive method, I have analysed, through her literary compositions, the iconographic references Marçal uses and the manner of this creative act. In this sense, the references to Aristotle's theoretical foundations and Hesiod's *Theogony*, contrasted with the use of Butler's perspective, have served to evidence that the very act of creating poetry necessitates the involvement of the subject with existing iconography and poetic structures. As a result, this chapter has illustrated the way in which writing poetry becomes, for Marçal, the particular mode of reconstructing her existence literarily.

Taking into account this particular point, in Chapter Three I have examined the spatial conditions of poetry and its potentiality of containing the processes (*in-stare*) analysed in the preceding chapter. These effects, underpinned by the concept of *mettere il mondo al mondo*, have asserted that Marçal's role as a poet engages with a corpo-real dimension, whereby experience is displayed poetically. The symbolic and cultural consequences of this action have uncovered the extent to which poetry serves as the space for reconfiguring reality. Given that reality has been understood from the perspective of sexual difference and supported theoretically by Diotima's theory of *mettere il mondo al mondo*, I have pursued the mechanisms whereby Marçal's approach to poetry and her poems are based upon the metaphorical implications of birth (*atopia*). This has been important in order to pursue my claim that Marçal, as a poet, becomes the founder of her own existence (*poietes*). Using the myths of the Legend of Saint George and the Birth of Athena, I have shown how the poet's agency emphasizes the need to rethink existing symbols from the perspective of sexual difference, whereby Marçal emerges from the tradition of Catalan literature. This emergence has testified not only that the female body, biologically predisposed to give birth, generates new significations but also that this creativity framed in the space of poetry reconfigures reality.

The fourth and final Chapter has examined this new symbolic world that Marçal has created poetically. This has been possible through unravelling the threads that constitute the interaction between the self and the other. This interaction, displayed in the poems through the theme of love, has allowed me to investigate the effects of loving the other who is the same as the self. These effects have drawn upon existing debates around the concept of love and related issues such as passion, eroticism, pleasure and desire. The direct involvement of the body in the poetic revelation of this experience has subsequently determined that to write about the love for the other as the same extends the boundaries of self and consolidates poetic writing as the alchemic action that drives the poet towards transcendence. The theoretical implications of *affidamento* have provided the theoretical support to my argument of how transcendence takes place in the poems. In this sense, the female poet has challenged her position as object of love, revealing that she is not a carrier of lack but a carrier of excess. This excess culminates in a consideration of desire as the drive that fuels this transcendence. Therefore, Chapter Four has illustrated that female desire is not located in the subject but from the subject. Desire is the movement that connects Marçal to both the social order, through the other, and the poetic world, through writing.

I conclude by stating that in Marçal's corpus poetry accomplishes two significant functions: symbolic and socio-communicative. Both functions question prevailing forms of *ser dona* and provide the means and the images whereby her poetic research takes place. In addition, her agency and poetic action contributes to the creation of alternative forms of representation. Marçal's proposal of *ser dona* is not based upon essentialist frameworks but upon dynamic relationships: with the space of poetry, with the other, and with existing iconography. This reveals that the female poet is a dynamic subject who actively participates in the process of creation, acts socially at the time she decides to write and ultimately contributes to the continuous formation of the history of poetry. In raising the question of the body in Marçal's poetry, we find that the function of poetry is elaborated through the theoretical support of *il pensiero della differenza sessuale*. Marçal explores the possibilities that poetry offers her literary project. This exploration emphasizes the qualities of symbolic function in the poems. This symbolic function asserts poetry as the space of epiphany, as it is within this space that Marçal elaborates herself culturally. In this sense, the action of writing walks hand in hand with life. For Marçal, to write poetry is to generate meaning. The poet demonstrates the means, the actions and modes of representation in the poems as principles that make up her feminine poetics. With this analysis, I have proposed and proved that Marçal provides the tradition of Catalan poetry with a poetics of the feminine. Her creativity is inseparable from her body, and this body generates new symbolic worlds that exceed the limits of the skin.

BIBLIOGRAPHY

Abelló, Montserrat, Neus Aguado and Josefa Contijoch, 1998. *Homenatge a Maria-Mercè Marçal* (Barcelona: Empúries)
——, 2000. 'Adrienne Rich, Sylvia Plath i Anne Sexton en l'obra de Maria-Mercè Marçal', in Pont and Guerrero, eds., *Llengua abolida, 1r. Encontre de creadors* (Lleida: La Paeria), pp. 88–92
——, 2008. 'Gosar poder triar. Sylvia Plath i la mort del pare', in Marçal and Llorca, eds., *II Jornades Marçalianes. Saba vella per a les fulles noves* (Sabadell: Fundació Maria-Mercè Marçal), pp. 171–86
Abrams, Sam, and Kathleen McNerney, 1995. 'Maria-Mercè Marçal', *Catalan Writing*, no. 14: 81–87
Accati, Luisa, 1991. 'En busca de las diversidades perdidas. Conceptos anglosajones y madres mediterráneas', *DUODA*, no. 2: 15–44
Adell, Joan-Elies, 2008. 'Quan el cos dóna la raó', *Reduccions*, no. 89–90: 262–73
Aguado, Neus, 1986. 'Un mundo sin límites', *La Vanguardia*, 7 Aug., p. 22
——, 2008. 'La llum de la paraula en una altra llengua', in Marçal and Llorca, eds., *II Jornades Marçalianes. Saba vella per a les fulles noves* (Sabadell: Fundació Maria-Mercè Marçal), pp. 55–70
Akhmàtova, Anna, 1990. *Rèquiem i altres poemes*, tr. Maria-Mercè Marçal and Monika Zgustová (Barcelona: Ed. 62)
Alcaraz, Joan, 1983. 'Un poeta universal, encara massa inconegut: J. V. Foix, en els seus noranta anys', *Full de la Cultura*, 24 Jan., no. 33: 1–2
Alonso, Vicent, 2010. 'Maria-Mercè Marçal o les raons de la literatura', *Reduccions*, no. 97: 133–45
Altés, Elvira, 1995. 'Maria-Mercè Marçal', *Avui Diumenge*, 15 Jan., pp. 28–29
Alzueta, Miquel, 1978. 'Maria-Mercè Marçal de classe baixa i nació oprimida', *Mundo Diario*, 6 July, pp. 6–7
——, 1979. 'Un llibre de poesia feminista', *Mundo Diario Cultura*, 8 Nov., p. 23
——, 1980. '"La nova poesia catalana": una aposta de futur', *Avui*, 13 July, p. 24
Amorós, Celia, 1991. *Hacia una crítica de la razón patriarcal* (Barcelona: Anthropos)
Anglada, Maria Àngels, 1988. *El mirall de Narcís. El mite grec en els poetes catalans* (Sabadell: Ed. Ausa Orientalia Barcinonensia)
Ardid i Borrás, Rosa, 2001. 'Maria-Mercè Marçal: un clàssic, una clàssica?: rao(ns) de gènere', *Serra d'Or*, no. 496: 72–75
Arenas Noguera, Carme, ed., 2006. *Joan Salvat-Papasseit. Obra completa* (Barcelona: Galàxia Gutenberg)
Arendt, Hannah, 1958. *The Human Condition* (Chicago: University of Chicago Press)
——, 1987. 'What is Authority?', *Between Past and Future: Eight Exercises in Political Thought* (New York: Penguin)
——, 2000. *Rahel Varnhagen: The Life of a Jewess*, ed., Liliane Weissberg (Baltimore: Johns Hopkins UP)

Ayén, Xavi and Rosa M. Piñol, 1998. 'La pasión según Maria-Mercè Marçal', *La Vanguardia*, 12 July, p. 51
Balasch, Ramon, 2007. '*Cau de llunes* des de 1969', in *Traginera de llunes i cançons, 30 anys de la irrupció poètica de Maria-Mercè Marçal*, *Urc*, no. 22: 27–42
——, 2008. 'Blake i la cega estrella', in Marçal and Llorca, eds., *II Jornades Marçalianes. Saba vella per a les fulles noves* (Sabadell: Fundació Maria-Mercè Marçal), pp.133–56
Barba, Carles, 1981. 'Maria-Mercè Marçal: Un día romperé con el verso y haré poemas en prosa', *El Correo Catalán*, 12 May, p. 30
Barthes, Roland, 1975. *The Pleasure of the Text*, tr. Richard Miller (London: Jonathan Cape)
——, 1979. *A Lover's Discourse* (New York: Hill and Wang)
Bartra, Agustí, 1980. *Sobre poesia* (Barcelona: Laia)
Bataille, George, 1985. *Visions of Excess, Selected Writings, 1927–1939* (Manchester: UP)
——, 1986. *Erotism: Death and Sensuality* (San Francisco: City Lights Books)
——, 1989. *The Tears of Eros* (San Francisco: City Lights Books)
Batista, Antoni, 1979. 'Des d'uns ulls de dona', *Treball*, 22 Nov., p. 12
——, 1986. 'Maria-Mercè Marçal, una intel·lectual del feminisme', *Avui Diumenge*, 23 Feb., p. 1–3
Benedetti, L., Julia L. Hairston and Silvia M. Ross, 1996. *Gendered Contexts: New Perspectives in Italian Cultural Studies* (New York: Peter Lang)
Bertolino, Elisabetta, 2008. 'Beyond Ontology and Sexual Difference: An Interview with the Italian Feminist Philosopher Adriana Cavarero', *Differences*, 19.1: 128–67
Birulés, Fina, 1992. *Filosofía y género. Identidades femeninas* (Pamplona: Pamiela)
——, 1997. 'Indicios y fragmentos: historia de la filosofía de mujeres', in Rosa M. Rodríguez Magda, ed., *Mujeres en la historia del pensamiento* (Barcelona: Anthropos), pp. 17–31
——, 1997. 'Fragmentos del discurso sobre la autoridad femenina', *Archipiélago*, no. 30: 56–67
Blanchot, Maurice, 1989. *The Space of Literature*, tr. Ann Smock (Lincoln, NE: University of Nebraska Press)
——, 1992. *El espacio literario*, tr. Vicky Palant and Jorge Jinkis (Barcelona: Paidós)
——, 2003. *The Book to Come*, tr. Charlotte Mandell (Stanford: UP)
——, 2005. *El libro por venir*, tr. Cristina de Peretti and Emilio Velasco (Madrid: Trotta)
Bloom, Harold, 1997. *The Anxiety of Influence* (Oxford: UP)
Blundell, Susan, 1995. *Women in Ancient Greece* (London: British Museum Press)
Bocchetti, Alessandra, 1991. 'The Indecent Difference', in Bono and Kemp, eds., *Italian Feminist Thought: A Reader* (Oxford: Basil Blackwell), pp.148–61
——, 1999. *Lo que quiere una mujer* (Valencia: Ediciones Cátedra)
Bock, Gisela, and Susan James, 1992. Beyond Equality and Difference: Citizenship, Feminist Politics and Female Subjectivity (London: Routledge)
Bonnin, Catalina, 1982. 'La trajectòria poètica de Maria-Mercè Marçal', *L 39*, no. 10–12: 4–6
Bono, Paola and Sandra Kemp, 1991. *Italian Feminist Thought: A Reader* (Oxford: Basil Blackwell)

——, 1993. *The Lonely Mirror: Italian Perspectives on Feminist Theory* (London and New York: Routledge)
Bordo, Susan, 1987. *The Flight to Objectivity: Essays on Cartesianism and Culture* (New York: State University of New York Press)
Bordons, Glòria, 2008. 'Maria-Mercè Marçal i Joan Brossa', in Marçal and Llorca, eds., *II Jornades Marçalianes. Saba vella per a les fulles noves* (Sabadell: Fundació Maria-Mercè Marçal), pp. 111–32
Borràs, Laura, 2008. 'La germana, l'estrangera: continuïtats i ruptures en Maria-Mercè Marçal', *Reduccions*, no. 89–90: 241–61
Braidotti, Rosi, 1994. *Nomadic Subjects: Embodiment and Sexual Difference in Contemporary Feminist Theory* (New York: Columbia UP)
Braidotti, Rosi, ed., 1991. *Patterns of Dissonance: a Study of Women in Contemporary Philosophy*, tr. Elizabeth Guild (Oxford: Polity)
Braidotti, Rosi and Judith Butler, 1994. 'Feminism by Any Other Name' (Interview), *Differences*, 6: 27–61
Broch, Àlex, 2003. 'Maria-Mercè Marçal o el camins de la llibertat' in *El meu amor sense casa* (Barcelona: Proa)
Brogger, Susan, 1978. *Y líbranos del amor* (Barcelona: Caralt)
Bru de Sala, Xavier, 2000. '"El Mall" 25 anys abans', in Pont and Guerrero, eds., *Llengua abolida, 1r. Encontre de creadors* (Lleida: La Paeria), pp. 41–51
Bull, Anna, Hannah Diamond and Rosalind Marsh, 2000. *Feminisms and Women's Movements in Contemporary Europe* (Basingstoke: Macmillan)
Busquets i Grabulosa, Lluís, 1978. 'Maria-Mercè Marçal i Xavier Bru de Sala, dos poetes', *El Correo Catalán*, no. 165: 19–20
——, 1980. 'Maria-Mercè Marçal, bruixa i fada el 1980' in *Plomes Catalanes Contemporànies* (Barcelona: Edicions del Mall), pp. 215–20
Butler, Judith, 1986. 'Sex and Gender in Simone de Beauvoir's Second Sex', *Yale French Studies*, no. 72: 35–49
——, 1990. *Gender Trouble: Feminism and the Subversion of Identity* (London: Routledge)
——, 1993. *Bodies that Matter: On the Discursive Limits of "Sex"* (London: Routledge)
——, 1994. 'Gender as Performance, an interview with Judith Butler', *Radical Philosophy*, no. 67: 32–39
——, 1995. 'Conscience Doth Make Subject of Us All', *Yale French Studies*, no. 88: 6–26
——, 1997. 'Further Reflections on Conversations of Our Time', *Diacritics*, 27.1: 13–15
——, 1998a. 'How Bodies Come to Matter: An Interview with Judith Butler', *Signs* 23.2: 275–86
——, 1998b. 'The Future of Sexual Difference: An Interview with Judith Butler and Drucilla Cornell', *Diacritics*, 28.1: 19–42
——, 1999. 'Preface (1999)', *Gender Trouble* (New York: Routledge)
——, 2001. '"There Is a Person Here!": An Interview with Judith Butler', *International Journal of Sexuality and Gender Studies*, 6.1–2: 7–24
——, 2005. *Giving an Account of Oneself* (Ashland, Ohio: Fordham UP)
Butler, Judith, Ernesto Laclau and Reinaldo Laddaga, 1997. 'The Uses of Equality', *Diacritic*, 27.1: 3–12

Buttarelli, Annarosa, Luisa Muraro and Liliana Rampello, 2004. *Dues mil dones que canvien l'Italia* (Valencia: Denes)
Cabré, Rosa, 2004. 'La passió segons Renée Vivien i el miratge-miracle del mirall', *Lectora*, no. 10: 173-90
Calafat, Francesc, 1997. 'Entre el llenguatge i la realitat: vint anys de poesia catalana', *Caplletra*, no. 22: 27-47
——, 2008. 'Donant la raó al cos', in Marçal and Llorca, eds., *II Jornades Marçalianes. Saba vella per a les fulles noves* (Sabadell: Fundació Maria-Mercè Marçal), pp. 87-100
Calvo, Lluís, 2008. 'Maria-Mercè Marçal o la fusió dels pols: cos, alteritat, desig', *Reduccions*, no. 89-90: 90-119
Camboni, Marina, 1993. 'Language in the crucible of the mind', in Bono and Kemp, eds., *Italian Feminist Thought: A Reader* (Oxford: Basil Blackwell), pp. 83-98
Campabadal, Jordi, 1981. 'Maria-Mercè Marçal, entre lluna, bruixa i mar', *Issauna*, no. 33: 10-12
Cantavella, Rosanna, 1983. 'Maria-Mercè Marçal: 'Cau de llunes' i altres', *L'Espill*, no. 19: 157-59
Carabí, Àngels, and Marta Segarra, 1996. *Amor e identidad* (Barcelona: Promociones y Publicaciones Universitarias)
Castellet Josep Maria i Joaquim Molas, 1963. *Poesia catalana del segle XX* (Barcelona: Ed. 62)
Castillo, David, 1986. 'Un pacte de sang', *El País*, 27 April, p. 6
——, 1989a. 'Una extraordinària potència lírica', *El Temps*, no. 270: 78
——, 1989b. 'M. Mercè Marçal, la vivència singular i l'estil personal', *Avui*, 23 July, p. 17
Cavarero, Adriana, 1991. 'The Need for a Sexed Thought', in Bono and Kemp, eds., *Italian Feminist Thought: A Reader* (Oxford: Basil Blackwell), pp. 181-85
——, 1992. 'Equality and Sexual Difference: Amnesia in Political Thought', in Bock and James, eds., *Beyond Equality and Difference: Citizenship, Feminist Politics and Female Subjectivity* (London: Routledge), pp. 28-42
——, 1993. 'Towards a theory of sexual difference', in Bono and Kemp eds., *Italian Feminist Thought: A Reader* (Oxford: Basil Blackwell), pp. 189-221
——, 1995. *In Spite of Plato: A Feminist Rewriting of Ancient Philosophy*, tr. Serena Anderlini-D'Onofrio and Áine O'Healy (New York: Routledge)
——, 1996. 'Decir el nacimiento', in Diotima, *Il pensiero della differenza sessuale* (Milan: La Tartaruga), pp. 115-46
——, 1997. 'Birth, Love, Politics', *Radical Philosophy*, no. 86: 19-23
——, 2000. *Relating Narratives: Storytelling and Selfhood*, tr. Paul A. Kottman (London: Routledge)
——, 2002a. *Stately Bodies: Literature, Philosophy and the Question of Gender*, tr. Robert de Lucca and Deanna Shemek (Michigan: University of Michigan Press)
——, 2002b. 'Who Engenders Politics?, in Parati and West, eds., *Italian Feminist Theory and Practice: Equality and Sexual Difference* (Madison, Teaneck: Fairleigh Dickinson UP), pp. 88-103
Caws, Mary Ann, 1986. 'The Conception of Engendering, the Erotics of Editing', in Miller, ed., *Poetics of Gender* (New York: Columbia UP), pp. 42-62
Centelles, Ester, 1977. 'Maria-Mercè Marçal: "Cau de llunes"', *Els Marges*, no. 11: 123

Chavarria, Adrià and Ivan Favà, 2006. 'Miscel·lània Maria-Mercè Marçal', *Rels*, no. 8
Cirera, Jorja, 1984. 'Les ones, la lluna, les bruixes, i algún bruixot; la mar, la sal, Heura', *Pamiela*, no.7: 14–20
Cigarini, Lia, and others, 1991. 'Entrustment enters the palace', in Bono and Kemp, eds., *Italian Feminist Thought: A Reader* (Oxford: Basil Blackwell), pp.126–29
——, 1995. *La política del deseo: la diferencia femenina se hace historia* (Barcelona: Icaria)
Cirlot, Juan Eduardo, 1971. *A Dictionary of Symbols* (London: Routledge)
Civil, M., 1995. 'Maria-Mercè Marçal: "Canviar de gènere, t'obre horitzons nous"', *El 9 nou*, 13 Jan
Cixous, Hélène, 1976. 'The Laugh of the Medusa', *Signs*, no. 1.4: 875–93
——, 1986. *The Newly Born Woman* (Manchester: UP)
Clarà, Irsael, 2005. *Mel de sucre i vidre. Maria-Mercè Marçal o l'encís de la feminitat* (Barcelona: Omicron)
Climent Raga, Laia, 2004. 'La literatura catalana femenina a partir dels vuitanta: el mestratge de Maria-Mercè Marçal', *Col.loqui Europeu d'Estudis Catalans* (Montpellier: Centre d'Études et de Recherches Catalanes Université Paul Valéry: Association Française des Catalanistes), no. 2: 95–110
——, 2006. 'Sal oberta a la paraula. El discurs de la corporalitat en la poètica marçaliana', *Rels*, no. 8: 28–38
——, 2007. 'Les textures del llenguatge: el procés evolutiu de la poètica marçaliana', in Marçal ed., 2007. *I Jornades Marçalianes. Llavor de cant, lluita en saó* (Sabadell: Fundació Maria-Mercè Marçal), pp. 89–126
——, 2008a. *Maria-Mercè Marçal, cos i compromís* (Valencia: Institut Interuniversitari de Filologia Valenciana)
——, 2008b. '"La dona de Lot". Anàlisi d'un poema de Marçal', *Reduccions*, no. 89–90: 287–98
——, 2008c. 'Maria-Mercè Marçal: dona i reivindació nacional', *Lluc*, no. 864: 41–44
——, 2010. 'Entre la investigació i l'experiència viva', *El Temps*, no. 1380: 17
Codina, Francesc, 2008. 'Fúria i forma: Una aproximación a la poètica de Maria-Mercè Marçal', *Reduccions*, no. 89–90: 218–29
Cònsul, Isidor, 1986. 'És perquè et sé estrangera que puc dir-te germana', *Avui*, 26 Jan., p. 4
Contijoch, Josefa, 2006. 'La claror (La paraula en Maria-Mercè Marçal)', *Rels*, no. 8: 25–27
De Beauvoir, Simone, 1988. *The Second Sex* (London: Pan Books)
De Lauretis, Teresa, 1989. 'The Essence of the Triangle or, Taking the Risk of Essentialism Seriously: Feminist Theory in Italy, the U.S., and Britain', *Differences*, 2: 1–37
——, 1990. 'The Practice of Sexual Difference and Feminist Thought in Italy: An Introductory Essay', in *Sexual Difference: A Theory of Social-Symbolic Practice* (Bloomington and Indianapolis: Indiana UP), pp. 1–21
——, 1994. *The Practice of Love: Lesbian Sexuality and Perverse Desire* (Bloomington and Indianapolis: Indiana UP)
——, 2000. *Diferencias. Etapas de un camino a través del feminismo* (Madrid: horas y HORAS)

—, 2002. 'Subjectivity, Feminist Politics, and the Intractability of Desire', in Parati and West, eds., *Italian Feminist Theory and Practice: Equality and Sexual Difference* (Madison, Teaneck: Fairleigh Dickinson UP), pp. 117–35
Delor, Rosa, 2002. 'La memòria de l'aigua', *Serra d'Or*, no. 511–512: 105
—, 2008. 'Primera aproximación a la poesía de Maria-Mercè Marçal', *Reduccions*, no. 89-90: 138–89
Demau Group (demystification of authority), 1991. *Manifesto*, tr. in Bono and Kemp 1991: 33–35
De Palol, Miquel, 1989. 'El cercle poètic de Maria-Mercè Marçal', *Avui Cultura*, 6 August, p. 19
De Rougemont, Denis, 1983. *Love in the Western World*, tr. Montgomery Belgion (New York: Schocken Books)
Derrida, Jacques, 1982. 'Différance', in *Margins of Philosophy*, tr. with additional notes Alan Bass (Chicago: The University of Chicago Press)
Descartes, René, 1989. *The Passions of the Soul*, tr. Stephen H. Voss (Indianapolis: Hackett)
Desclot, Miquel, 2001. *El jardí de les malícies: de la poesia eròtica universal* (Manresa: Angle)
Díaz Vicedo, Noelia, 2004. *Maria-Mercè Marçal: An Exploration of the Feminine Poetics in the Work of a Late 20th Century Catalan Poet*, Cuadernos de Trabajo de Investigación, 9 (Alacant: Centre d'Estudis de la Dona)
Diotima, 1987. *Il pensiero della differenza sessuale* (Milan: La Tartaruga)
—, 1989. *Mettere al mondo il mondo: Oggetto e oggetività alla luce della differenza sessuale* (Mila: La Tartaruga)
—, 1992. *Il cielo stellato dentro di noi* (Milan: La Tartaruga)
—, 1995. *Oltre uguaglianza. Le radici femminili dell'autorità* (Naples, Italy: Liguori)
—, 1996a. *Traer al mundo el mundo: Objeto y objetividad a la luz de la diferencia sexual*, tr. María Milagros Rivera Carretas (Madrid: Icaria)
—, 1996b. *La sapienza di partire da sé* (Naples, Italy: Liguori)
Dominijanni, Ida, 1991. 'Radicality and Asceticism', in Bono and Kemp, eds., *Italian Feminist Thought: A Reader* (Oxford: Basil Blackwell), pp.129–38
Echauz, Pau, 1986. 'Maria-Mercè Marçal o la poesía de cada día', *Segre, Cultura*, 11 April, p. 12
Edmunson, Mark, 1995. *Literature Against Philosophy, Plato to Derrida: A Defence of Poetry* (Cambridge: UP)
Eliot, T.S., 1921. 'Tradition and the Individual Talent', in *The Sacred Wood: Essays on Poetry and Criticism* (New York: Alfred A. Knopf), pp. 42–53
Everly, Kathryn A., 2003. *Catalan Women Writers and Artists: Revisionist Views from a Feminist Space* (London: Associated University Presses)
Farrés, Ernest, 1994. 'Maria-Mercè Marçal', *Esment. Revista catalana de poesia*, no. 1: 13–14
Farwell, Marilyn R., 1988. 'Toward a Definition of the Lesbian Literary Imagination', *Signs*, no. 14.1: 100–18
Faulí, Josep, 1980. 'De las "llunes" a la "bruixa"', *La Vanguardia*, 28 Febr., p. 42
—, 1982. 'Poemas de lírica amorosa actual' *La Vanguardia*, 14 Oct., p. 42
Favà, Ivan and Adrià Chavarria, 2006. 'Miscel.lània Maria-Mercè Marçal', *Rels*, no. 8: 6–9

Fernández Ardanaz, Santiago, 1987. 'Evolución del pensamiento hebreo sobre el hombre', *Revista Catalana de Teología*, XII.2: 263–311

Fernàndez, Josep-Anton, 2004. 'Subversió, transició, tradició: política i subjectivitat a la primera poesia de Maria-Mercè Marçal', *Lectora*, no. 10: 201–16

Foix, J.V., 1987. *Les irreals omegues* (Barcelona: Edicions dels Quaderns Crema)

——, 1991. *Sol i de dol* (Barcelona: El Observador)

Frazer, Sir James George, 1911. *The Golden Bough: A Study on Magic and Religion* (London: Macmillan)

Freud, Sigmund, 1991. 'The question of Lay Analysis', in *The Essential of Psycho-Analysis: By Sigmund Freud*, selected and introduced by Anna Freud (London: Penguin), pp. 5–74

Frye, Marilyn, 1996. 'The Possibility of Feminist Theory', in Garry and Pearsall, eds., *Women, Knowledge and Reality: Explorations in Feminist Philosophy* (New York and London: Routledge), pp. 34–47

Fuster, Joan, 1972. *Literatura catalana contemporània* (Barcelona: Curial)

Galarza José, 1995. 'Parlant amb Maria-Mercè Marçal', *Lambda*, no. 23: 20–21

Garí, Blanca, 2008. 'Un forat a l'infinit', in Marçal and Llorca, eds., *II Jornades Marçalianes. Saba vella per a les fulles noves* (Sabadell: Fundació Maria-Mercè Marçal), pp.157–70

Garry, Ann and Marilyn Pearsall, 1996. *Women, Knowledge and Reality: Explorations in Feminist Philosophy* (New York and London: Routledge)

Giardini, Federica, 1999. 'Public Affects. Clues towards a Political Practice of Singularity', *The European Journal of Women's Studies*, no. 6: 149–59

Gilbert, Sandra and Susan Gubar, 1996. *The Norton Anthology of Literature by Women* (New York; London: Norton)

Gimferrer, Pere, 2000a. 'Pròleg', in *Raó del cos* (Barcelona: Ed. 62-Empúries), pp. 7–9

——, 2000b. 'Raó del cos', *Avui Cultura*, 16 March, p. 7

Godayol, Pilar, 2008. 'Entre Atenea i la Medusa: les mares literàries de Maria-Mercè Marçal', *Reduccions*, no. 89–90: 190–206

Gómez Sánchez, Lucía and Ana Belén Martín Sevillano, 2006. 'Experience, Subjectivity and Politics in the Italian Feminist Movement', *European Journal of Women's Studies*, 13.4: 343–55

Gomila, Andreu, 2002. 'Mossegar la vida', *Avui Cultura*, 2 May, p. 10

——, 2004. 'Marçal, dins la cambra pròpia', *Avui Cultura*, 27 May, p. 5

Goujon, Jean-Paul, 1998. 'De Renée Vivien a Maria-Mercè Marçal', in Abelló, Aguado and Contijoch 1998: 105–09

Granell, Marc, 1980. *Materials per a una mort meditada* (Gandia: Ajuntament de Gandia)

Graves, Robert, 1960. *The Greek Myths*, vol.1 and vol.2 (Harmondsworth: Penguin)

Griffin, Gabriele, 1993. *Heavenly Love: Lesbian Images in Twentieth-Century Women's Writing* (Manchester: UP)

Griffin, Gabriele and Rosi Braidotti, eds., 2002. *Thinking Differently: A Reader in European Women Studies* (London: Zed)

Grosz, Elizabeth, 1994. *Volatile Bodies: Toward a Corporeal Feminism* (Bloomington: Indiana UP)

——, 1995. *Space, Time and Perversion: Essays on the Politics of Bodies* (London: Routledge)

Gubar, Susan, 1981. "The Blank Page" and the Issues of Female Creativity', *Critical Inquiry*, no. 8.2: 243–63
Guillamon, Julià, 1998. 'Muere a los 45 años Maria-Mercè Marçal, la más destacada autora feminista catalana', *La Vanguardia*, 6 July, p. 31
——, 2004. 'Maria-Mercè Marçal, crítica y brillante', *La Vanguardia*, 16 June, p. 6
Halpein, David M., John J. Winkler and Froma I. Zeitlin, ed., 1990. *Before Sexuality: The Construction of Erotic Experience in the Ancient Greek* (Princeton: UP)
Heinämaa, Sarah, 2003. *Toward a Phenomenology of Sexual Difference, Husserl, Merleu-Ponty and Beauvoir* (Oxford: Rowman and Littlefield)
Hesiod, 2006. *Theogony; and Works and Days*, tr. and ed. Catherine Schlegel and Henry Weinfield (Ann Arbor: University of Michigan Press)
Hillman, James, 1995. 'Salt: A Chapter in Alchemical Psychology', in Marlan 1995: 145–79
Homans, Margaret, 1980. *Women Writers and Poetic Identity: Dorothy Wordsworth, Emily Brontë, and Emily Dickinson* (Princeton: UP)
Homer, 2004. *The Iliad*, ed. Michael M. Silk (Cambridge: UP)
Hurwitt, Jeffrey, M., 1999. *The Athenian Acropolis: History, Mythology, and Archeology from the Neolithic Era to the Present* (Cambridge: UP)
Ibarz, Mercè, 2000. 'Maria-Mercè Marçal al castell de la comtessa Valença', in Pont and Guerrero, eds., *Llengua abolida, 1r. Encontre de creadors* (Lleida: La Paeria), pp. 77–82
——, ed., 2004. *Maria-Mercè Marçal. Sota el signe del drac: Proses 1985–1997* (Barcelona: Proa)
Irigaray, Luce, 1985a. *Speculum of the Other Woman*, tr. Gillian C. Gill (Ithaca, NY: Cornell UP)
——, 1985b. *This Sex which is not One*, tr. Catherine Porter and Carolyn Burke (Ithaca, NY: Cornell UP)
——, 1989. *Il tempo della differenza. Diritti e doveri civili per i sessi. Per una rivoluzione pacifica* (Rome: Editori Riuniti)
——, 1992. *Elemental Passions*, tr. Joanne Collie and Judith Still (New York: Routledge)
——, 1993a. *An Ethics of Sexual Difference*, tr. Carolyn Burke and Gillian C. Gill (London: Athlone Press)
——, 1993b. *Sexes and Genealogies*, tr. Gillian C. Gill (Ithaca, NY: Cornell UP)
——, 1994. *Thinking the Difference: For a Peaceful Revolution*, tr. Karin Montin (London: Athlone Press)
——, 1995. 'The Question of the Other', *Yale French Studies*, no. 87: 7–19
——, 2004. *The Way of Love* (London: Continuum)
Jaggar, Alison M., 1996. 'Love and Knowledge: Emotion in Feminist Epistemology', in Garry and Pearsall, eds., *Women, Knowledge and Reality: Explorations in Feminist Philosophy* (New York and London: Routledge), pp. 166–90
James, Susan, 1997. *Passion and Action: the Emotions in Seventeenth-Century Philosophy* (Oxford: Clarendon Press)
Jay, Karla, 1995. *Lesbian Erotics* (New York: UP)
Jones, Ernest, 1951. 'The Symbolic Significance of Salt in Folklore and Superstition', in Marlan, ed., 1995. *Salt and the Alchemical Soul* (Woodstock, CT: Spring Publications), pp. 47–144

Jong, Erica, 1979. 'Creativity vs. Generativity: The Unexamined Lie', *The New Republic*, no. 180: 27
Julià, Lluïsa and Maria-Mercè Marçal, 1998. 'En dansa obliqua de miralls: Pauline M. Tarn (Renée Vivien), Víctor Català (Caterina Albert), Maria Antònia Salvà', in *Cartografies del desig* (Barcelona: Proa), pp. 21–56
Julià, Lluïsa, 1998. 'Contra les llengües abolides', *Serra d'Or*, no. 467: 23–26
——, 2000. 'Utopia i exili en la poesia de Maria-Mercè Marçal', in *El Gai Saber*, ed. Josep-Anton Fernàndez (Barcelona: Llibres de l'Índex), pp. 353–72
——, 2004. 'Cap a l'ordre simbòlic femení: La passió segons Renée Vivien', *Lectora*, no. 10: 161–71
——, ed., 2007a. 'Traginera, de llunes i cançons. 30 anys de la irrupció poètica de Maria-Mercè Marçal', *Urc*, no. 22
——, 2007b. 'Mujer y escritura: una construcción de sentido en la literatura catalana actual', *Ínsula*, no. 62.729: 16–18
——, 2008a. 'Mots preliminars', in Sant-Celoni i Verger, ed., *Eròtiques i despentinades* (Barcelona: Arola), pp. 9–10
——, 2008b. 'De Brossa als trobadors i a Ausiàs March. Maria-Mercè Marçal, el diàleg amb la pròpia tradició', in Marçal and Llorca, eds., *II Jornades Marçalianes. Saba vella per a les fulles noves* (Sabadell: Fundació Maria-Mercè Marçal), pp. 37–54
——, 2008c. 'Set autògrafs. Imatges, poemes, versions de Maria-Mercè Marçal', *Reduccions*, no. 89–90: 11–21
Jung, C. G., 1963. 'Sal, Salt as the Arcane Substance' in *Mysterium Coniunctionis*, tr. R. F. C. Hull (London: Routledge and Kegan Paul), pp. 183–91
Kauffman, Linda. S., 1986. *Discourses of Desire: Gender, Genre, and Epistolary Fictions* (Ithaca and London: Cornell UP)
Keown, Dominic, 1996. *Sobre la poesia catalana contemporània* (Valencia: 3i4)
Kingston, Stephen, 2002. *Dilemmas of British and Italian Feminist Movements and Critical Social Theory: Reflexive Critiques* (Birmingham: University of Birmingham)
Kristeva, Julia, 1980. *Desire in Language: A Semiotic Approach to Literature and Art*, tr. Leon S. Roudiez (New York: Columbia UP)
——, 1984. *Revolution in Poetic Language*, tr. Leon S. Roudiez (New York: Columbia UP)
——, 1989. *Tales of Love*, tr. Leon. S. Roudiez (New York: Columbia UP)
——, 1991. *Strangers to Ourselves*, tr. Leon S. Roudiez (New York: Columbia UP)
——, 1996. 'Women's Time', in Garry and Pearsall, eds., *Women, Knowledge and Reality: Explorations in Feminist Philosophy* (New York and London: Routledge), pp. 61–83
Lacan Jacques, 1982a. 'The Meaning of the Phallus', in Rose and Mitchell 1982: 74–85
——, 1982b. 'God and the Jouissance of The Woman', in Rose and Mitchell 1982: 137–48
——, 1998. 'A Love Letter (*une lettre d'âmour*)', in *Book XX Encore 1972–3: On Feminine Sexuality, the Limits of Love and Knowledge*, tr. Bruce Fink (London: Norton), pp. 78–89

Laurenzi, Elena, 1996. '"Nacer por sí misma". Naixement i renaixement en la filosofia de María Zambrano', *DUODA*, no. 11: 97–112
Lazzaro-Weis, Carol. 2002. 'The Concept of Difference in Italian Feminist Thought: Mothers, Daughters, Heretics', in Parati and West, eds., *Italian Feminist Theory and Practice: Equality and Sexual Difference* (Madison, Teaneck: Fairleigh Dickinson UP), pp. 31–49
Lesbofemminismo, 1991. 'Suggestions from Irigaray', in Bono and Kemp, eds., *Italian Feminist Thought: A Reader* (Oxford: Basil Blackwell), pp.177–80
Lévinas, Emmanuele, 1999. *Alterity and Transcendence*, tr. Michael B. Smith (New York: Columbia UP)
Levi-Strauss, Claude, 1955. 'The Structural Study of Myth', *Journal of American Folklore*, no. 68.270: 428–44
Libreria delle donne di Milano, 1987. *Non credere di avere dei diritti. La generazione della libertà femminile nell' idea e nelle vicende di un gruppo di donne* (Torino: Rosenberg and Sellier)
——, 1990. *Sexual Difference: A Theory of Social-Symbolic Practice*, tr. and ed. Teresa de Lauretis (Bloomington and Indianapolis: Indiana UP)
——, 1991. 'More Women than Men', in Bono and Kemp, eds, *Italian Feminist Thought: A Reader* (Oxford: Basil Blackwell), pp. 110–22
——, 2006. *La cultura patas arriba, 'Selección de la Revista Sottosopra con el final del patriarcado 1973-1996'* (Madrid: Horas y HORAS)
Lonzi, Carla, 1981. *Escupamos sobre Hegel. La mujer clitórica y la mujer vaginal*, tr. Francesc Parcerisas (Barcelona: Anagrama)
——, 1991. *Sputiamo su Hegel. La donna clitoridea e la donna vaginale, e altri scritti*, in Bono and Kemp, eds., *Italian Feminist Thought: A Reader* (Oxford: Basil Blackwell), pp. 40–58
Lorde, Audre, 1988. 'Uses of the Erotic: The Erotic as Power', in *The Audre Lorde Compendium: Essays, Speeches and Journals* (London: HarperCollins), pp. 106–12
Lunati, Montserrat, 2005. "El salt a l'interior de la consciència mòrbida" o qui és l'Altre/l'Altra a la narrativa d'Imma Monsó', in *Los hábitos del deseo*, ed. Carme Riera, Meri Torras, Isabel Clúa and Pau Pitarch (Valencia: excultura), no. 2: 423–34
Lundgren-Gothlin, Eva, 1996. *Sex and Existence: Simone de Beauvoir's The Second Sex* (London: Athlone)
Llorca Antolín, Fina, 2002. 'La solitud i el mirall de l'altre/a segons Maria-Mercè Marçal', in *II Jornades d'estudi. Vida i obra de Caterina Albert i Paradís (Víctor Català), 1869-1966* (Barcelona: Abadia de Montserrat), pp. 283–97
——, 2004. 'Terra on arrelar: la construcció de la genealogia literària femenina segons Maria-Mercè Marçal', *Lectora*, no. 10: 217–31
——, 2008. 'Set paraules en la poesia de Maria-Mercè Marçal', in Marçal, ed., *I Jornades Marçalianes. Llavor de cant, lluita en saó* (Sabadell: Fundació Maria-Mercè Marçal), pp.17–36
Macià, Albert, 1987. 'Maria-Mercè Marçal: Poesia amb vistes de Mai i Enlloc', *Regió 7*, 16 Aug., pp. 4–5
MacKeon, Richard P., 1954. *Thought, Action and Passion* (Chicago: UP)
Magli, Patrizia, 1993. 'The Discourse of Passion', in Kemp and Bono, eds., *The Lonely Mirror: Italian Perspectives on Feminist Theory* (London and New York: Routledge), pp. 31–37

Magué i Pegueroles, Jordi, 2007. *Mites clàssics en la literatura catalana moderna i contemporània* (Barcelona: Publicacions i Edicions de la Universitat de Barcelona)
McNerney, Kathleen, 2004. 'Joys and Sorrows of Literary Translation: A Tale of Two Poets', *Lectora*, no. 10: 233–38
Marçal, Heura, ed., 2007. *I Jornades Marçalianes. Llavor de cant, lluita en saó* (Sabadell: Fundació Maria-Mercè Marçal)
Marçal, Heura and Fina Llorca, ed., 2008. *II Jornades Marçalianes. Saba vella per a les fulles noves* (Sabadell: Fundació Maria-Mercè Marçal)
Marçal i Serra, Maria-Mercè, 1977. *Cau de llunes*, in Marçal 1989b, *Llengua abolida (1973–1988)* (Valencia: Poesia 3i4), pp. 17–78
——, 1979. *Bruixa de dol*, in Marçal 1989b, *Llengua abolida (1973–1988)*, pp. 79–170
——, 1982a. *Sal oberta*, in Marçal 1989b, *Llengua abolida (1973–1988)*, pp. 171–274
——, 1982b. 'La tenebra i el far', *Reduccions*, no. 15: 9–14
——, 1982c. *Terra de Mai*, in Marçal 1989b, *Llengua abolida (1973–1988)*, pp. 291–325
——, 1983. 'J.V.Foix, en els seus noranta anys: Un poeta universal, encara massa inconegut', *Full de la Cultura*, 24 Jan., no. 33: 1–2
——, 1985a. *La germana, l'estrangera*, in Marçal 1989b, *Llengua abolida (1973–1988)*, pp. 291–416
——, 1985b. 'Pròleg', in *La germana, l'estrangera* (Barcelona: Edicions del Mall), pp. 7–9
——, 1986. 'Per deixar d'ésser inexistents', in *Les dones i la literatura catalana* (Barcelona: IEC, sèrie seminaris), pp. 33–37
——, 1989a. 'Sota el signe del drac', in Marçal 1989b, *Llengua abolida (1973–1988)*, pp. 7–11
——, 1989b. *Llengua abolida (1973–1988)* (Valencia: Poesia 3i4)
——, 1989c. 'Viratges, reminiscències', in Ibarz, ed., *Maria-Mercè Marçal. Sota el signe del drac: Proses 1985–1997* (Barcelona: Proa, 2004), pp. 25–34
——, 1989d. *Desglaç*, in Marçal 1989b *Llengua abolida (1973–1988)*, pp. 417–518
——, 1991. 'Anna Dodas', in Ibarz, ed., *Maria-Mercè Marçal. Sota el signe del drac: Proses 1985–1997* (Barcelona: Proa, 2004), pp. 103–19
——, 1993. 'Meditacions sobre la fúria', in Ibarz, ed., *Maria-Mercè Marçal. Sota el signe del drac: Proses 1985–1997* (Barcelona: Proa, 2004), pp. 133–54
——, 1994a. 'La passió amorosa', in Ibarz, ed., *Maria-Mercè Marçal. Sota el signe del drac: Proses 1985–1997* (Barcelona: Proa, 2004), pp. 171–84
——, 1994b. 'Un lloc per a l'entusiasme. Sobre Salvat-Papasseit', in Ibarz, ed., *Maria-Mercè Marçal. Sota el signe del drac: Proses 1985–1997* (Barcelona: Proa, 2004), pp. 91–93
——, 1994c. *La passió segons Renée Vivien* (Barcelona: Columna)
——, 1994d. 'Cop d'ull a l'actual literatura catalana de dona', *Paper de dona* no. 19: 13–21
——, 1995a. 'Llengua abolida: Poesia, gènere, identitat', in Ibarz, ed., *Maria-Mercè Marçal. Sota el signe del drac: Proses 1985–1997* (Barcelona: Proa, 2004), pp. 189–200
——, 1995b. 'Qui sóc i per què escric', in Ibarz, ed., *Maria-Mercè Marçal. Sota el signe del drac: Proses 1985–1997* (Barcelona: Proa, 2004), pp. 21–24
——, 1995c. 'Joc de màscares', in *Dones soles* (Barcelona: Editorial Planeta), pp. 73–92

——, 1995d. 'El retorn', Àrnica, no. 27: 167–75
——, 1995–96. 'Entre dones', in Ibarz, ed., Maria-Mercè Marçal. Sota el signe del drac: Proses 1985–1997 (Barcelona: Proa, 2004), pp. 201–03
——, 1996a. 'Més enllà i més ençà del mirall de la Medusa', in Ibarz, ed., Maria-Mercè Marçal. Sota el signe del drac: Proses 1985–1997 (Barcelona: Proa, 2004), pp. 155–66
——, 1996b. 'Elogi del drac', in Ibarz, ed., Maria-Mercè Marçal. Sota el signe del drac: Proses 1985–1997 (Barcelona: Proa, 2004), pp. 35–39
——, 1997. 'Fragments del discurs sobre l'autoritat femenina', in Ibarz, ed., Maria-Mercè Marçal. Sota el signe del drac: Proses 1985–1997 (Barcelona: Proa, 2004), pp.167–69
——, ed., 1998a. Cartografies del desig. Quinze escriptores i el seu món (Barcelona: Proa)
——, 1998b. 'Pròleg', in Marçal ed., Cartografies del desig. Quinze escriptores i el seu món (Barcelona: Proa), pp. 5–10
——, 1998c. 'En dansa obliqua de miralls: Pauline M. Tarn (Renée Vivien) — Caterina Albert (Víctor Català) — Maria Antònia Salvà', in Marçal, ed., Cartografies del desig. Quinze escriptores i el seu món (Barcelona: Proa), pp. 21–52
——, 1998d. 'Com en la nit, les flames, Anna Akhmàtova — Marina Tsvetàieva', in Marçal, ed., Cartografies del desig. Quinze escriptores i el seu món (Barcelona: Proa), pp.157–92
——, 1999a. 'Pròleg' to Memòria de l'aigua. Onze escriptores i el seu món, ed. Lluïsa Julià (Barcelona: Proa), pp. 9–12
——, 1999b. Paisatge emergent: trenta poetes catalanes del segle XX (Barcelona: Proa)
——, 2000. Raó del cos, ed. Lluïsa Julià (Barcelona: Ed. 62 and Empúries)
——, 2001. Contraban de llum, ed. Lluïsa Julià (Barcelona: Proa)
Marçal i Serra, Maria-Mercè and Lluïsa Julià, 2006. 'Diferència i/o normalització: la poesia catalana dels darrers trenta anys', Rels, no. 8: 39–56
Maria i Miriam, 1995. 'Entrevista a Maria-Mercè Marçal', Barcelona Rosa, no. 36: 10–11
Marlan, Stanton, ed., 1995. Salt and the Alchemical Soul (Woodstock, CT: Spring Publications)
Martínez Muñoz, Mado, 2006. 'Maria Mercè Marçal: Mi sexo y yo en el espejo. Poemas seleccionados de La germana, l'estrangera', Espéculo, no. 32: http://www.ucm.es/info/especulo/numero32/mercemar.html> [accessed 20 March 2009]
Marx, Karl, 1975. Early Writings (London: Penguin)
Massip, Francesc J., 1982. 'Maria-Mercè Marçal, fetillera del vers', Canigó 778: 8–9
Meese, Elizabeth, 1992. (Sem)Erotics, Theorising Lesbian: Writing (New York: UP)
Melandri, Lea. 2002. 'From Gender Difference to the Individuality of Male and Female', in Parati and West, eds., Italian Feminist Theory and Practice: Equality and Sexual Difference (Madison, Teaneck: Fairleigh Dickinson UP), pp. 104–16
Miceli Jeffries, Giovanna, 1994. Feminine Feminists: Cultural Practices in Italy (Minneapolis and London: University of Minnesota Press)
Miller, Nancy. K., ed., 1986. The Poetics of Gender (New York: Columbia UP)
Moi, Toril, 1986. The Kristeva Reader (Oxford: Blackwell)

——, 1999. 'Is Anatomy Destiny?: Freud and Biological Determinism', in *What is a Woman?: And Other Essays* (Oxford: UP), pp. 369-96
Montagut, Maria Cinta, 1979. 'Les paraules sense història', *Avui Diumenge*, 9 Dec., p. 21
Montefiore, Jan, 1987. *Feminism and Poetry: Language, Experience, Identity and Women's Writing* (London and New York: Pandora)
Montero, Anna, 1985. 'Experiència i paraula', *Daina*, no. 1: 115-16
——, 1994. 'Maria-Mercè Marçal. La poesia és el gènere més independent de les pressions reals', *Caràcters*, 15 June, p. 3
——, 2004. 'Anna Montero entrevista Maria-Mercè Marçal', *Lectora*, no. 10: 259-84
——, 2008a. 'La triple lluna i el mirall. "Cau de llunes" i "Bruixa de dol"', *Reduccions*, no. 89-90: 230-40
——, 2008b. 'Cos i paraula. Cartografies de la passió', in Marçal and Llorca, eds., *II Jornades Marçalianes. Saba vella per a les fulles noves* (Sabadell: Fundació Maria-Mercè Marçal), pp.101-10
Moreno, Maite and Joan Vilalta, 1980. *Maria-Mercè Marçal. Programa 'Solcant l'aire'* (Radio San Boi, 22 Nov.), Radio interview, in *Fundació Maria-Mercè Marçal*: <http://www.fmmm.cat/autora.html> [accessed 5 July 2008]
Mota, Guillermina, 1997. *Maria-Mercè Marçal. Programa 'Al cap dels anys'* (Catalunya Radio, 26 Oct.), Radio interview, in *Fundació Maria-Mercè Marçal*: <http://www.fmmm.cat/autora.html> [accessed 5 July 2008]
Moulton, Janice, 1996. 'A Paradigm of Philosphy: the Adversary Method', in Garry and Pearsall, eds., *Women, Knowledge and Reality: Explorations in Feminist Philosophy* (New York and London: Routledge), pp.11-25
Muntaner, Maria, 2006. 'L'escriptura que escriu', *Rels*, no. 8: 65-67
Muñoz, Jordi. 1997. 'Maria-Mercè Marçal', *Illacrua*, no. 42: 8-11
——, 1998. '"La poesia et porta a l'ull de l'huracà". Entrevista a Maria-Mercè Marçal', in *Homenatge a Maria-Mercè Marçal* (Barcelona: Empúries), pp. 169-76
Muraro, Luisa, 1991a. 'Hacer política, escribir historia', *DUODA*, no. 2: 87-97
——, 1991b. *L'ordine simbolico della madre* (Roma: Editori Reuniti)
——, 1992. 'Sobre la autoridad femenina', in Birulés, ed., *Filosofía y género. Identidades femeninas* (Pamplona: Pamiela), pp. 51-63
——, 1994a. *El orden simbólico de la madre*, tr. Beatriz Albertini (Madrid: Horas y HORAS)
——, 1994b. 'Female Genealogies', in Burke and Schor, eds., *Engaging with Irigaray: Feminist Philosophy and Modern European Thought*, (New York: Columbia UP), pp. 317-34
——, 1994c. 'Autoridad sin monumentos', *DUODA*, no.7: 86-100
——, 1996a. 'Nuestra capacidad común de infinito', in Diotima, ed., *Traer al mundo el mundo: Objeto y objetividad a la luz de la diferencia sexual*, tr. María Milagros Rivera Carretas (Madrid: Icaria), pp. 79-94
——, 1996b. 'The Narrow Door', in Benedetti, Hairston and Ross, eds., *Gendered Contexts: New Perspectives in Italian Cultural Studies* (New York: Peter Lang), pp. 7-17
——, 1998. 'La alegoría de la lengua materna', *DUODA*, no. 14: 17-36
——, 1998b. 'Una lezione di poesia', in Abelló, Aguado and Contijoch, eds., *Homenatge a Maria-Mercè Marçal* (Barcelona: Empúries), pp. 133-34

——, 2000. 'Love as a Political Practice: the Example of the Love for the Mother', in Bull, Diamond and Marsh, eds., *Feminisms and Women's Movements in Contemporary Europe* (Basingstoke: Macmillan), pp. 79-85
——, 2001a. 'Más mujeres que feministas', *DUODA*, no. 21: 27-34
——, 2001b. 'La mestra de Sòcrates', *Transversal*, no. 15: 24-29
——, 2002. 'The Passion of Feminine Difference beyond Equality', in Parati and West, eds., *Italian Feminist Theory and Practice: Equality and Sexual Difference* (Madison, Teaneck: Fairleigh Dickinson UP), pp. 77-87
——, 2007. 'El pensamiento de la experiencia', *DUODA*, no. 33: 41-46
Nadal, Marta, 1989. 'Converses literàries: Maria-Mercè Marçal, els confins de la identitat', *Serra d'Or*, no. 352: 24-28
——, 1995. 'Maria-Mercè Marçal. Escriptora del Mes. La paraula, principi ordenador', *Serra d'Or*, no. 421: 10-11
Nussbaum, Martha. C., 1990. *Love's Knowledge: Essays on Philosophy and Literature* (Oxford: UP)
Ostriker, Alicia, 1982. 'The Thieves of Language: Women Poets and Revisionist Mythmaking', *Signs*, no. 8.1: 68-90
Otero, Vidal, Mercè, 2008. 'La tradició popular i feminista en l'obra de Maria-Mercè Marçal', in Marçal and Llorca, eds., *II Jornades Marçalianes. Saba vella per a les fulles noves* (Sabadell: Fundació Maria-Mercè Marçal), pp. 71-86
Palau i Fabre, Josep, 1952. *Poemes del alquimista* (Barcelona: Triadú-Pereira)
——, 1976. *Quaderns de l'alquimista* (Barcelona: Pòrtic)
——, 1983. *Nous quaderns de l'alquimista* (Barcelona: Edicions del Mall)
——, 1991. *Quaderns inèdits de l'alquimista* (Barcelona: Ed. 62)
Pàmias, Jordi, 1986. 'L'última obra poètica de Maria-Mercè Marçal', *El Segre*, 27 April, p. 14
Pané i Sants, Francesc, 1977. 'Maria-Mercè Marsal: un Carles Riba femení i transcendent' *La Mañana*, 12 Febr., p. 11
Panyella, Vinyet, 1998. '. . . en el mirall fidel del teu poema', *Serra d'Or*, no. 467: 27-30
Papetti, Violi, 1993. 'The Erotic Woman Writer: a Special case of Hypokrites', in Bono and Kemp, eds., *The Lonely Mirror: Italian Perspectives on Feminist Theory* (London and New York: Routledge), pp. 55-65
Parati, Gabriela and Rebecca West, 2002. *Italian Feminist Theory and Practice: Equality and Sexual Difference* (Madison, Teaneck: Fairleigh Dickinson UP)
Parer, Josep, 1982. 'Maria-Mercè Marçal: "La bruixa, símbol de la dona solidària"', *Grama*, no. 263: 23
Pascual, Teresa, 2006. 'Maria-Mercè Marçal: genealogia de la diversitat', *Rels*, no. 8: 15-18
——, 2008. 'Bachmann-Marçal: una forma de mort', in Marçal and Llorca, eds., *II Jornades Marçalianes. Saba vella per a les fulles noves* (Sabadell: Fundació Maria-Mercè Marçal), pp.187-04
Paz, Octavio, 1993. *La llama doble: amor y erotismo* (Barcelona: Seix Barral)
Pérez Boluda, Adrián, 2007. '"Terra de Mai": ejercicio de hermenéutica erótica en un poemario de Maria-Mercè Marçal', in Adrienne L. Martín and José Ignacio Díez, eds., *Venus venerada II. Literatura erótica y modernidad en España*, (Madrid: Universidad Complutense), pp. 245-64

Pérez i Vallverdú, Eulàlia, 1990. 'Maria-Mercè Marçal, *Llengua abolida*', *Els Marges*, no. 42: 127
Pérez Montaner, Jaume, 1985. *Poesia eròtica de Vicent Andrés Estellés* (Barcelona: Laia)
Piussi, Anna, 2000. 'Partir de sí, necesidad y deseo', *DUODA*, no. 19: 107–26
Pladevall, Antoni, 2008. 'L'empremta dels clàssics grecollatins en la poesia de Maria-Mercè Marçal', in Marçal and Llorca, eds., *II Jornades Marçalianes. Saba vella per a les fulles noves* (Sabadell: Fundació Maria-Mercè Marçal), pp. 21–36
Plato, 2008. *Republic*, tr. Robin Waterfield (Oxford: UP)
Pons, Arnau, 2006. 'Raó de l'obra (o "La lladre és l'escriptura")', *Rels*, no. 8: 10–14
——, 2007. 'Matriu desnonada- homeniqueu nonat', in Marçal, ed., *I Jornades Marçalianes. Llavor de cant, lluita en saó* (Sabadell: Fundació Maria-Mercè Marçal), pp. 37–78
Pont, Jaume, 1977. 'Las lunas de Maria-Mercè Marçal', *Destino*, 10 Aug., p. 37
——, 1991. 'Maria-Mercè Marçal: l'hora del mirall', *Urc*, no. 4–5: 91–93
Pont, Jaume and Joaquim Marco, 1980. 'La nova poesia catalana: una aposta de futur', *Avui*, 13 July, p. 24
Pont, Jaume and Manel Guerrero, 2000. *Llengua abolida, 1r. Encontre de creadors* (Lleida: La Paeria)
Probyn, Elspeth, 1995. 'Lesbians in Space: Gender, Sex and the Structure of Missing', *Gender, Place and Culture*, no. 2.1: 77–84
Rafart, Susanna, 2008a. 'Les poetes venim a morir: aproximació a la poesia de Maria-Mercè Marçal', *Reduccions*, no. 89–90: 120–37
——, 2008b. 'Visió de Maria-Mercè Marçal', *El Temps*, no. 1238: 57
Rahola, Pilar, 1988. 'L'erotisme, un plat de mal pair', *Serra d'Or*, no. 348: 41
——, 1998. 'A Maria Mercè Marçal, dona, catalana, compromesa', *Avui*, 14 May, p. 19
Ranger, Terence O., 1992. *The Invention of Tradition* (Cambridge: UP)
Re, Lucia, 1996. 'Feminist Thought in Italy: Sexual Difference and the Question of Authority', in *Italian Criticism: Literature and Culture* (Ann Arbor: University of Michigan), pp. 61–86
——, 2002. 'Diotima's Dilemmas: Authorship, Authority and Authoritarianism', in Parati and West, eds., *Italian Feminist Theory and Practice: Equality and Sexual Difference* (Madison, Teaneck: Fairleigh Dickinson UP), pp. 50–76
Rendé i Masdéu, Joan, 1981. 'Maria-Mercè Marçal, una sensibilitat alada', *Avui*, 17 May, p. 19
Rich, Adrienne, 1976. *Of Woman Born: Motherhood as Experience and Institution* (New York: Norton)
——, 1979a. 'It is the Lesbian in Us. . .', in *On Lies, Secrets and Silence: Selected Prose 1966–1978* (New York: Norton), pp. 199–202
——, 1979b. 'When We Dead Awaken: Writing as Re-vision', in *On Lies, Secrets and Silence: Selected Prose 1966–1978* (New York: Norton), pp. 33–50
——, 1980. 'Compulsory Heterosexuality and Lesbian Existence', *Signs*, no. 5.4: 631–60
Riera, Carme, 2004. 'Maria-Mercè Marçal, autora de contes', *Lectora*, no. 10: 251–58
——, 2008. 'Maria-Mercè Marçal, més enllà de la tradició', in Marçal and Llorca, eds., *II Jornades Marçalianes. Saba vella per a les fulles noves* (Sabadell: Fundació Maria-Mercè Marçal), pp. 205–16

Rius Gatell, Rosa, 2004. 'De llibertat, autoritat i in/dependències (a la vida i l'obra de Maria-Mercè Marçal), *Lectora*, no. 10: 239-49
Rivera Garretas, María Milagros, 1994. *Nombrar el mundo en femenino* (Barcelona: Icaria)
——, 2003. 'Historia de una relación sin fin: la influencia en España del pensamiento italiano de la diferencia sexual (1987-2002)', *DUODA*, no. 24: 19-37
Roig, Montserrat, 1980. *¿Tiempo de mujer?* (Barcelona: Plaza y Janés)
Rose, Jacqueline and Juliet Mitchell, ed., 1982. *Feminine Sexuality: Jacques Lacan and l'école freudienne* (London: MacMilan)
Rosen, Stanley, 1988. *The Quarrel between Philosophy and Poetry: Studies in Ancient Thought* (New York: Routledge)
Rosich, Albert, 1985. *Poesia eròtica i pornogràfica catalana del segle XVIII* (Barcelona: Quaderns Crema)
Ross, William David, 1924. *The Works of Aristotle Vol. XI* (Oxford: Clarendon)
Sabadell, Joana, 1998. 'Allà on literatura i vida fan trena: conversa amb Maria-Mercè Marçal sobre poesia i feminisme', *Serra d'Or*, no. 467: 12-21
——, 2000. 'Escribirse en verso: las poetas catalanas del s. XX', in Myriam Diaz-Diocaretz and Iris Zavala, eds., *Breve historia feminista de la literatura española (en lengua catalana, galega y vasca,* (Barcelona: Anthropos), no. 4: 108-20
——, 2001. 'Maria-Mercè Marçal: The Passion and Poetry of Feminism', in Lisa Wollendorf, ed., *Recovering Spain's Feminist Tradition*, (New York: The Modern Language Association of America), pp. 357-73
——, 2004. 'Domesticacions, domesticitats i altres qüestions de gènere', *Lectora*, no. 10: 191-99
Sala-Valldaura, Josep-Maria, 1977. *Antologia de la poesia eròtica catalana* (Barcelona: Proa)
——, 1980. 'La poesia de Maria-Mercè Marçal', *Serra d'Or*, no. 249: 44-45
——, 1989. 'Poesia catalana i erotisme', *L'Avenç*, no. 123: 14-17
——, ed., 2008a. 'La poesia de Maria-Mercè Marçal', *Reduccions*, no. 89-90
——, 2008b. 'Maria-Mercè Marçal: un espai entre', *Reduccions*, no. 89-90: 87-89
Salvador, Vicent, 2000. 'La metàfora en la poesia de Maria-Mercè Marçal', in Pont and Guerrero, eds., *Llengua abolida, 1r. Encontre de creadors* (Lleida: La Paeria), pp. 71-76
——, 2003. 'Cos i mirada en l'escriptura de la dona: la literatura segons Maria-Mercè Marçal', in *Professor Joaquim Molas: memòria, escriptura, història* (Barcelona: Universitat de Barcelona), no. 2: 931-46
San Martín, Ángel, 1994. *Fi de segle. Incerteses davant un nou mil·leni* (Gandia: Ajuntament de Gandia)
Sant-Celoni i Verger, Encarna, 2008. *Eròtiques i despentinades* (Barcelona: Arola)
Sartori, Diana, 1996. 'Nacimiento y nacer en la acción. A partir de Hannah Arendt', *DUODA*, no. 11: 135-57
——, 2004. 'Entre el deseo y la realidad. La tentación del bien', in *DUODA*, no. 27: 89-107
Schatzki, Theodore R. and Wolfgang Natter, ed., 1996. *The Social and Political Body* (London and NY: The Guildford Press)
Schor, Naomi and Elizabeth Weed, 1994. *The Essential Difference* (Bloomington: Indiana UP)

Sebastián, Santiago, ed., 1985. *Alciato Emblemas* (Madrid: Akal)
Segarra, Marta, ed., 2004. 'Monogràfic Maria-Mercè Marçal', *Lectora*, no. 10
Segura, Cristina, 1986. 'Maternitat i plenitud de l'amor a "La germana, l'estrangera"', *La Mañana Cultura*, 12 April, p. 21
Segura, Cristina, 1987. 'Maria-Mercè Marçal, la expresión de la poesía en cada vivencia', *La mañana*, 5 April, pp. 27–30
Sempere, Màrius, 2002. 'La poesia i el caos', *Reduccions*, no. 75: 75–79
Servidei, Brunella, 2007. 'Maria-Mercè Marçal: el do de la paraula', in Marçal, ed., *I Jornades Marçalianes. Llavor de cant, lluita en saó* (Sabadell: Fundació Maria-Mercè Marçal), pp. 79–88
Showalter, Elaine, 1981. 'Feminist Criticism in the Wilderness', *Critical Inquiry*, no. 2: 179–205
Simó, Isabel-Clara, 1995. 'Dones i literatura', *L'Illa*, no. 13: 7–10
Simonides, of Amorgos, 1975. *Females of the Species: Semonides on Women*, ed. Hugh Lloyd-Jones (London: Duckworth)
Singer, Irving, 2009. *The Nature of Love: From Plato to Luther* (Chicago: University of Chicago Press)
Sistac, Dolors, 2001. *Líriques del silenci. La cançó de dona a Safo, Renée Vivien i Maria-Mercè Marçal* (Lleida: Pagès Editors)
Stanford Friedman, Susan, 1987. 'Creativity and the Childbirth Metaphor: Gender Difference in Literary Discourse', *Feminist Studies*, no. 13.1: 49–82
Stone, Alison, 2007. 'Birth', in *An Introduction to Feminist Philosophy* (Cambridge: Polity), pp. 167–191
Subirana, Jaume. 2008. 'Tres voltes rebel. 10 anys de la mort de Maria-Mercè Marçal', *Avui Cultura*, 5 July, p. 11
Suleiman, Susan R., 1985. '(Re)Writing the Body: The Politics and Poetics of Female Eroticism', *Poetics Today*, no. 6.1-2: 43–65
Sullà, Enric, 1974. 'La poesia catalana jove: una alternativa al realisme', *Els Marges*, no. 1: 118–25
Sunyer, Magí, 2006. *Els mites nacionals catalans* (Vic: Eumo editorial)
Surís, Paloma, 1982. 'Parece que exite hay un "boom" de literatura escrita por mujeres', *Última hora*, 23 Sept., p. 25
Tanesini, Alessandra, 1996. 'Whose Language', in Garry and Pearsall, eds., *Women, Knowledge and Reality: Explorations in Feminist Philosophy* (New York and London: Routledge), pp. 353–66
Tarrés i Vallespí, Anna, 1992. 'Entrevista a Maria-Mercè Marçal. La seva obra. La seva vida', *L'Arbós. Tornaveu literari*, no. 51: 4–6 (Complete interview can be found in Fons Maria-Mercè Marçal at Biblioteca Catalunya, 17/3, 16 pages)
Tarrés i Canimas, Irene, 2010. 'Germanes, estrangeres, Anna Akhmàtova i Marina Tsvetàieva en l'obra de Maria-Mercè Marçal', *Serra d'Or*, no. 606: 43–47
Tarrida, Joan, 1990. 'Maria-Mercè Marçal, Bruixa de dol', *Catalan Writing*, no. 5: 87
Terry, Arthur, 2003. *A Companion to Catalan Literature* (Woodbrige: Tamesis)
Tommasi, Wanda, 1996. 'Simone Weil: darle cuerpo al pensamiento', in Diotima, ed., *La sapienza di partire da sé* (Naples, Italy: Liguori), pp. 95–111
——, 2000. '¿Segundo sexo o autoridad femenina?', *DUODA*, no. 18: 69–86
——, 2002. *Filósofos y mujeres. La diferencia sexual en la Historia de la Filosofía* (Madrid: Narcea)

——, 2004. 'Prácticas y teorías: un saber de experiencia', *DUODA*, no. 27: 49–55
Tsvetàieva, Marina, 1992. *Poema de la fi*, tr. Maria-Mercè Marçal and Monika Zgustová (Barcelona: Ed. 62)
Vegetti Finzi, Silvia, 1992. 'Female Identity between Sexuality and Maternity', in Bock and James, eds., *Beyond Equality and Difference: Citizenship, Feminist Politics and Female Subjectivity* (London: Routledge), pp. 117–37
Viladot, Guillem, 1979. 'Maria-Mercè Marçal amb bicicleta', *Avui Diumenge*, 9 Dec., p. 21
——, 1988. 'Catàleg d'una sexualitat', *Cultura Idees*, 5 June, p. 5
Vintges, Karen, 1996. *Philosophy as Passion: the Thinking of Simone de Beauvoir* (Bloomington: Indiana UP)
Violi, Patrizia, 1992. 'Gender, Subjectivity and Language', in Bock and James 1992: 153–65
Walker, Cheryl, 1990. 'Literary Criticism and the Author', *Critical Inquiry*, no. 16.3: 551–71
Wittig, Monique, 1986. *The Lesbian Body* (Boston: Beacon Press)
Wittig, Monique, 1992. *The Straight Mind and Other Essays* (London: Harvester)
Woolf, Virginia, 1966. 'Women and Fiction', in *Collected Essays Vol. II* (London: The Hogarth Press), pp. 141–48
——, 1994. *A Room of One's Own* (London: Flamingo)
Yanal, Robert J., 1982. 'Aristotle's Definition of Poetry', *Noûs*, no. 16.4: 499–525
Yorke, Liz, 1991. *Impertinent Voices: Subversive Strategies in Contemporary Women's Poetry* (London: Routledge)
Zamboni, Chiara, 1991. 'Acció política i contemplació', *DUODA*, no. 2: 129–40
——, 1996. 'Prefazione', in *La sapienza di partire da sé* (Naples, Italy: Liguori)
——, 2000. 'La vía simbólica en la relación materna y el cortejo de las imágenes del yo', *DUODA*, no. 19: 89–104
Zambrano, María, 1993a. *El hombre y lo divino* (Madrid: Fondo de Cultura Económica)
——, 1993b. *Filosofía y poesía* (Madrid: Fondo de Cultura Económica)
——, 1997. *Delirio y destino* (Madrid: Editorial Universitaria Ramón Areces)
Zerilli, Linda M.G., 2004. 'Refiguring Rights through the Political Practice of Sexual Difference', *Differences*, no. 15.2: 15–90
Zimmermann, Marie-Claire, 2008. 'Lectura d'un poema de Desglaç: l'art de Maria-Mercè Marçal', *Reduccions*, no. 89–90: 274–86

INDEX

Adorno, Theodor W., 55
Ad-stare, 123,130, 189
Aesthetics, 12, 12, 22, 24, 25, 150, 189
Affidamento, 13, 22, 24, 139, 143, 144, 173, 174, 180, 191
Affidataria, 49, 139, 143, 144, 173
Akhmatova, Anna 50, 53 n. 26, 181 n. 11
Alchemy, 175, 176, 180
Arendt, Hannah, 49, 120, 121, 155
Aristotle, 15, 34, 54–57, 59, 190
Arnaut, Daniel, 141, 149, 160
Athena, 27–29, 41–42, 112, 119, 120, 125–31, 190
Atopia, 105, 110, 112, 115–23, 131, 190

Balasch, Ramon, 2, 8, 9, 63 112
Bartra, Agustí, 126, 135 n. 45
Bataille, George, 159, 163, 170
Baudelaire, Charles, 113, 134 n. 24
Birth, 10, 27–28, 34, 59, 69–70, 82, 83, 88, 110, 112, 115, 117, 119–28, 130, 137, 167, 168, 170, 178, 180, 190
Blanchot, Maurice, 6, 140, 176
Blasphemy, 146, 168, 169
Blood, 83–86, 115, 117, 129, 134 n. 31, 140
Blundell, Sue, 27, 53 n. 13, 129, 136 n. 52
Bocchetti, Alessandra, 65, 75, 76, 89, 165, 166, 168, 171
Brogger, Susan, 154
Brossa, Joan, 2, 3, 113, 141, 149
Butler, Judith, 9, 10, 12, 13, 15, 16, 19–21, 32–38, 52, 54–56, 90–95, 190

Carner, Josep, 126
Catalan Literary tradition, 69, 101, 102, 121, 125, 150
Caterina, Albert, 98 n. 33, 135 n. 41, 151
Cavarero, Adriana, 15, 18–19, 58–60, 103–05, 116, 118–22, 155, 156
Chaos, 29, 54, 58–60, 78, 89, 102, 118, 178
Cigarini, Lia, 47, 81
Collocazione simbolica, 23, 55, 58–60, 93, 95, 102
Corporeality, 2, 12, 14, 33, 34, 36, 38, 51, 52, 101, 104, 188
Co-stare, 123, 138, 172, 180, 189

Death, 1, 3, 27, 47, 74, 78, 87–89, 113, 115, 117, 119, 128–29, 131, 142, 159, 165, 170, 171, 177, 178, 180
Demau, 16
Differenza sessuale, 6, 7, 9, 11 n. 14, 13, 16, 17, 31, 36, 38, 51, 52, 54, 55, 57, 91, 93, 95, 99 n. 47, 132 n. 3, 189, 191
Diotima, 6, 7, 10, 13, 46, 50, 52 n. 4, 53 n. 11, 57, 96 nn. 4 & 5, 101, 102, 105, 120, 123, 132 n. 3, 173, 181 n. 15, 190
Dominijanni, 64, 86

Écriture féminine, 5, 20 134 n. 33, 185 nn. 56 & 64
El Mall, 2, 7, 63, 112–14
Entrustment (see also *affidamento*), 7, 13, 16, 22–24, 35, 39, 44–46, 49, 50, 52, 95, 98 n. 41, 139, 144, 145
Eros, 140, 157 160 177–80
Estellés, V. A., 161
Everly, Kathryn A., 117
Excess, 29, 140, 152, 168, 171, 173, 177, 179–80, 191
Ex-sistere, 96 n. 11, 102, 104,119, 134 n. 35, 140, 141, 157

Index

Faulí, Josep, 149
Female creativity, 51, 131, 181 n. 10
Female erotics, 149, 152, 153, 156, 157, 158, 160, 163, 165, 166–80
Female genealogy, 24, 25, 29, 45
Female identity, 7, 9, 28, 100, 173
Female sexuality, 41, 58, 80, 163–64, 167
Female symbolic, 22–24, 38, 43–47, 81
Feminine poetics, 1, 5, 56, 190, 191
Feminine subject, 4, 6, 9, 68–69, 92, 102–04, 112, 117 120 142
Feminism and poetry, 8, 9, 12, 25, 26, 30, 125, 135 n. 43
Ferrater, Gabriel, 2, 161
Foix, J. V., 2, 3, 113–14
Foucault, Michel, 5, 37, 55, 99 n. 46
Francoist dictatorship, 2, 15, 65
Freud, Sigmund, 60, 125, 172

Genesis, 169–70
Grosz, Elizabeth, 15, 98 n. 37

Hesiod, 27, 59, 96 n. 10, 135 n. 45, 178, 190
Hesiod, 27, 59, 178, 190
Heterosexuality, 37

Identity
  female, 7, 28, 100, 173
  gendered, 34, 38, 60
  sexual, 31, 32, 36, 102, 104, 107
In-stare, 105, 123, 137, 189, 190
Irigaray, Luce, 5, 6, 14, 16, 27, 34, 35, 37, 52, 53 n. 18, 99 n. 47, 127, 134 n. 34, 135 n. 43, 139, 166, 180 nn. 1 & 6, 181, 183 n. 42, 185 nn. 56 & 64, 186 n. 74
Ivy, 62, 71, 83

Kristeva, Julia, 5, 15, 96 n. 12, 186 n. 73

Lacan, 13, 23, 31–33, 37, 39, 93, 172
Lesbian, 26, 37, 80, 97 n. 19, 138, 139, 167, 181 n. 10, 185 n. 66,
Lesbian erotics, 167
Lesbofemminismo, 162, 167

Lévinas, Emmanuel, 55, 181 n. 16
Libreria delle donne di Milano, 6–8, 11 n. 14, 13, 17, 19, 22– 25, 41, 42, 52 nn. 4 & 7, 53 nn. 11 & 27, 58, 63, 96 n. 4, 139
Lluïsa, Julià, 2, 3, 5, 25, 26, 161
Lonzi, Carla, 17, 18, 52 n. 5

Mallarmé, Stéphane, 113, 134 n. 24
Marçal, Antoni, 3, 8, 87
March, Ausiàs, 3, 97 n. 24, 126
Martí i Pol, Miquel, 2, 112
Marx, Karl, 16, 21, 52 n. 8
Maternity, 3, 20, 41, 75, 79, 84, 85, 122, 123
Medusa, 2, 7, 28, 29, 42 119, 126–31
Meta-empirical, 162, 171, 176
Meta-physical, 171, 176
Metis, 28, 126–31
Mettere al mondo il mondo, 101–04, 118–20, 137
Montefiore, Jan, 125, 132 nn. 2 & 43
Moon, 42, 51, 53 n. 21, 56, 61–63, 71–76, 79, 80, 81, 83–86, 90, 98 n. 29, 104, 116–18, 140, 144, 145, 165, 186 n. 76
Motherhood, 3, 71, 75, 78
Muraro, Luisa, 5–7, 13, 15, 45–50, 110
Mythology, 29, 53 n. 13, 77, 115, 125, 126, 135 nn. 42 & 43, 136 n. 49

Partire da sé, 6–8
Palol, Miquel de, 10 n. 4, 112
Paz, Octavio, 159, 160, 163, 170
Pinyol, Ramon, 10 n. 3, 63, 97 n. 15, 145
Plath, Sylvia, 87, 133 n. 18
Plato, 15, 34, 155–56, 161, 172
Pleasure, 66, 140, 155, 162–72, 174–75, 177, 179–80, 191
Pound, Ezra, 113, 149

Riba, Carles, 2, 73, 126
Rich, Adrienne, 87, 96 n. 8, 131, 135 n. 36, 151, 181 n. 10
Riera, Carme, 2, 151

Rivera Garretas, María Milagros, 11 n. 14, 102, 132 n. 3
Roíç de Corella, Joan, 126

Saint George, 96 n. 13, 112, 115–18, 131, 134 n. 27, 190
Sala-Valldaura, J. M., 5, 161
Salt, 62, 77–79, 140, 171, 174–77, 179, 186 nn. 75 & 76, 187 n. 79
Salvà, Maria Antònia, 135 n. 41, 151
Salvat-Papasseit, Joan, 161
Same-sex love, 62, 138, 150–51
Same-sex passion, 10, 150, 153, 156–58, 165
Sant-Celoni, Encarna, 161
Sappho, 151, 157
Self-transcendence 137, 140, 155, 173–74, 177, 180
Serpent, 169–70
Sestina, 2, 62, 80–82, 109, 112, 139–41, 144, 148, 149, 152, 153, 156, 157, 158, 160, 163, 165, 166–80
Sexuality, 20, 23, 164–65, 167
Shadow, 61–63, 67, 72, 76–80, 84–90, 93, 104
Solitude, 65, 66, 69, 114, 134 n. 26, 138, 180 n. 2
Sun, 71, 73, 140

Symbolic Barth, 110, 112, 120
Symbolic placement, see *collocazione simbolica*
Symbolic transcendence, 121, 123, 128, 153, 179

Tommasi, Wanda, 15, 96 n. 5, 118, 132 n. 6
Transgression, 44, 60, 88, 140, 145, 162, 168–71, 183 n. 35,
Tsvetaieva, Marina, 50, 53 n. 26, 181 n. 11

Verdaguer, Jacint, 126
Violi, Patrizia, 58, 60–62, 73, 74

Witch, 62, 71, 77, 79, 85, 104, 140, 146
Wittig, Monique, 15, 135 n. 43
Woman and writing, 26, 40, 41, 53 n. 12, 56

Xavier, Bru de Sala, 2, 112

Yourcenar, Marguerite, 47, 183 n. 40

Zambrano, María, 26, 134 n. 34, 183 n. 36, 186 n. 78, 187 n. 78
Zeus, 28, 41, 126–31

www.ingramcontent.com/pod-product-compliance
Lightning Source LLC
Chambersburg PA
CBHW071439150426
43191CB00008B/1178